Lecture Notes in Computer Science 3294

Commenced Publication in 1973
Founding and Former Series Editors:
Gerhard Goos, Juris Hartmanis, and Jan van Leeuwen

C. Neville Dean   Raymond T. Boute (Eds.)

Teaching
Formal Methods

CoLogNET/FME Symposium, TFM 2004
Ghent, Belgium, November 18-19, 2004
Proceedings

 Springer

Volume Editors

C. Neville Dean
Anglia Polytechnic University
East Rd, Cambridge, CB1 1PT, UK
E-mail: c.n.dean@apu.ac.uk

Raymond T. Boute
INTEC, Ghent University
Sint-Pietersnieuwstraat 41, B-9000 Ghent, Belgium
E-mail: raymond.boute@intec.UGent.be

Library of Congress Control Number: 2004113937

CR Subject Classification (1998): D.2, F.3, F.2, F.4, D.1, E.1, K.3

ISSN 0302-9743
ISBN 3-540-23611-2 Springer Berlin Heidelberg New York

Springer is a part of Springer Science+Business Media

springeronline.com

© Springer-Verlag Berlin Heidelberg 2004
Printed in Germany

Typesetting: Camera-ready by author, data conversion by PTP-Berlin, Protago-TeX-Production GmbH
Printed on acid-free paper   SPIN: 11339786   06/3142   5 4 3 2 1 0

Preface

"Professional engineers can often be distinguished from other designers by the engineers' ability to use mathematical models to describe and analyze their products."[1]

This observation by Parnas describes the de facto professional standards in all classical engineering disciplines (civil, mechanical, electrical, etc.). Unfortunately, it is in sharp contrast with current (industrial) practice in software design, where mathematical models are hardly used at all, even by those who, in Holloway's words[2] "aspire to be engineers." The rare exceptions are certain critical applications, where mathematical techniques are used under the general name formal methods.

Yet, the same characteristics that make formal methods a necessity in critical applications make them also advantageous in everyday software design at various levels from design efficiency to software quality.

Why, then, is education failing with respect to formal methods?

 - failing to convince students, academics and practitioners alike that formal methods are truly pragmatic;
 - failing to overcome a phobia of formality and mathematics;
 - failing to provide students with the basic skills and understanding required to adopt a more mathematical and logical approach to software development.

Until education takes these failings seriously, formal methods will be an obscure byway in software engineering, which in turn will remain severely impoverished as a result.

These proceedings record the papers presented at the Symposium on Teaching formal methods (TFM 2004) held at the University of Ghent in Belgium, 18–19 November 2004. This symposium served as a forum to explore the failures and successes of formal methods education, to consider how the failings might be resolved, to learn from the successes, and to promote cooperative projects to further the teaching and learning of formal methods (FMs). The symposium was instrumental in bringing together

 - formal methods educators, both actual and potential;
 - other computer science and software engineering educators;
 - industrial practitioners and project managers;
 - technical and scientific publishers.

---

[1] David L. Parnas, "Predicate Logic for Software Engineering", *IEEE Trans. SWE 19*, 9, pp. 856–862 (Sept. 1993)

[2] Michael Holloway, "Why Engineers Should Consider Formal Methods", *Proc. 16th. Digital Avionics Systems Conference* (Oct. 1997),
http://techreports.larc.nasa.gov/ltrs/PDF/1997/mtg/
NASA-97-16dasc-cmh.pdf

The response to the Call for Papers was very encouraging, and it was possible to select a number of high-quality contributions.

The conference was also blessed with three excellent invited speakers: David Gries from Cornell University, Leslie Lamport from Microsoft Corporation, and Peter Pepper from the Technische Universität Berlin.

September 2004
Neville Dean
Raymond Boute

Program Committee

The following people were members of the TFM 2004 program committee and reviewed papers for the symposium:

Neville Dean (*Program Chair*), Anglia Polytechnic University, UK
Vicki Almstrum, University of Texas at Austin, USA
Roland Backhouse, University of Nottingham, UK
Wolfgang Grieskamp, Microsoft Research, USA
Henri Habrias, Université de Nantes, France
Andrew Martin, University of Oxford, UK
José Oliveira, Universidade do Minho, Braga, Portugal
Elvinia Riccobene, Università di Catania, Italy

External Referees

The program committee members are grateful to the following people who assisted them in the reviewing of papers:

Bernhard Aichernig, UNU-IIST, Macao, SAR China
Franco Barbanera, Università di Catania, Italy
L. Soares Barbosa, Universidade do Minho, Braga, Portugal
Giampaolo Bella, Università di Catania, Italy
Egon Boerger, Università di Pisa, Italy
Giuseppe Difazio, Università di Catania, Italy
Angelo Gargantini, Università di Catania, Italy
Jeremy Gibbons, Oxford University Computing Laboratory, UK
Yuri Gurevich, Microsoft Research, Redmond, USA
Marc Guyomard, ENSAT, Université de Rennes, France
John Jacky, University of Washington, Seattle, USA
Steve McKeever, Oxford University Computing Laboratory, UK
Giuseppe Pappalardo, Università di Catania, Italy
J. Sousa Pinto, Universidade do Minho, Braga, Portugal
Pascal Poizat, Université d'Evry, France
Patrizia Scandurra, Università di Catania, Italy
S. Melo de Sousa, Universidade da Beira Interior, Portugal
Nikolai Tillmann, Microsoft Research, Redmond, USA
Guy Vidal-Naquet, Ecole Supérieure d'Electricité, Paris, France

Support

Financial support from the following was instrumental in making the symposium possible:

CoLogNET
Fonds voor Wetenschappelijk Onderzoek (FWO) Vlaanderen

Organization

Many thanks must also go to Prof. Jean-François Raskin (Local Organization Chairman) and Bernadette Becue (Financial Administration INTEC) for their roles in organizing and running the symposium.

Finally, thanks are due to Dines Bjørner for instigating the symposium and for his help.

Table of Contents

A Beginner's Course on Reasoning About Imperative Programs   1
   Kung-Kiu Lau

Designing Algorithms in High School Mathematics   17
   Sylvia da Rosa

Motivating Study of Formal Methods in the Classroom   32
   Joy N. Reed, Jane E. Sinclair

Formal Systems, Not Methods   47
   Martin Loomes, Bruce Christianson, Neil Davey

A Practice-Oriented Course on the Principles of Computation,
Programming, and System Design and Analysis   65
   Egon Börger

Teaching How to Derive Correct Concurrent Programs
from State-Based Specifications and Code Patterns   85
   Manuel Carro, Julio Mariño, Ángel Herranz,
   Juan José Moreno-Navarro

Specification-Driven Design with Eiffel and Agents
for Teaching Lightweight Formal Methods   107
   Richard F. Paige, Jonathan S. Ostroff

Integrating Formal Specification and Software Verification
and Validation   124
   Roger Duke, Tim Miller, Paul Strooper

Distributed Teaching of Formal Methods   140
   Peter Pepper

An Undergraduate Course on Protocol Engineering –
How to Teach Formal Methods Without Scaring Students   153
   Manuel J. Fernández-Iglesias, Martín Llamas-Nistal

Linking Paradigms, Semi-formal and Formal Notations   166
   Henri Habrias, Sébastien Faucou

Teaching Formal Methods in Context   185
   Jim Davies, Andrew Simpson, Andrew Martin

Embedding Formal Development in Software Engineering   203
   Ken Robinson

Advertising Formal Methods and Organizing Their Teaching:
Yes, but 214
   Dino Mandrioli

Retrospect and Prospect of Formal Methods Education in China 225
   Baowen Xu, Yingzhou Zhang, Yanhui Li

A Survey of Formal Methods Courses in European Higher Education 235
   The FME Subgroup on Education (Convenor: J.N. Oliveira)

Author Index 249

A Beginner's Course on
Reasoning About Imperative Programs

Kung-Kiu Lau

Department of Computer Science, University of Manchester
Manchester M13 9PL, United Kingdom
kung-kiu@cs.man.ac.uk

Abstract. Formal Methods teaching at undergraduate level has been going on at
Manchester for a good number of years. We have introduced various courses based
on different approaches. We have experienced the usual problems. To combat these
problems, our approaches and our course contents have evolved accordingly over
the years. In this paper we briefly trace this evolution, and describe the latest
course, on reasoning about simple imperative programs, for first-year students
who are half-way through our introductory programming course.

1 Introduction

Formal Methods teaching at undergraduate level has been going on at Manchester for a
good number of years. We have run an introductory programming course which taught
students how to read, and program from, VDM-like specifications. We have also had
various courses on reasoning about programs which taught first-order logic, program
specification and verification, and theorem proving techniques. On these courses, we
have experienced the usual problems: the perception of Formal Methods as being too
mathematical, too complex and completely impractical, coupled with an aversion to all
things mathematical. To combat these problems, our approaches and our course contents
have evolved accordingly over the years. In this paper we briefly trace this evolution, and
describe the latest course, on reasoning about simple imperative programs, for first-year
students who are half-way through our introductory programming course. We briefly
trace its evolution, evaluate its success, and discuss the lessons learnt.

Apart from sharing our experience and the contents of our current course, we wish
to convey the message that with suitable motivation and tool support, we believe it is
possible to make the rudiments of Formal Methods accessible to beginner programmers.
Moreover, it is highly desirable for such novices to be shown that testing alone is not
sufficient for ensuring program correctness, and that Formal Methods are required for
accomplishing the task properly.

2 Previous Courses

The current course has evolved from earlier courses on reasoning about programs. The
latter courses started after a previous course on introductory programming using Pascal
and VDM dropped out of the syllabus. In this section, we briefly describe all these
courses.

C.N. Dean and R.T. Boute (Eds.): TFM 2004, LNCS 3294, pp. 1–16, 2004.
© Springer-Verlag Berlin Heidelberg 2004

2.1   Introductory Programming with Pascal and VDM

At first we had an introductory programming course for first-year students, where students were taught how to read specifications written in a notation similar to VDM [8], and how to write Pascal programs from these specifications. This was a compulsory course that ran for the full year. As an introductory programming course it had to teach beginner programmers the Pascal programming language from scratch. At the same time, the students were taught to read specifications written in a notation based on VDM. This notation was rather informal and not proper VDM at all. Even so, the students were not required to write any specifications, they only had to read specifications given to them. The course thus combined teaching Pascal programming with teaching the programming process of going from requirements, expressed as specifications, to program design and coding. To achieve this combination, special course material was developed that integrated the VDM-like notation into a programming process using Pascal. This material was published as a textbook [9] (shortly before the course was dropped from the syllabus! See below).

The course profile was as follows:

Lectures	72 lectures (3 a week)
Labs	10 lab sessions, 8 exercises
Tools	None
Exam	3 hours, answer 4 questions

This course was dropped eventually when the syllabus for the whole first-year in our department was revised, replacing Pascal with SML as the first programming language. Although various versions of the course appeared subsequently as optional (half-year or one-semester) units in the third-year and second-year syllabi, eventually they disappeared altogether.

2.2   Reasoning About Programs I

In the new first-year syllabus, we introduced an optional half-year course on reasoning about programs. This consisted of 2 parts: (i) program verification; (ii) logic. Part (i) covered the specification and verification of a simple imperative language (with assignments, sequential composition, conditional commands, and while loops) and a simple functional language. For imperative programs, the semantics were based on predicate transformers: program specifications were expressed as assertions that represented pre- and post-conditions, and loop invariants were expressed by suitably defined assertions.

The emphasis was on proving correctness. For imperative programs, proof rules were given for the various constructs, and for functional programs, proof by induction was taught. There were no labs, however, so all verification exercises were done on paper only.

Part (ii) was not a continuation of Part (i). Instead it was a separate section that covered the basic concepts of first-order logic: formulae and their truth tables, normal forms, logical consequence, equivalence, validity, etc. The teaching was supported by labs based on Tarski's World (see Section 4.1) for first-order logic.

The course profile was as follows:

Lectures	24 lectures (2 a week)
Labs	5 lab sessions, 4 exercises in logic, none in program verification
Tools	Tarski's World for logic
	No tool for program verification
Exam	2 hours, answer 3 questions

2.3   Reasoning About Programs II

With the switch from Pascal to SML as the first programming language, it was felt that the imperative language part should be taken out of the Reasoning about Programs course. This duly happened, and to replace this part, theorem proving was introduced. However, the course profile remained unchanged.

At first the theorem proving technique that was taught was natural deduction. Later, this was changed to the tableau method. There were no labs for theorem proving, however, and all verification exercises remained pen-and-paper only.

2.4   Reasoning About Programs III

When the whole world went Java-mad, our first-year syllabus was revised again, adopting Java as the introductory programming language. Consequently, the Reasoning about Programs course had to re-focus on imperative languages. However, it was felt that the material on functional programs, in particular proof by induction, was generally useful, and so it was retained. First-order logic was also retained, but theorem proving was dropped, to make way for a more substantial section on imperative programs, based om material from [5]. So the course contents became:

1. First-order Logic.
2. Reasoning about Functional Programs.
3. Reasoning about Imperative Programs.

The course profile was as follows:

Lectures	22 lectures (2 a week)
Labs	4 lab sessions, 4 exercises in first-order logic, none in reasoning about functional programs, none in reasoning about imperative programs
Tools	Tarski's World for first-order logic
	No tool for reasoning about functional programs
	No tool for reasoning about imperative programs
Exam	2 hours, answer 3 questions

3   The Current Course: Reasoning About Programs IV

Now we describe the current course on Reasoning about Programs. In this section, we trace its evolution from its predecessor, state its aims and objectives, and outline the course contents. In subsequent sections, we will elaborate on the material for different parts of the course.

In the previous versions of the course, the lack of tools for reasoning about imperative programs had always been felt to be unsatisfactory, especially from the students' point of view. Finding a suitable tool that would fit into the scope of the Reasoning about Programs course was no easy task, either. However, recently we came across SPARK [2] and its tools, and decided to adopt it for the course.

This meant that there would be no room for functional programs, but in fact this suited us very well. With Java firmly ensconced by now as the introductory programming language, the material on functional programs looked increasingly irrelevant, so we welcomed the opportunity to lose it.

With some additional material on SPARK, the course contents are now as follows:

1. First-order Logic.
2. Reasoning about Imperative Programs (Part1: Principles).
3. Reasoning about Imperative Programs (Part 2: Practice).

The course profile is now as follows:

Lectures	14 lectures (2 a week)
Labs	4 lab sessions, 2 exercises in first-order logic, 2 in reasoning about imperative programs
Tools	Tarski's World for first-order logic
	SPARK tools for reasoning about imperative programs
Exam	$1\frac{1}{2}$ hours, answer 2 questions
Assessment	Exam 70%, labs 30%

Now that we have tool support for the entire course, we have made the course more lab-based than before. So labs now contribute 30% of the assessment, and the exam's contribution has been reduced from 100% (the norm) to 70%. Accordingly, the exam in now shorter (by $\frac{1}{2}$ hour), and the number of lectures has also been reduced by 30%. This development is in line with the move in our department to re-appraise the traditional approach of using lectures as the only means of course material delivery.

3.1 Aims and Objectives

The aim of the course is stated in the published course description as follows:

The aim of this module is to introduce students to the principles and practice of reasoning about simple imperative programs. The principles will be based on first-order logic, and the practice will be provided by the imperative language SPARK and its tools.

The objectives are stated as the following learning outcomes:

1. Students should have a basic knowledge of first-order logic and should be able to understand sentences in first-order logic.
2. Students should be able to write sentences in first-order logic and translate them to and from English sentences.

3. Students should be able to understand first-order logic specification of simple properties of imperative programs.
4. Students should be able to reason informally about simple imperative program properties specified in first-order logic.
5. Students should be able to reason about SPARK programs.
6. Students should be able to use Tarski's World in the lab to create universes and reason about them in first-order logic.
7. Students should be able to use SPARK tools in the lab to write SPARK programs and reason about them.

3.2 Course Contents

The published syllabus is the following:

- Introduction
  - Introductory Example
  - Proving versus Testing
  - Introduction to First-order Logic
- Reasoning about Imperative Programs (Part 1: Principles)
  - Pre-post-condition Specifications
  - Commands as Predicate Transformers
    * Assignments
    * Sequential Composition
    * Conditional Commands
    * Iterative Commands
  - Weakest Pre-Conditions
- Reasoning about Imperative Programs (Part 2: Practice)
  - SPARK: An Introduction
  - The SPARK Tools
  - Path Functions
  - Verification Conditions
  - Using SPARK Tools in the Lab

In the introductory part, the students are introduced to first-order logic. They learn (in the lab) how to write and reason about first-order logic sentences. This knowledge will enable them to write pre-post-condition specifications later.

For reasoning about programs, there are two parts: principles and practice. In the principles part, the course uses a simple made-up imperative language (with assignments, sequential composition, conditional commands, and iterative commands) as a running example to introduce and illustrate predicate transformer semantics for imperative languages. The students learn the principles of how to reason about the correctness of given programs with pre-post-condition specifications.

In the practice part, the course introduces SPARK and its tools, and shows how the principles of predicate transformer semantics can be applied in practice to reasoning about SPARK programs. The SPARK tools provide automated help for correctness verification, so the students not only learn how to write SPARK programs (with pre-post-condition specifications) but also how to use the tools (in the lab) to prove the correctness of these programs.

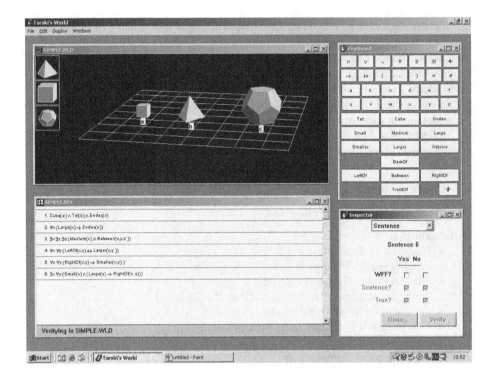

Fig. 1. Tarski's World: the GUI

4   First-Order Logic

The first part of the course gives an introduction to first-order logic. The students are introduced to Tarski's World right from the start, to learn the basics of first-oder logic. In this section, we describe Tarski's World and how our students use it to learn first-order logic.

4.1   Tarski's World

Tarski's World is an award-winning package for teaching beginners first-order logic. The package consists of a text book [3] and a graphical tool, and is supported by a web site [14]. The graphical tool, in particular, provides a very accessible way of learning the basics of first-order logic. Our students rely almost solely on this tool to learn how to write and reason about simple first-order logic sentences.

The GUI of Tarski's World is shown in Fig. 1. It consists of four sub-windows:

1. the World window (top left);
2. the Keyboard (top right);
3. the Sentence window (bottom left);
4. the Inspector (bottom right).

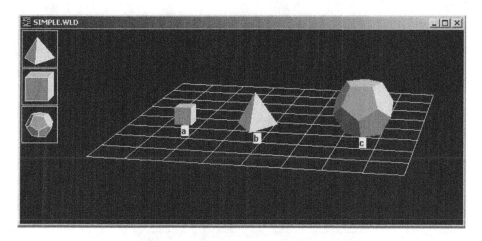

Fig. 2. Tarski's World: the World window

The World window, displays a *world* of objects called *blocks* that are simple geometric shapes, viz. tetrahedrons (tet), cubes and dodecahedron (dodec). Blocks can be large, medium or small in size, and can be labelled. A *world* consists of a 2-D grid (of fixed size) with a set of blocks placed on it. The World window allows a world to be constructed interactively, saved to a file, or reloaded from a saved file. For example, the SIMPLE world (in the file SIMPLE.WLD) in Fig. 2 consists of a small cube a, a medium tetrahedron b and a large dodecahedron c, placed in a line on the grid, as shown.

The Keyboard, Fig. 3, provides keys for logical symbols. These are laid out as follows, going from top to bottom: quantifiers and connectives, constant symbols (a,b,c, d,e,f), variable symbols (u,v,w,x,y,z), and predicate symbols (Tet, Cube, Dodec, ..., BackOf, ...FrontOf).[1] The Keyboard is used for constructing sentences in the Sentence window.

The Sentence window shows first-order logic sentences about the blocks in the chosen world, i.e. the world displayed in the World window. It allows sentences to be constructed interactively (using the keys provided by the Keyboard), saved to a file, and reloaded from a saved file. For example, Fig. 4 shows an example set of sentences (in the file SIMPLE.SEN) for the SIMPLE world. These sentences are:

1. Cube ∧ Tet(b) ∧ Dodec(c)
2. ∀ x (Large(x) → Dodec(x))
3. ∃ x ∃ y ∃ z (Medium(x) ∧ Between(x,y,z))
4. ∀ x ∀ y (LeftOf(x,y) ↔ Large(x,y))
5. ∀ x ∀ y (RightOf(x,y) → Smaller(x,y))
6. ∃ x ∀ y (Small(x) ∧ (Large(y) → RightOf(x,y)))

The Inspector is used for inspecting the world in the World window and the associated sentences in the Sentence window. Using the Inspector, it is possible to add a label to a block, or change the label, and to change the size of a block. The Inspector can also be used to check if a formula being constructed in the Sentence window is well-formed

---

[1] There are no function symbols in Tarski's World.

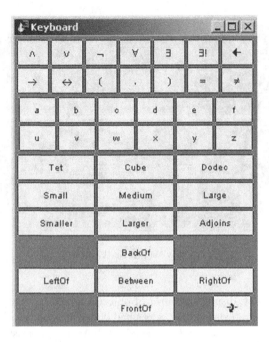

Fig. 3. Tarski's World: Keyboard

and therefore is indeed a sentence. The main purpose of the Inspector, however, is to verify the truth or falsehood of sentences in the Sentence world. For a chosen sentence, Tarski's World performs the verification automatically, and displays the resulting truth value against the sentence in the Sentence window. For example, in Fig. 5, part (b) shows the result of using the Inspector to verify sentence 6 in SIMPLE.SEN. Part (a) shows the truth values of all the sentences in the Sentence window which have been verified. It is obvious that sentences 1 to 3 are true and sentences 4 to 6 are false, so the Sentence window in Part (a) shows the following:

T   1. Cube $\wedge$ Tet(b) $\wedge$ Dodec(c)
T   2. $\forall$ x (Large(x) $\rightarrow$ Dodec(x))
T   3. $\exists$ x $\exists$ y $\exists$ z (Medium(x) $\wedge$ Between(x,y,z))
F   4. $\forall$ x $\forall$ y (LeftOf(x,y) $\leftrightarrow$ Large(x,y))
F   5. $\forall$ x $\forall$ y (RightOf(x,y) $\rightarrow$ Smaller(x,y))
F   6. $\exists$ x $\forall$ y (Small(x) $\wedge$ (Large(y) $\rightarrow$ RightOf(x,y)))

Lab Exercises. In the lab, the students do exercises in writing first-order logic sentences and reasoning about them in worlds, i.e. writing and verifying sentences in worlds that they have been given or have created themselves. These exercises can be classified into the following categories:

1. write well-formed formulas that are correct translations of given English sentences, with no reference to any world;

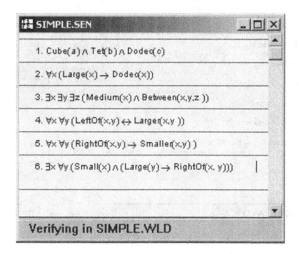

Fig. 4. Tarski's World: the Sentence window

2. write well-formed formulas that are correct translations of given English sentences, and verify them in a given world;
3. create a world such that a given set of sentences (in English or first-order logic) has specified truth values.
4. edit an existing world such that a given set of sentences (in English or first-order logic) has specified truth values.

5 Reasoning About Imperative Programs

Reasoning about imperative programs is split into two parts: principles and practice. The first part gives an introduction to predicate transformer semantics of imperative commands and programs, and hence their specifications by pre- and post-conditions. In particular weakest pre-conditions are explained and used. The second part uses SPARK and its tools as an example of doing reasoning on real imperative programs. In this section, we outline these two parts.

5.1 Principles: Predicate Transformer Semantics

The material for the principles of predicate transformer semantics is based on the standard text [5]. Pre-post-condition specifications, and programs as predicate transformers are first explained. Then a simple but representative imperative language is used as a running example. The language contains the following constructs:

– Assignment
– Sequential Composition
– Conditional Command
– Iterative Command.

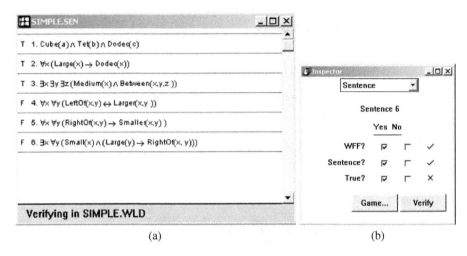

Fig. 5. Tarski's World: the Inspector

Each of these commands is defined as a predicate transformer. For iterative commands, loop invariants are defined and explained. Weakest pre-conditions ar then introduced, and the semantics of the commands of the simple language are re-stated in terms of weakest preconditions.

All this is of course well-known, standard material, so we will not elaborate on it any further here.

5.2 Practice: SPARK and Its Tools

To put the principles of reasoning about imperative programs using predicate transformer semantics into practice, we then introduce a real imperative language SPARK and its tools. SPARK has a textbook [2] and a website [12].

SPARK is a subset of Ada, but on our course, we use a simple subset of SPARK which our students can pick up straightaway, since it is really no different from a similar subset of Java. What our students have to learn is the set of SPARK tools used for proving correctness, and the principles behind them.

SPARK: The Language. In SPARK a basic program unit is a *package*, which could be a *procedure* or a *function*. A package has a *specification* part and an *implementation* part, the package *body*. SPARK has various *annotations* (denoted by --#). In particular, these include *pre-conditions* (--# pre) and *post-conditions* (--# post) that can be put in the specification part of a package, and *assertions* (--# assert) that can be inserted anywhere in the body of a package. For instance, *loop invariants* in the body are represented by suitable assertions.

Example 1. In the package Div, the procedure Divide divides an integer X by another integer Y, yielding a quotient Q and a remainder R.

```
1   package Div
2   is
3   procedure Divide(X, Y : in Integer;
4                    Q, R : out Integer);
5     --# derives Q, R from X,Y;
6     --# pre (X >= 0) and (Y > 0);
7     --# post (X = Q * Y + R) and (R < Y) and (R >= 0);
8   end Div;
9   package body Div
10  is
11  procedure Divide(X, Y : in Integer; Q, R : out Integer)
12     is
13     begin
14        R := X;
15        Q := 0;
16        loop
17           --# assert (X = Q * Y + R) and (R >= 0);
18           exit when R < Y;
19           R := R - Y;
20           Q := Q + 1;
21        end loop;
22     end Divide;
23  end Div;
```

The SPARK Examiner. SPARK has a tool, the SPARK Examiner, for generating *path functions* and their corresponding *verification conditions.*[2] For path analysis, a program is cut into sections without loops and sections that are just loops. For every path found, its pre- and post-conditions are generated from the annotations in the program. For example, the pre-condition of the first path is just the pre-condition of the program, and the post-condition of the last path is the post-condition of the program. A loop is regarded as one path, with its loop invariant as both its pre- and post-conditions.

For each path, with pre-condition p and post-condition q, the SPARK Examiner generates a verification condition. This is obtained by first generating the weakest pre-condition w for q, by hoisting q backwards through the commands in the path to the beginning of the path. The verification condition for this path is then $p \rightarrow w$. The Examiner outputs this in the form *Hypothesis* $\rightarrow$ *Conclusion*, or $H \rightarrow C$.

For example, for Example 1, the Examiner will generate the following paths and their verification conditions:

```
procedure Div.Divide

For path(s) from start to assertion of line 17:

procedure_divide_1.
H1:    x >= 0 .
H2:    y > 0 .
```

---

[2] The Examiner first performs syntax checks and flow analysis, but these are not of interest here.

```
          ->
C1:     x = 0 * y + x .
C2:     x >= 0 .
```

For path(s) from assertion of line 17 to assertion of line 17:

```
procedure_divide_2.
H1:     x = q * y + r .
H2:     r >= 0 .
H3:     not (r < y) .
          ->
C1:     x = (q + 1) * y + (r - y) .
C2:     r - y >= 0 .
```

For path(s) from assertion of line 17 to finish:

```
procedure_divide_3.
H1:     x = q * y + r .
H2:     r >= 0 .
H3:     r < y .
          ->
C1:     x = q * y + r .
C2:     r < y .
C3:     r >= 0 .
```

The SPARK Simplifier. SPARK also has a tool, the SPARK Simplifier, for simplifying or reducing verification conditions. For example, for Example 1, the Simplifier will reduce all verification conditions to true, thus (trivially) completing the correctness proof completely automatically!

```
procedure Div.Divide
```

For path(s) from start to assertion of line 17:

```
procedure_divide_1.
*** true .            /* all conclusions proved */
```

For path(s) from assertion of line 17 to assertion of line 17:

```
procedure_divide_2.
*** true .            /* all conclusions proved */
```

For path(s) from assertion of line 17 to finish:

```
procedure_divide_3.
*** true .            /* all conclusions proved */
```

In general, of course the result of applying the Simplifier to a set of verification conditions is just another set of verification conditions, albeit reduced or simplified in complexity. This set of verification conditions has then to be verified using a theorem prover. SPARK also provides such a tool. Our students do not have to do any theorem proving, so they do not use this tool (see below).

Lab Exercises. In the lab, our students have to run the SPARK Examiner and Simplifier on given programs, and then write and prove their own program using these tools. The program they have to write is described in English in the lab manual, so the students have to write annotations (pre- and post-conditions) that faithfully capture this specification. The program also requires a loop invariant, so the students have to define this and insert it as an assertion in a suitable place in the loop.

The students are not required to do any theorem proving, however. To ensure this, the exercises are chosen so that they are simple enough for the Simplifier to be able to reduce all verification conditions to true completely automatically, as in Example 1.

To emphasise the importance of proving correctness, as opposed to testing, no compiler for SPARK is provided in the lab. So the students cannot resort to running the program to show correctness by testing. Of course, this does not stop them from writing, running and testing Java programs which they believe to be equivalent to the SPARK program, and then translating the former, after testing, to the latter. However, they still have to prove the SPARK program correct.

6   Motivation

On the previous courses, at the beginning of the course, it had been hard to explain the motivation for the course material. This was principally due to the difficulty of showing the relevance of Formal Methods to beginner programmers, which is what our students are. This is compounded by the fact that we did not use a real programming language.

So on the current course, apart from using a real programming language, we provide motivation along the following lines:

Safety-critical Applications. It is hard to motivate the use of Formal Methods for general applications, so on this course, we motivate the use of Formal Methods for safety-critical applications only. Further motivation is provided by citing well-known examples of expensive and disastrous software failures in safety-critical applications, e.g. Ariane 5.

Hardware Verification. We point out that verification has been accepted as necessary by the hardware industry and is done routinely nowadays. This suggests that sooner or later software verification will (have to) follow suit.

Proving versus Testing. We make the point that to show program correctness, testing alone is not complete, and it is necessary to use proving. Of course at this stage, our students only know about testing, and they use it in the labs for all courses to demonstrate that their programs work correctly. So to be told that correctness needs to be proved does make an impact.

The Praxis Prize. So far, the best motivation we have come up with (we hope) is an annual prize for the best SPARK program written and proved by the students in the lab. This is kindly donated by Praxis Critical Systems. At the time of writing, this prize is so new that it has not even been awarded, so it is too early to assess its impact just yet.

7   Evaluation

The current format of the course came into being in 2003. The course is an optional course in the second semester of our first-year programme. Take-up is good, with around 130 students.

On the whole, the current course has been a qualified success. Both tools, Tarski's World and the SPARK tools, are well received, and students have no problems doing the lab work using them. Tarski's World has a nice GUI, and is accessible even to the maths phobic students. SPARK tools have a less fancy user interface, but do not look strange to the students because they have similar 'look and feel' to the Java development environment that they use. Both Tarski's World and the SPARK tools are also stable and reliable, and cause no problems in the running of the labs.

The SPARK language is simple enough not to need any teaching at all, so the students are not put off by having to learn another language just for this course. The principles behind the SPARK tools do need teaching, but they are not too difficult to learn. Undoubtedly, using the tools in the lab really helps the students to understand this material.

Reducing the number of lectures, and making the course more lab-based have also worked well. Students are not forced to sit through an unnecessary number of 'dense' lectures on stuff that they will not apply in the lab.

The effect of the prize is not known at the time of writing, but I expect in the long term it will be a big plus.

On the down side, the course does not teach a whole Formal Method, even though it may be debatable whether it is advisable to do so. Students only learn to write simple logic specifications for simple SPARK programs, and to prove the programs correct using the SPARK tools. For beginners, this may be the right level to aim for, but it barely scratches the surface of proper Formal Methods like VDM [8], Z [13] or B [1].

8   Lessons Learnt

The lessons we have learnt are probably the obvious ones:

1. Students like tools.
2. Students like lab work.
3. Students do not like theory.
4. Integration with other, in particular core, courses, e.g. introductory programming or software engineering courses, is important.
5. Relevance to the real world is important.

These lessons are probably universal, since we believe our students are no different from students elsewhere. However, it should be pointed out that the lessons are only impressions based purely on observation and subjective feelings, rather than any objective study or analysis.

In order to motivate students to learn Formal Methods, demonstrating relevance to the real world is probably the biggest challenge, and integration with core courses in a crowded study programme is at best problematic (see the Conclusion for our own experience). Computer science students' dislike for maths or theory in general is a hurdle that seems increasingly insurmountable, with most computer science degrees not including maths in their admissions requirements.

To make a Formal Methods course accessible, clearly it is good to make the course lab-based. In general, lectures are no longer the best way, and definitely should not be the only way, to deliver course material. For less popular topics, such as Formal Methods, lecture-only courses would be a non-starter. Lab-based courses with good tools would be a much more sensible alternative with a better chance of success.

9   Conclusion

We have described a course that teaches beginner programmers the rudiments of Formal Methods. We have experienced the usual problems faced by Formal Methods teaching, but we believe our course represents a reasonable effort to overcome these problems, chiefly by making the course more lab-based and by using good tools in the lab to support learning.

Integration with core courses remains a problem for us. Our course, which runs in the first year, is not linked to, or followed up, by any of our core courses in the second year. Our course is run by the Formal Methods group in the department. In the second year, our Software Engineering group teaches Z [13] as part of their software engineering course, which is a core course. Unfortunately, however, from the Formal Methods point of view, Z specifications are not used in the development process. The Unified Software Development Process [6] with UML [11] is used instead. So the material of our Reasoning about Programs course is not used by this, or indeed any other, course.

It would be reasonable to expect our course to be better integrated with the core introductory programming course if we used Java instead of SPARK. However, in our view, this is not feasible since formal reasoning about object-oriented programs in general is the subject of on-going research, and is far more complex than formal reasoning about non-object-oriented imperative programs. In particular, Java reasoning tools, e.g. JML [7] and ESC Java [4], are not yet mature enough. Even if they were, we suspect that for novices in both programming and Formal Methods, they would be too difficult to master.

With Formal Methods perceived as a fringe rather than a core subject, it remains hard to get an opportunity to teach a whole Formal Method, especially in an undergraduate computer science programme that has hardly enough room for competing core topics. Overcoming this fringe status is, we feel, the biggest stumbling block facing Formal Methods teaching.

Finally, should you be interested in finding out more about our Reasoning about Programs course, the material for this course can be found on the web page [10].

Acknowledgements. I am indebted to my colleagues Peter Aczel and John Latham at Manchester for providing information about the previous courses. I would also like to publicly thank Praxis Critical Systems Limited for their generosity in donating a prize for this course.

References

1. J.R. Abrial. *The B-Book: Assigning Programs to Meanings*. Cambridge University Press, 1996.
2. J. Barnes. *High Integrity Software: The SPARK Approach to Safety and Security*. Addison-Wesley, 2003.
3. J. Barwise and J. Etchemendy. *The Language of First Order Logic*. CSLI, 3rd edition, 1993.
4. Extended Static Checking for Java Home Page.
   http://research.compaq.com/SRC/esc/.
5. D. Gries. *The Science of Programming*. Springer-Verlag, 1981.
6. I. Jacobson, G. Booch, and J. Rumbaugh. *The Unified Software Development Process*. Addison-Wesley, 1999.
7. The Java Modeling Language (JML) Home Page.
   http://www.cs.iastate.edu/~leavens/JML.html.
8. C.B. Jones. *Systematic Software Development Using VDM*. Prentice Hall, second edition, 1990.
9. J.T. Latham, V.J. Bush, and I.D. Cottam. *The Programming Process: An Introduction using VDM and Pascal*. Addison-Wesley, 1990.
10. K.-K. Lau. CS1112: Reasoning about Programs.
    http://www.cs.man.ac.uk/~kung-kiu/cs1112/.
11. J. Rumbaugh, I. Jacobson, and G. Booch. *The Unified Modeling Language Reference Manual*. Addison-Wesley, 1999.
12. SPARKAda, Praxis Critical Systems Limited.
    http://www.praxis-cs.co.uk/sparkada/.
13. J.M. Spivey. *The Z Notation: A Reference Manual*. Prentice Hall, second edition, 1992.
14. Tarski's World. http://wwwcsli.stanford.edu/hp/Tarski1.html.

Designing Algorithms in High School Mathematics

Sylvia da Rosa

Instituto de Computación - Facultad de Ingeniería
Universidad de la República
Montevideo, Uruguay
darosa@fing.edu.uy

Abstract. Teaching formal methods in software construction has often been a concern of several computer science educators. In our opinion, the origin of most of the difficulties in learning formal methods in computer science and software engineering does not lie in computer science courses but in the mathematical background of the students. Moreover, there are numerous obstacles to learning basic concepts noted by both computer science and mathematics educators. To change this situation it is necessary to integrate the work of mathematics and computer science educators. That is, the main focus should be the creation of new educational approachs nourished by two components: a *theoretical* one (formally introducing discrete mathematics concepts) and an *experimental* one (implementing those concepts in a suitable programming language). In this paper, using examples from a discrete mathematics course for high school teachers, we describe the main characteristics of our approach.

1 Introduction

Computer Science is developing in many directions. Its influence on other sciences expands each day, new paradigms of programming languages are created, more and more sophisticated tools and applications in diverse fields of society and industry become available. At the same time, new ideas, concepts and theories arising from scientific advances have to be integrated into social knowledge that is transmitted to new generations through the educational system. However, the mathematics currently taught has not caught up with the information age - it is primarily based upon the continuous mathematics of the physical sciences. Mathematics focus, methodology of research and education has evolved from these sciences. It has not adapted to the mathematics of the information age - mainly discrete mathematics. For educators, this implies a shift of focus from pedagogical issues mainly stressing the development of students' calculation and symbolic manipulation skills - often neglecting the understanding of important concepts - to ones encouraging the active participation of students in acquiring knowledge on their own in contexts where mathematics seems more useful and applicable. We are convinced that this transformation requires the assembled work of both mathematics and computer science educators. This would provide

C.N. Dean and R.T. Boute (Eds.): TFM 2004, LNCS 3294, pp. 17–31, 2004.

not only a thorough grounding in computer science, but also would benefit the mathematical background for *all students.*

We have been teaching courses in functional programming and discrete mathematics as part of the curriculum of computer science studies at Universidad de la República and Universitario Autónomo del Sur. Here we observed a need for the adequate preparation of entering students. Accordingly, one of our recent projects involves the preparation of high school mathematics teachers [1], in particular, introducing them to topics in discrete mathematics using a programming language to reinforce important concepts. In this project, the teachers are required to introduce a selected topic in their own classes applying these ideas and using the language. Our methodology supports self-study, active learning and collaborative work, as well.

This paper is organized as follows. In section 2, the theoretical framework supporting our ideas is briefly described. In section 3, several examples illustrating our methodology of carrying these ideas out are developed. Finally, some general conclusions are presented.

2   Theoretical Framework

Computer science and mathematics education face important challenges from scientific and social changes. Scientific research in education [6] [7], has provided sufficient evidence of the failure of the traditional educational system and observed that serious research in education, requires understanding of the learning process. Effective teachers require experience, a grasp of the subject matter and an epistemological framework within which their proposals, projects, experiments, etc, are developed. For instance, in the traditional educational system of today the pedagogical issues are characterized by the belief that students learn by listening and/or imitating. Consequently, that knowledge has been transferred and that expected responses indicate effective learning.

Piaget's theory of genetic epistemology provides a satisfactory epistemological framework [8]. His theory provides reasonable explanations regarding the central questions of the development of the process of acquiring knowledge. That is, the learning process consists in a mental construction governed by laws and tenets similar to those that govern the biological development of human beings.

Although the work of Piaget is in great part devoted to the development of the intelligence of children, he stated that the mechanisms and general laws involved in the construction of the cognitive structures are similar from the early stages of development to those of the more advanced theories [8] [9]. In particular his studies and research about mathematical thought cover all aspects from the genesis of the concepts of number, order relations, space, etc, until the most refined forms of mathematical theories.

---

[1] The term high school refers to two years which follow secondary school and prepare students for University-level studies. In our country, the topics described in this paper are introduced in high school courses, but our proposal is appropriate to University courses, as well.

Piaget's theory of genetic epistemology is not about pedagogy which was not the main focus in his work (despite 40 years as director of Bureau of Education). However, the pedagogical implications of his theory and experiments, cannot be ignored in scientific studies about learning-teaching issues. Many researchers in these areas have interpreted Piaget's ideas giving rise to different theories (for instance, radical constructivism, social constructivism, constructivism, APOS theory, Theory of Generalization [1] [2] [3] [4] [5]).

In our work we apply Piaget's ideas to teaching computer science concepts, by means of identifying the processes and laws described in his works when the students are required to design algorithms for solving problems.

In our work, we concentrate on the process by which knowledge constructed by the students in solving a problem or class of problems is transformed into general conceptual knowledge. The latter is formalized in a universal system of symbols (mathematics) and implemented in a programming language, providing an experimental context in which mathematical objects can be manipulated.

3   Examples

Selected examples are taken from a discrete mathematics course for high school mathematics teachers. The main goals of this course are:

- to explain the relationship between computer science and discrete mathematics through concepts common to both disciplines - logic, functions, algorithms, inductive definitions, etc,
- to stress the process of abstraction through the development of problem solutions from their specifications,
- to reinforce the importance of logic to understanding definitions, properties, proofs, etc,
- to demonstrate the benefits of using a programming language. For instance, requiring the precise expressions of definitions and developing other skills such as solving a problem by focusing on what must be accomplished rather than how to accomplish it,
- to demonstrate that computer science involves interesting mathematical activities.

The problems and exercises posed in the course are selected from the current high school mathematics curriculum. Our methodology consists of contrasting the differences between solving problems using our approach and the traditional way. At the same time emphasizing that the students have to discover their own techniques of solving problems and then transforming their informal solutions into algorithmic specifications in natural language. These specifications are put into correspondence with formal mathematical definitions and finally, these mathematical definitions are implemented in a programming language. All these stages occur in an interactive way and the effective participation of students is encouraged. It is worth remarking that in most of the cases, the students already know how to apply an algorithm to particular cases. For instance, they know how to find the gcd of two natural numbers using Euclid's algorithm or they know how to sort the elements of a given set according to an order relation. However, to abstract a general algorithmic solution for these problems, formalize it in a mathematical function definition and implement it in a programming language are stages of the learning process that take place with the help of the teacher.

Finally, teachers are required to introduce one discrete math topic in their high school classes applying this approach - including a programming exercise. Following each example below are comments from teachers regarding their experiences.

3.1   Counting Problems

Counting techniques are described in discrete mathematics books from the point of view of deriving formulas to get the number of different combinations of sets of objects. One of these cases is to count the number of ways of selecting m elements without replacement from a set of n elements.

The point is usually illustrated by building general observation from small problems. For example counting the number of words of three letters without repetitions from four letters a, b, c, d.

Whichever algorithm is used in class to solve the problem, it is traditionally considered a means of deriving a formula for the case and introducing the general calculation formula of k-permutations $P(n, k) = n \times (n-1) \times ... \times (n-k+1)$, where n is the number of elements of the set from which groups of k elements are selected. The traditional way of teaching counting techniques, does not take into account the algorithms themselves as objects of study.

However, in developing the algorithm the students acquire a fundamental knowledge, called in our epistemological framework *knowledge in the plane of actions*, which is the source of both the conceptualization and the formalization of the algorithm.

The Stage of Conceptualizing

Conceptualizing means to represent the knowledge acquired in a lower plane of actions or mental representations from which higher concepts will be constructed. The psychological process taking place has been defined by Piaget as *reflective abstraction* [10].

To induce this process, several questions about the algorithms are formulated focusing in what has been done to achieve a result. The students have to describe their answers in natural language as precisely as possible, likely generating new questions.

Regarding the problem stated above, the students commonly tend to join a letter with the pairs formed with the other ones without repetitions. After several attempts their actions can be summarized as:

I) take the first letter in the set and *add it to each of the pairs of letters without repetition not containing the first letter,*

II) take the second letter in the set and *do the same* as in I) but adding it to the pairs without repetition not containing the second letter,
III) do this until there are *no more letters in the set.*

Observe that it is very common that the students refer to "the first letter, the second, etc" of the set, although there is no order in a set. Algorithmically speaking, sets are often treated as sequences and actually, in our examples, we use sequences with no repetitions to represent sets.

The students are induced to discover subproblems in their descriptions. Marked in italics in point I above is the following subproblem: given a letter and a sequence of pairs, select from the latter those pairs not containing the given letter, and add it to them. What is marked in italics in points II and III is the subproblem above with respect to each of the letters of the sequence.

Finally, the students are induced to discover that to solve the problem of forming words of three letters, they use *the solution of the "previous" problem* represented by *the pairs (words of two letters) without repetition* of point I, to which they add each letter.

The most important fact here is that the students become aware that these subproblems *are already present in their descriptions*, which naturally permits the following refinement:
1. take the first letter x in the sequence A,
2. select from the previous solution the words that do not contain x,
3. add x to those words,
Reflecting about what has to be done after working out the first letter in the sequence A, the students strive to:
4. do the same with the remaining letters of A until no letters remain,
5. construct the sequence of all obtained words (the new solution).

Observe that point 5 above is the only one not included in students' descriptions. This is actually not rare, because what matters in mathematics while solving this problem is to count the words and not to construct the sequence of all of them. In our approach on the contrary, the sequence of words is constructed and the computer is used to count the number of its elements.

The Stage of Formalizing

The meaning of formalizing is to put into correspondence mental constructions (concepts) with some universal system of symbols [11]. Traditionally, in computer science teaching algorithms are described using different formalisms (pseudo-codes, diagrams, flow-charts). But these formalisms are not universal systems of symbols, while mathematics is. Mathematical objects representing computer science concepts can be implemented in almost any programming language. Most importantly, the mathematical methods can be used to prove properties about them, for instance, correctness. Actually, one of the goals of functional programming has been to bring programming closer to mathematics [12]. Our approach takes a step in the opposite direction, getting mathematics closer to programming. This implies, among many things, to adopt a notation suitable for describing computer science concepts in mathematical language. The following concepts, defined and used in our course, are denoted as follows:

Sets

> $Seq(A)$ denotes the inductively defined set of all sequences of elements taken from a set A.
>
> $Seq^+(A)$ denotes the set of non empty sequences of elements of a set A.
>
> N denotes the inductively defined set of natural numbers.
>
> N^+ denotes the natural numbers ≥ 1.
>
> $Bool$ denotes the set of Booleans values, true and false.
>
> - and $\cap$ stand for set difference and set intersection respectively.
>
> $\#X$ stands for the number of elements of a set X.

Sequences

> The symbol $[\,]$ denotes the empty sequence and $[x]$ denotes a sequence whose unique element is x.
>
> *cons* stands for the constructor function for sequences, that is to say, $cons(x,s)$, with $x \in A$ and $s \in Seq(A)$ denotes a non empty sequence.
>
> *head* denotes the function taking a non empty sequence and returning its first element.
>
> *tail* denotes the function taking a non empty sequence and returning the sequence without its first element.
>
> $++$ denotes the function (used as infix operator) taking two sequences s_1 and s_2 and returning a sequence with the elements of s_1 followed by the elements of s_2.
>
> *map* denotes the function taking a function $f : A \to B$ and a sequence $s \in Seq(A)$ and returning a sequence $\in Seq(B)$ formed by the applications of f to the elements of s.
>
> *filter* denotes the function taking a predicate $p : A \to Bool$ and a sequence $s \in Seq(A)$ and returning a sequence $\in Seq(A)$ with the elements of s satisfying the predicate p.
>
> *elem* denotes the function taking an element x and a sequence s and returning the value of $x \in s$.
>
> *length* denotes the function that given a sequence returns its number of elements.
>
> $[1 \,..\, n]$ stands for the sequence of consecutive natural numbers from 1 to n, being $n \geq 1$.

The symbol $=$ stands for testing equality and the symbol $\stackrel{\text{def}}{=}$ stands for introducing definitions.

High order functions are defined and used as in functional programming. For instance, $(elem\ x)$ is a function taking a sequence y and returning the value of $x \in y$.

Formalizing the Algorithm

Recall the specification of the algorithm given at the end of the section about conceptualization, composed using 5 steps. Steps two and three can be represented by the following function g, that given an element x and a sequence ss of sequences, adds x to all the sequences of ss not containing x:

$$g: A \times Seq(Seq(A)) \to Seq(Seq(A))$$
$$g(x,ss) \stackrel{\text{def}}{=} \underbrace{map \; (add \; x)}_{3} \; \underbrace{(filter \; (not \circ (elem \; x)) \; ss)}_{2}$$

where $add \; x \; y \stackrel{\text{def}}{=} y \mathbin{+\!\!+} [x]$

Function f below takes a sequence s_1 and a sequence of sequences ss_2 and returns the result of applying g to all the elements of s_1 and ss_2. It completes the formalization of steps 1, 4 and 5 of the algorithm:

$$f : Seq(A) \times Seq(Seq(A)) \to Seq(Seq(A))$$

$$f(s_1, ss_2) \stackrel{\text{def}}{=} \begin{cases} [\,] & ; \quad if \; \underbrace{s_1 = [\,]}_{4} \\[2mm] g(\underbrace{x}_{1}, ss_2) \underbrace{\mathbin{+\!\!+}}_{5} \underbrace{f(tail(s_1), ss_2)}_{4} & ; \quad otherwise \end{cases}$$

where $x \stackrel{\text{def}}{=} head(s_1)$

The general problem of obtaining all the subsequences of k elements, $k \neq 0$, from a given non-empty sequence s can be solved by function $subs$ below:

$$subs : (Seq^{+}(A)) \times (N^{+}) \to Seq(Seq(A))$$

$$subs(s, k) \stackrel{\text{def}}{=} \begin{cases} [[x] \mid x \in s] & ; \quad if \; k = 1 \\ f(s, subs(s, k - 1)) & ; \quad otherwise \end{cases}$$

That is, function $subs$ takes a non-empty sequence s and a natural number $k \neq 0$ and returns the result of applying f to s and the previous solution for $k - 1$.

Applying $subs$ to $[1..n]$ and k, a sequence of sequences of k elements without repetition formed from n elements, is computed. So, the function that computes the number $P(k, n)$ of k-permutations is defined by:

$$perm : N^{+} \times N^{+} \to N$$
$$perm \; (k,n) \stackrel{\text{def}}{=} length \; (subs([1..n],k))$$

Once the functions are defined and implemented, they are used to solve other instances of the problem and experiment with other types of problems as well. Teachers comment that since the sequences are available (and not just the number of them, which, if necessary, can always be calculated by the function length), the students themselves *propose* different problems, and use the computer to *calculate* their solutions. For instance, with respect to the problem of 3-permutations above, sequences holding a certain property are selected. For example, all sequences containing 'a' are obtained with *filter (elem 'a') (subs (['a','b','c','d'],3))*.

This type of activity illustrates the role of the computer as a helpful tool in making calculations and the role of the student as solutions designer, in our new educational framework. One of the most relevant aspects of software construction is the emphasis on the process of abstraction, by which a name is given to the group of steps of an algorithm allowing to refer to it as an entire object.

3.2   Sorting

Sorting a set of elements according to some order relation is a common problem in real life. Most people have, at one time or another, solved this problem for some particular case (sorting objects according to their size, children to their heights, pictures to their colors, sorting words lexicographically, numbers in increasing order, etc). The question is thus, to conceptualize and formalize this "know how". We have already described our methodology in the example about counting techniques, therefore in this example we present just the main points of the process.

The students are asked to solve some instances of the problem:
Given the following sets, construct sets with their elements sorted according to each of the indicated order relationships.

$\{3,2,-1,0,4,-3\}$ and $\leq$
$\{b,f,d,y,z,a,m\}$ and the lexicographic order
$\{\{a,b,c\},\{\},\{b\},\{a,b\}\}$ and $\subseteq$
$\{\{0,1,2\},\{a\},\{True, False\}\}$ and $\#X \leq \#Y$

Then, they are induced to reflect upon their methods and to abstract an algorithm for the general problem. Basically, the algorithm described by the students is:

1. take the least element in the set and put it first,
2. take the least element in the remaining set and put it next,
3. do the same than in 2. until there are no more elements in the set,
4. construct the result as a sequence.

Point 1 states a subproblem: given a finite and not empty set X and an order relation R, obtain the least element of the set, that is, the element x of X such that, forall elements y in X, x R y holds. To solve this problem the students define a function, (say ordR), taking a non-empty sequence X and an order relation R and returning the head of a sequence whose unique element is the "least" element of X according to R. This question poses the problem of representing a binary order relation so that it can be an argument of a function. It is represented by a function : (A x A) → Bool taking a pair of elements and returning true if the pair belongs to the relation, false otherwise.

ordR is defined as follows[2]:

$$ordR : (Seq^+(A)) \times ((A \times A) \to Bool) \to A$$
$$ordR\ (X,R) \overset{def}{=} head\ [x : x \in X \mid \forall y \in X,\ x\ R\ y]$$

The following definition of sort is the formalization of the algorithm's four steps, which are indicated by a corresponding number below each subexpression.

---

[2] Recall that we use sequences without repetitions as sets.

$$sort : Seq(A) \times (A \times A \to Bool) \to Seq(A)$$

$$sort(X, R) \stackrel{\mathrm{def}}{=} \begin{cases} [\,] & ; \quad if \underbrace{X = [\,]}_{3} \\ \underbrace{cons}_{4}(\underbrace{x}_{1}, \underbrace{sort}_{3} \underbrace{(X - [x], R)}_{2}) & ; \quad otherwise \end{cases}$$

$$where \; x \stackrel{\mathrm{def}}{=} ordR(X,R)$$

Once implemented, the algorithm is applied to each of the instances above.

Teachers comment that they are not accustomed to defining functions either involving logical terms or taking order relations as arguments - consequently neither are their students. Moreover, teachers remark that, at first, the students refuse to believe that this kind of activities are mathematical activities. In our opinion, this problem is an appropriate vehicle to counter the idea that mathematics is always continuous.

3.3   Euclid's Algorithm

In this example, functions like mod, div, divisors, is-prime, commonly used in programming languages are introduced as mathematical functions. Observe that concepts such as the quotient and the remainder of a division, the divisors of a number and prime numbers are widely used in mathematics courses, and the students know how to compute each for given values. However, these concepts are seldom introduced *as functions*, that is to say, as general methods to be applied to particular cases. This difference in focus contributes, in our opinion, to the introduction of formal methods in software construction from ground levels, so that mathematics makes sense to the students.

The case of the functions *div* and *mod* calculating the quotient and the remainder of the division of two natural numbers respectively, is illustrative: all students know how to compute the result; however when asked to present a general method for any values, they have difficulties. After several attempts, they arrive at a satisfactory description of the algorithms in natural language. The mathematical meaning of this description yields the following definitions:

$$div : N \times N^+ \to N$$

$$div(n, m) \stackrel{\mathrm{def}}{=} \begin{cases} 0 & ; \quad if \; n < m \\ div(n - m, m) + 1 & ; \quad otherwise \end{cases}$$

$$mod : N \times N^+ \to N$$

$$mod(n, m) \stackrel{\mathrm{def}}{=} \begin{cases} n & ; \quad if \; n < m \\ mod(n - m, m) & ; \quad otherwise \end{cases}$$

$$division : N \times N^+ \to N \times N$$
$$division \; (n, \; m) \stackrel{\mathrm{def}}{=} (div(n,m), \; mod(n,m))$$

$divisors : N \rightarrow Seq(N)$

$divisors\ (n) \overset{\text{def}}{=} [x : x \in [1\ ..\ n] \wedge n\ mod\ x = 0]$

The teachers present Euclid's algorithm and propose various activities. The students experiment with different cases until they understand how the algorithm works. As in the previous examples, they are first asked to specify it in natural language and step by step, arriving at a definition of a function that computes it:

$$gcd : Z \times Z \rightarrow Z$$

$$gcd(a,b) \overset{\text{def}}{=} \begin{cases} b & ; \quad if\ a\ mod\ b = 0 \\ gcd(b, a\ mod\ b) & ; \quad otherwise \end{cases}$$

The teachers comment that using this approach, permits students to pay attention to properties and not to the details of the operations. For example, the students were able to define the operation of division in Z: $\forall a, b \in Z,\ b > 0,\ \exists c, r \in Z \mid a = b \times c + r$ with $0 \le r < b$, and to observe which are the possible remainders according to the divisor. They observed that the condition of r ≥ 0 guarantees that the results are unique, as well.

The teachers also comment that they informally discuss the concept of recursion in class, recalling the importance of the base case and the application of the function to, in some sense, "smaller" arguments, in order to reach the base case guaranteeing termination of the program. This concept is formally introduced later.

3.4   Properties and Proofs

The reader may wonder about our approach with respect to proofs. We agree with [13] and we think, that to some extent, we apply a similar methodology to definitions, while in [13] the focus is on proofs. From definitions, the students are capable of stating properties and become aware of the need for proofs. For instance, in the case of Euclid's algorithm, the students are asked about the meaning of "the greatest common divisor of two numbers" and are encouraged to derive another definition of the function accordingly. Defining an instance of ordR in which the order relation is "x is greater or equal than y", the maximum value of a set of numbers can be obtained. The new definition of gcd, say gcd', is straightforward:

$gcd': Z \times Z \rightarrow Z$

$gcd'\ (a,b) \overset{\text{def}}{=} max\ (divisors(a) \cap divisors(b))$

Having two definitions of the function that computes the greatest common divisor of two integers, the need for arguing the behavioral equivalence of two definitions naturally arises, that is to say, the proof of equivalence:

$\forall\ a,\ b \in Z,\ gcd(a,b) = gcd'\ (a,b)$, that is to say:

$\forall\ a,\ b \in Z,\ gcd(a,b) = max(divisors(a) \cap divisors(b))$

Proofs are presented in the usual way.

In our opinion, terms like algorithm, relationship, function, definition, property, etc, become understandable and the need for proofs is much clearer.

The Stage of Implementing

Although functional programming languages are the most suitable for our purpose, languages from other programming paradigms can be used.

We have been using Haskell[3] in discrete mathematics courses of computer science University studies [15]. In discrete mathematics courses for high school teachers we have been using Isetl [4](which is not functional)[17]. Discussing about these alternatives is beyond the context of this paper.

We include the implementation of the functions in Haskell because it is more understandable. Some of the features of Haskell are: it is a strong typed language, equational definitions of functions using pattern matching are allowed, as well as users defined algebraic types.

Some of the predefined functions in Haskell are implemented by students (for instance, forall, gcd), others are not (for instance div and mod).

Sets Functions:

```
--intersection of two sequences
inter :: Eq a => [a] -> [a] -> [a]
inter [] _ = []
inter _ [] = []
inter (x:xs) ys = case (elem x ys) of
                    True  -> x : inter xs ys
                    False -> inter xs ys


-- removing a given element from a sequence
remove :: Eq a => a -> [a] -> [a]
remove x [] = []
remove x (y:ys) = if x == y then remove x ys else y:remove x ys


-- checking if all elements of a sequence hold a given property
forall :: (a -> Bool) -> [a] -> Bool
forall p [] = True
forall p (x:xs) = (p x) && (forall p xs)
```

k-Permutations Example:

```
g :: Eq a => (a ,[[a]]) -> [[a]]
g (x,xss) = map (add x) (filter (not.(elem x))) xss)
            where add x xs = xs ++ [x]


f :: Eq a => [a] -> [[a]] -> [[a]]
```

---

[3] http://www.haskell.org
[4] http://isetlw.muc.edu/isetlw/

```
f [] 11 = []
f (x:l) 11 = (g (x,11)) ++ (f l 11)

subs :: Eq a => ([a], Int) -> [[a]]
subs (xs,1) = [[x] | x <- xs]
subs (xs,k) =  f xs (subs (xs,k-1))

perm :: (Int,Int) -> Int
perm (k,n) = length (subs([1..n],k))
```

Sorting Example:

```
ordR :: [a] -> (a -> a -> Bool) -> a
ordR xs r = head [x | x <- xs, forall (r x) xs]

-- sort is predefined in Haskell, so sorti is used instead.
sorti :: Eq a => (a -> a -> Bool) -> [a] -> [a]
sorti r [] = []
sorti r xs = y : sorti r (remove y xs)
                where y = ordR xs r
```

Euclid's Algorithm Example:

```
-- divisors is defined for integers different from 0.
divisors :: Int -> [Int]
divisors 0 = error "infinite list"
divisors n = [x | x <- [1..abs(n)]++[-abs(n)..(-1)], mod n x == 0]

-- gcd is predefined in Haskell, so mcd is used instead.
mcd :: (Int,Int) -> Int
mcd (n,m)
    | mod n m == 0   = m
    | otherwise      = mcd (m,mod n m)

-- max is predefined in Haskell, so may is used instead.
may :: Ord a => [a] -> a
may (xs) = ordR xs maxi
            where maxi x y = x >= y

mcd' :: (Int,Int) -> Int
mcd' (a,b) = may(divisors(a) `inter` divisors(b))
```

After implementing the functions above, the students are encouraged to pose different types of questions and to investigate properties, as well. Some examples are: Which is the result of perm (k,n) in which k > n? Which are the divisors of 0 according to the mathematical definition? Why the case of 0 returns an error message in the divisors program? These questions provide the opportunity for discussing the limitations of the computer. Why does Haskell use the == symbol instead of = like mathematics? The use in mathematics traditional teaching of the same symbol = with different meanings (defining and testing equality) unconsciously confuses the students. A programming language avoids this type of confusion and provides the opportunity for discussing the semantics of languages.

Observe that in the stages we do not care about efficiency issues. Our goal is to induce thinking about the methods (algorithms) that the students make contact with in many problems of mathematics courses.

4   Related Work

We agree with opinions regarding the need for improving education as a means of contributing to increasing software development quality. Teaching formal methods in computer science constitutes a valuable effort in this direction, in particular works relating mathematics and computer science education.

However, in most of the cases, the authors base their works on their own intuition and experiences of teaching courses. High failure rates in introductory courses frequently motivate them to implement changes in the delivery of the courses, emphasizing the importance of mathematical thinking to the study of computer science [19] [18]. Examples of introductory discrete mathematics textbooks for computer science are [22] [21] [23] [20].

We took a similar approach in early works [15] [16] which evolved into the ideas described in this paper: although sharing of ideas and techniques for teaching is relevant to the progression of computer science education, what makes the research in this area an academic discipline is the connection with pedagogical and epistemological theories.

On the other hand, in [24] some evidence is presented about deficiencies in proof skills of computer science students. In [13] the authors claim that the origin of the problem lies, at least partially, in high school mathematics, with which we agree.

The proposal described in [14] consists in designing a computer science course teaching discrete mathematics concepts for high school students. The way of teaching algorithms is similar to ours, although mathematics is not explicitly considered for algorithms representation.

Finally, another main difference between our approach and those of the mentioned authors is the stress we put on the integrated work of mathematics and computer science educators.

5   Conclusions

Our motivation arises from the observation that courses in computer based mathematics offered in high school provide a suitable context in which formal methods can be introduced. Not only for demonstrating properties [13], but also for *the careful construction of definitions of methods (algorithms)*. Accordingly, all students, not just computer science students, would benefit from an updated curriculum addressing social and scientific development. At the same time, computer science education would be released from teaching basic mathematical concepts.

The computer science community, especially computer science educators, should play a central role in such transformations of the educational system.

In our opinion, to introduce the conceptualization of algorithms and to describe how to formalize them is *at least as important* as the derivation and application of calculation formulas. The examples included in this paper illustrate how our ideas are put into practice. Although we have not gathered data about results of our work in a systematic way, we can draw some initial conclusions:

- mathematics teachers recognize that the discrete mathematics topics of interest are present in high school curriculum (e.g., sets, relations, functions, sequences, etc.). Our approach supplements and reinforces the existing curriculum so additional intricate mathematical knowledge is not required of students,
- teachers have also remarked that *this kind of mathematics* (discrete with computer science approach) is much more interesting to the students than what they are exposed to in traditional courses. Consequently, obstacles due to math phobia are considerably diminished,
- the increasing complexity of computer science subjects demands more time and efforts, both from educators and students. Updating mathematics curriculum to support current educational needs provides a solid foundation for the new knowledge and skills that will be required of students in the twenty-first century,
- the role of the computer is clearly established as a *powerful tool* which calculates *what the student has designed* as a solution of a problem. The importance to developing skills in formally doing these designs (programs) is evident.

Finally, it is worth remarking that we feel it is very important to explicitly adopt an epistemological framework of doing research in education. That is, a theoretical support for understanding how the processes involved in learning take place. Accordingly, designing supporting instructional material is essential. Our view is that taking epistemological issues into consideration is in some sense analogous to applying formal methods in doing research in the area of education.

Acknowledgements. I thank Peter B. Henderson for his comments on draft versions of the paper. The comments of the anonymous referees are gratefully acknowledged.

References

1. M.Asiala, Ed Dubinsky et. al.: A Framework for Research and Curriculum Development in Undergraduate Mathematics Education. Research in Collegiate Mathematics Education II, CBMS Issues in Mathematics Education, 6 1-32 (1999)

2. Mordechai Ben-Ari: Constructivism in Computer Science Education. Journal of Computers in Mathematics and Science Teaching (2001)
3. Ed Dubinsky and Philip Lewin: Reflective Abstraction and Mathematics Education: The Genetic Decomposition of Induction and Compactness. The Journal of Mathematical Behavior 5. 55–92 (1986)
4. W.Dörfler: Forms and Means of Generalization in Mathematics. Unpublished (1991)
5. P.Ernest: Social Constructivism as a Philosophy of Mathematics: Radical Constructivism Rehabilitated? (Unpublished) (2000)
6. Battista Michael: How Do Children Learn Mathematics? Research and Reform in Mathematics Education. Talk in Conference "Curriculum Wars: Alternative Approaches to Reading and Mathematics." Harvard University (1999)
7. Schoenfeld Alan H.: Making Mathematics Work for All Children: Issues of Standards, Testing, and Equity. Educational Researcher, Vol. 31, No. 1 (2002)
8. Piaget Jean and Rolando Garcia: Psychogenesis and the History of Sciences. Columbia University Press, New York (1980)
9. Piaget Jean and Evert Beth: Mathematical Epistemology and Psychology. D.Reidel Publishing Company, Dordrecht-Holland (1966)
10. Piaget Jean et. al.: Recherches sur la Généralisation. Presses Universitaires de France (1978)
11. Piaget Jean: L'équilibration des Structures Cognitives, Problème Central du Développement. Presses Universitaires de France (1975)
12. R. Bird and P. Wadler: Introduction to Functional Programming. Prentice-Hall (1988)
13. Back Ralph-Johan and von Wright Joakim: Structured Derivations: a Method for Doing High-School Mathematics Carefully. TUCS Technical Report No 246 (1999)
14. Viera K. Proulx: The Role of Computer Science and Discrete Mathematics in the High School Curriculum. DIMACS Series in Discrete mathematics and Theoretical Computer Science V.36 (1997)
15. Sylvia da Rosa and Gustavo Cirigliano: Matemática y Programación. Congreso Iberoamericano de Educación Superior en Computación (1998) (In Spanish)
16. Sylvia da Rosa and Gustavo Cirigliano: Ensayo sobre Matemática aplicada a Computación. Congreso Iberoamericano de Educación Superior en Computación (1999) (In Spanish)
17. Sylvia da Rosa: The Role of Discrete Mathematics and Programming in Education. Workshop: Functional and Declarative Programming in Education (2002)
18. Peter B. Henderson: Functional and Declarative Languages for Learning Discrete Mathematics. Workshop: Functional and Declarative Programming in Education (2002)
19. Rex L. Page: Software is Discrete Mathematics. ICFP'03 (2003)
20. Allen B.Tucker: Fundamentals of Computing I: Logic, Problem Solving, Programs and Computers. Mc Graw-Hill Series in Computer Science (1995)
21. H.Abelson, G.J. Sussman and J.Sussman: Structure and Interpretation of Computer Programs. The MIT Press (1996)
22. Cordelia Hall and John O'Donnell: Discrete Mathematics using a Computer. Springer Verlag (2000)
23. M.Felleisen, R.B.Findler,M.Flat and S.Krishnamurthi: How to Design Programs. An Introduction to Computing and Programming. The MIT Press (2003)
24. Pieter H. Hartel, Bert van Es, Dick Tromp: Basic Proof Skills of Computer Science Students. LNCS 1022 (1995)

Motivating Study of Formal Methods in the Classroom

Joy N. Reed[1] and Jane E. Sinclair[2]

[1] Armstrong Atlantic State University, Savannah Ga, US
jreed@armstrong.edu
[2] University of Warwick, Coventry, UK
jane@dcs.warwick.ac.uk

Abstract. One challenge to Formal Methods educators is the need to motivate students both to choose our courses and to continue studying them. In this paper we consider the question of motivation from two angles. Firstly, we provide small examples designed to overcome the "mental resistance" often found in typical students studying introductory formal methods courses. The examples illustrate advantages of a formal approach, and can be appreciated by both novice and experienced programmers. The second part of the paper considers the questions of motivation more generally and raises for debate a number of relevant issues.

1   Introduction

One of the problems encountered by Formal Methods educators is that of motivating students. Evidence emerging at the recent Teaching Formal Methods Workshop [D+03] suggests that Formal Methods modules are increasingly classed as optional and that attracting and retaining students on such modules is a significant problem. In contrast to those students who by studying an option have taken a positive decision to be there, students in core courses are locked into a subject about which they definitely need convincing. The difficulty of interesting students in Formal Methods is by no means new. In 1981 Dijkstra wrote in his foreword to Gries' book "The science of Programming" [Gri81]: "we get a glimpse of the educational challenge we are facing: besides teaching technicalities, we have to overcome the mental resistance always evoked when it is shown how the techniques of scientific thought can be fruitfully applied to a next area of endeavour". Nearly a quarter of a century later, the discipline of Formal Methods has evolved considerably, but the educational challenge appears to be as great as ever.

Authors of Formal Methods texts and papers often make assumptions about the most effective motivational approaches. Dijkstra emphasised the need for appropriate "choice and order of examples" as well as "the good taste with which the formalism is applied". Today it is perhaps more usual to see greater weight placed on factors such as suitable tool support and relevant industrial case studies. It is also suggested that the mathematical nature of the topic may

C.N. Dean and R.T. Boute (Eds.): TFM 2004, LNCS 3294, pp. 32–46, 2004.

be off-putting to students. All of the suggestions seem to be plausible, yet little seems to be known about the degree to which any of these factors actually influence students or whether our assumptions as to what motivates students are justified.

At the other end of the spectrum, the question of motivating and retaining students has been studied in general terms by educational researchers. This research has tended to focus on primary and secondary level education, with the assumption being made that students at a post-compulsory level are already highly motivated. But, particularly with increasing student numbers, the situation has changed. As noted by Race [Rac98, p47]: "When only a small fraction of the population entered Higher Education, it could more or less be taken for granted that students had a strong source of motivation, and would mostly succeed. Now, both drop-out and failure rates give cause for concern." The prospects for Formal Methods seem to be even more gloomy in that many students who tackle a range of challenging Computer Science courses seem reluctant to engage with Formal Methods.

Those of us who believe that Formal Methods are an important area to teach are faced with the challenge of attracting students onto our courses and then maintaining their interest. The harsh reality for optional courses is that failure to convert our own enthusiasm to numbers enrolled could jeopardise the existence of the course. Retention can be just as difficult as recruitment. If students find the subject too difficult, or if they are unable to see the benefit of using Formal Methods, other modules may beckon. There can be a tension between introducing and explaining enough of a method to support meaningful and convincing examples, and maintaining students' interest and concentration.

The first part of this paper looks at some small examples which we have found useful in the early stages of teaching Formal Methods. Both authors have been involved in Formal Methods education for many years and the examples presented here are a selection of ones which proved to be particularly interesting and inspirational to students. Whilst we might like to think that this is a result of our excellent teaching, these examples appear to be demonstrating areas which are fundamental in raising student awareness of the benefits of Formal Methods. We have observed that these small examples can be very beneficial in helping students to "overcome the mental resistance". Some examples (not necessarily novel, but ones which have stood the test of time) are presented together with consideration of the features which make them interesting. The examples we have chosen are all very simple to explain and can be readily understood by novice programmers. It is not suggested that such examples can be seen as solving the wider problem of motivation: issues such as scalability are not tackled at all and must be addressed if the topic is to be credible. However, we have found that such examples can be of real practical benefit, either as part of a general introduction or as students are starting to apply Formal Methods.

In pointing to the usefulness of such examples we are obviously agreeing with Dijkstra's view that choice of example is important. However, it can often be the case that examples carefully selected to introduce and extend knowledge of a particular topic can be mathematically very appropriate and yet fail to engage our students. For example, specifying a library system or a game may be a very useful vehicle for introducing a number of concepts in the method, but students may view it as being of little real benefit. The point is that while many excellent formal methods test books exist with beautiful examples which illustrate perfectly the topics they address, students can still feel dissatisfied and unconvinced. They like to see the subject applied in areas which allow them to do something necessary which they would not otherwise have done, or to enable them to do it better. A similar point is made by Boerger [Boe03] who stresses the motivational benefit of demonstrating how use of Formal Methods can reveal errors and omissions in real-life systems. This is certainly one aspect that students find convincing, but there are others too. These include the ability to write better, clearer code; the insight that a formal description can provide into the way a system works; the detection of errors at an earlier stage of development. Unfortunately, it can be difficult to provide real-life examples early on in a course when the need for motivation is greatest.

The examples of Section 2 are offered as a selection of useful introductory studies, with some brief comments on the points that they illustrate. The examples given are generally well-known, but we restate them as they are ones to which our students have responded particularly favourably. We relate these examples to the motivational aspects mentioned in the previous paragraph.

Readers may well have many examples of their own to offer which they have found to be particularly well-received. It has been suggested in the past that sharing educational resources such as project ideas, cases studies etc is extremely useful, and some useful sites, such as the Formal Methods Educational Resources page [FME] exist. A bank of specific examples endorsed by those who have tried and tested them could be a very useful addition.

The final section of this paper moves to a more general view of the position of Formal Methods in education and raises for discussion some of the broader issues affecting students' motivation and the study of Formal Methods.

2   Motivating with Examples

C.A.R. Hoare has observed that within every complex program is a simple one struggling to come out.[1] Novice programmers, and often experienced ones too, typically produce convoluted solutions to even simple programming tasks. Writing programs which are simple and elegant requires considerable skill. Also, recognising program constructions which are overly complex requires a comparable level of skill, sophistication, and maturity.

The first two examples below illustrate how a pre/post style of formal specification leads the programmer towards simple and elegant programming code. Each example shows good and bad styles: a naive approach compared to a disciplined one. In each case, the disciplined solution, derived from a formal speci-

---

[1] This has become known as Hoare's Law of Large Programs, with various related corollaries.

fication, is significantly superior. The formal specifications provide insight as to why simplicity and elegance goes hand-in-hand with clarity.

2.1   Example 1: Fibonacci Numbers

The nth Fibonacci number is typically defined:

$$F(n) = \begin{cases} 1 & \text{if } n = 0 \text{ or } n = 1 \\ F(n-2) + F(n-1) & \text{if } n \geq 2 \end{cases}$$

An obvious program strategy to calculate the nth Fibonacci number is to use a loop which calculates the kth Fibonacci by adding together the two previous ones. Let us first examine program P1 found in Figure 1. It is very typical of programs developed by students who write loops *before* formulating loop invariants. A pre/post style specification for $PRE \;\hat{=}\; n \geq 0$ and $POST \;\hat{=}\; fib = F(n)$ is

$$\{PRE\} \text{ P1 } \{POST\}$$

It would seem that the following predicate INV1 should be a natural invariant relationship for the while loop.

$$INV1 \;\hat{=}\; fib = F(k) \text{ and } fib_1 = F(k) \text{ and } fib_2 = F(k-1) \text{ and } 0 \leq k \leq n$$

However the predicate is not true initially, since the variable fib is not initialised until the first time through the loop. Thus the invariant must be expressed with the more complex and less pleasing, predicate $INV2$:

$$INV2 \;\hat{=}\; k > 1 \Rightarrow$$
$$fib = F(k) \text{ and } fib_1 = F(k) \text{ and } fib_2 = F(k-1) \text{ and } 0 \leq k \leq n$$

Now let us take another approach and derive the program from its specification, by formulating the invariant before writing the loop. We observe that for $GUARD \;\hat{=}\; k < n$, we have

$$INV1 \text{ and } \neg\ GUARD \Rightarrow POST$$

which strongly suggests that there is a strategy based on the simpler invariant $INV1$. Clearly, we want to initialise the variables in such a way that they immediately satisfy the invariant. By doing so, we are able to handle the boundary conditions seamlessly as part of the loop operations, and hence, the surrounding if-else construct is not required.

If we define $F(-1) = 0$, it follows that the statements labelled initVars in the program P2 of Figure 1 satisfy the loop invariant $INV1$. Thus we can establish the desired postcondition with the simpler and more satisfying program P2. By judiciously initialising all the variables to satisfy the invariant immediately, not only do we benefit from a simpler invariant but we happily have omitted an unnecessary level of nesting. For $n = 0$ or $n = 1$, P2 does cost 3 more

```
P1:  if n < 2                          P2:  fib := 1;  fib₁ := 1;
        fib := 1;                           fib₂ := 0;   k := 0;
     else                                   while k < n
        fib₁ := 1;  fib₂ := 1;  k := 1;        fib := fib₁ + fib₂;
        while k < n                            fib₂ := fib₁;
           fib := fib₁ + fib₂;                 fib₁ := fib;
           fib₂ := fib₁;                       k := k + 1;
           fib₁ := fib;                     end;
           k := k + 1;
        end;
     end;
```

Fig. 1. Two programs to compute the nth Fibonacci number

assignment operations to initialise the unused variables, rendering it three times less efficient. But for all other values of n, P2 is more efficient than P1 because of the boolean evaluation in P1 in its if-else statement.

Lesson Learned: Constructing specifications and invariants before writing code produces simpler and more efficient programs.

2.2 Example 2: Integer Division

The while construct is equivalent to an if construct conjoined with itself:

while B *stmt*; ≡ **if** B *stmt* **while** B *stmt*;

Thus it is often the case that constructs containing one of if-else and while embedded in the other can be flattened. We illustrate with two programs to compute $a \bmod b^2$.

For integers a and b with $b > 0$, the *mod* relation is defined:

$$a \bmod b = r \Leftrightarrow \exists q : int \mid a = q * b + r \text{ and } 0 \le r < b$$

Consider the program P3 of Figure 2 (originally suggested by an experienced programmer) which uses the strategy of iteratively adding b to a (if $a < 0$)or subtracting b from a (if $a \ge 0$)until t he remainder r gets bounded by 0 and b. The appropriate invariant for the loop in P3 is the rather cumbersome

$(((r \ge 0) \text{ and } (delta = -b) \text{ and } (delta < 0))$
      $\text{or } ((r < 0) \text{ and } (delta = b) \text{ and } (delta > 0))) \text{ and}$
$\exists q : integer \mid a = q * b + r$

Experience tells us that the invariant need not be so complicated, which is comforting since the above would quite drive students to their daydreams. Re-examining the definition and splitting the constraint on r into two, we have

$$a \bmod b = r \Leftrightarrow \exists q : int \mid a = q * b + r \text{ and } 0 \le r \text{ and } r < b$$

[2] Professor Richard Bird of Oxford University first pointed out this example to the authors several years ago.

By breaking the above relationship into a natural invariant and now two guards, it clearly follows that the invariant and the negation of the guards imply our desired postcondition. That is

$$INV \text{ and } \neg\, GUARD1 \text{ and } \neg\, GUARD2 \Rightarrow POST$$

for

INV: $\exists\, q : integer \mid a = q * b + r$
GUARD1: $r < 0$
GUARD2: $r \geq b$
POST: $\exists\, q : integer \mid a = q * b + r \text{ and } 0 \leq r < b$

Now the programmer is led to

```
{b > 0}
r := a;
{INV}
while r < 0
    r := r + b;
{INV and 0 ≤ r}
while r ≥ b
    r := r − b;
{INV and 0 ≤ r and r < b}
{POST}
```

Comparing the two programs in Figure 2, we see that P3 and P4 are comparable in efficiency, yet P4 is more elegant and simpler to understand because by design it is simpler to reason about.

```
P3:  r := a;                 P4:  r := a;
     if r ≥ 0                      while r < 0
         delta := −b;                  r := r + b;
     else                         while r ≥ b
         delta := b;                   r := r − b;
     while ¬ (0 ≤ r < b)
         r := r + delta;
```

Fig. 2. Two programs to compute $a \bmod b$

Lesson Learned: (Yet again.) Constructing specifications and invariants before writing code produces simpler and more efficient programs.

A *while* statement incorporates some *if − else* semantics, and this can sometimes remove the need for other nested *if − else* statements.

2.3   Example 3: Invariants and Understanding

Sometimes even small programs can be difficult to understand. The formal statements necessary to verify a piece of code can allow us not only to prove it correct but also to explain and illuminate the way in which the program works and what it achieves.

Gries [Gri81, p142] gives an example of a small but difficult to understand program. Another algorithm which similarly makes perfect sense when considered in its own right but may be confusing if an implementation is seen without explanation, is Knuth's SX method [Knu69, p399][3]. A program for this is given in Figure 3.

```
a := A;  b := B;  c := 1;                    (B ≥ 0)
while b ≠ 0
        while b mod 2 ≠ 0
            a := a * a;
            b := b div 2
    end;
    b := b − 1;
    c := c * a
end
```

Fig. 3. A mystery program

Even students experienced in programming find it hard to see what this program is intended to do. It can be presented as an exercise in code maintenance in which the students are trying to find where a bug has occurred in some existing software. Some students will come up with an answer but find it difficult to convince others that it is correct.

Suppose that documentation is "found" which states that the code sets c to A^B. Again, testing various values may lead to a belief that it *is* doing this, but how can we be sure for all values? However, the situation changes dramatically if the documenter has left us the key to the puzzle in the form of an invariant: $a^b * c = A^B$. The idea of an invariant can be discussed: what it is and how, if this property really is invariant, it can be used in conjunction with the guard to show that the stated result is established. The process of showing that the property really is invariant helps explain how the algorithm is working. The idea of using a variant function to show termination can also be introduced. Even with the discussion at a fairly informal level, the use of the invariant provides the way in to understanding what is going on.

Lesson Learned: Even a small program using simple constructs can be very difficult to understand. Knowing what a program is supposed to do may not give

---

[3] Thanks to the anonymous reviewer who pointed out this reference.

us much insight into how to establish whether or not it really does achieve its goal. The use of formal statements (in particular, invariants) can both illuminate the working of the code and allow us to prove it correct.

2.4   Example 4: The Needham-Schroeder Protocol

Students like to see relevant, real-life examples where using Formal Methods can help us do things we would otherwise find very difficult, or where the result is clearly better with the use of Formal Methods. However, to use such examples early on in a course they must be easy to explain. The Needham-Schroeder security protocol has been analysed by Lowe [Low96] demonstrating clearly how a seemingly innocent 3-line authentication protocol can be shown to be prone to attack. The protocol had existed for many years before formal analysis detected possible flaws. The example can be used with a specific method, such as a process algebra, or can be described in general terms as another introductory study.

The relevant part of the protocol can be simply described in 3 lines. It is intended to provide mutual authentication between two parties (A and B say) who wish to communicate. The sequence of exchanges in Figure 4, labelled $NS1$ to $NS3$, describes the protocol.

$$
\begin{array}{lll}
NS1: & A \rightarrow B: & \{N_A, A\}_{K_B} \\
NS2: & B \rightarrow A: & \{N_A, N_B\}_{K_A} \\
NS3: & A \rightarrow B: & \{N_B\}_{K_B}
\end{array}
$$

Fig. 4. The Needham-Schroeder authentication protocol

In the first step, A sends to B a message containing A's nonce and identity. This is encrypted using B's public key (indicated by the bracketed terms subscripted with K_A). B's reply in message 2 sends back A's nonce and flags B's own identity encrypted with A's public key. The final confirmation from A sends back B's nonce, encrypted for B.

The way the protocol works can be discussed (and enacted) by the students. Issues such as the way authentication is achieved and the use of public key cryptography are generally well-received, and the protocol is seen to be performing a useful task. The protocol is so simple that it is easy to believe that we understand it fully. A counter-example such as that given in Figure 5 comes as a surprise.

Here, I is a user within the system, but is prepared to subvert the system if possible (for example, a user of an on-line bank who has their own legitimate communications with the bank but who should not be allowed access to other peoples' accounts). The notation I_A indicates user I pretending to be A. The figure shows two interleaved runs of the protocol: the one on the left is A communicating with I. The one on the right shows I_A running the protocol with B.

$NS1:$	$A \rightarrow I:$	$\{N_A, A\}_{K_I}$

$NS1':$	$I_A \rightarrow B:$	$\{N_A, A\}_{K_B}$
$NS2':$	$B \rightarrow: I_A$	$\{N_A, N_B\}_{K_A}$

$NS2:$	$I \rightarrow A:$	$\{N_A, N_B\}_{K_A}$
$NS3:$	$A \rightarrow I:$	$\{N_B\}_{K_I}$

$NS3':$	$I_A \rightarrow B:$	$\{N_B\}_{K_B}$

Fig. 5. Breaking the Needham-Schroeder authentication protocol

I reuses the nonce sent by A and sends it to B. The crucial step is that I can obtain B's reply and send it to A to be decrypted. The protocol concludes with B believing they are talking to A, and hence authentication has failed.

Again, this example can be used at an introductory stage and described in an informal way. It can also be shown in a formal notation, such as CSP [Hoa85]. In this case, the FDR tool [For] and interface Casper [Low98] can be used to show how security properties may be checked automatically. The output gives a trace of counter-examples found.

Lesson Learned: This is another small example, and one which is recognised as being useful and relevant. Despite the size, it is very difficult to spot possible flaws. The use of formal analysis finds errors which were not previously detected. The subject area is also one in which such errors are potentially very serious. Tool support has been essential in this work.

2.5 Example 5: A Development Through to Code

A specification which can be verified and refined down to code shows how Formal Methods can be incorporated into the development process. Doing this by hand shows what is being done but is laborious and unconvincing for students as a viable approach. A small example which can be developed, refined and implemented with the aid of tool support shows how the different aspects of the process fit together. To do this, we have used the B method [Abr96], supported by the B-Toolkit [BTo] (also supported by Atelier B [Ate]). A small, easily-understood specification can be investigated using the tool's animation and proof facilities. Deficiencies can be spotted and corrected at this level. Refinement steps can be added and verified, with code generated automatically once all constructs are implementable.

To use the tools effectively requires understanding of the underlying method. It would be misleading to represent the tools as a substitute for this. However, a small introductory, start-to-finish example can motivate the different areas to be studied and demonstrate what we are aiming at. A specific example has not been included in this section as it would take a good deal of space to work through. Also, the important point here is not so much the specific example, but the ability of a tool to support a full development. Suitable examples for the B method can be found in the literature (for example, Schneider's text book [Sch01] is an excellent source of material), at various course websites, or from the tool developers.

Lesson Learned: Formal Methods can be used throughout the development process. Effective tool support exists. Errors can be detected at the specification level.

3 Discussion

The previous section has suggested some examples which have been found to engage and interest students and to motivate them in the study of Formal Methods. Used in conjunction with other approaches, such as linking to realistic industrial examples, integrating with other areas of the syllabus, use of appropriate tool support and an awareness of the need for good teaching, the effect in terms of student engagement and interest is seen to be positive. However, despite these efforts the position appears to be that in many places courses are dwindling. A survey conducted at the Teaching Formal Methods Workshop [D+03] showed that many courses were running with very small numbers. Our attempts to motivate students through teaching are useless if the students do not enrol in the first place.

One of the main reasons often cited for lack of participation is "maths phobia". Students who are weak in mathematics may assume (however the course is pitched) that it will be too hard for them. Students with a poor mathematical background certainly challenge the course designer. There is also the suggestion that, within the UK at least, the situation is becoming worse. Finney [Fin03] cites a 20% fall in the number of students taking mathematics at A level in 2003. This, combined with an increase in recent years to many universities' allocation of Computer Science students, means it is likely that students with less mathematical preparation will be accepted.

Although the maths problem presents a challenge for Formal Methods education, it would be wrong to focus on this as the sole reason for the low numbers. Some Computer Science degrees have A level maths as an entry requirement, and may even demand an A grade. The degree program itself can also include further mathematics-based courses which present little difficulty for the majority of students. Yet even within this population of students with a proven capability for mathematical subjects, the resistance to Formal Methods can be quite high. Students who quite happily deal with abstraction in many other areas can seem unwilling to engage in formal program development.

Perhaps one problem here is a prevailing culture of wanting to achieve quick results. For example, the use of agile program methodologies such as XP [Bec99] has proved very popular with students who now often cite this as their project development methodology. Some authors (such as Baumeister [Bau02] and Herranz and Moreno-Navarro [AHMN]) have suggested that agile programming and Formal Methods are not so contrary as they may at first appear and that a combination of the two might be achieved, with formal specification used in the role of the test. This may be so, but unfortunately students who claim to be using an agile methodology are often not following the structure of that methodology but using it as a convenient justification for hacking. This is not the fault of the methodology, but shows the eagerness of students to legitimise a way of working which they like and with which they are familiar.

Many students encountering Formal Methods for the first time have already been involved with programming, either through their own exploration or via an introductory course. The use of Formal Methods challenges them to work in a new way. Using Formal Methods is generally not part of students' expectation, who often see the subject in quite a different way. Changing students' view of what the subject is about and their idea of what they could and should be studying may prove difficult. If their view is shaped by the public face of the computing industry, it may be somewhat limited. Of course, this is part of what going to university should be about. Again, the traditional image of a student is of someone with a passionate interest for the subject they are studying: someone who is interested in the pursuit of knowledge and who is able to appreciate the beauty of their subject. The elegance of Formal Methods has often been noted (cf: "Beauty is our business" [FvGGM90,Int]). It is a source of great disappointment to realise that one's students are not impressed!

Perhaps it is naive to picture students as thirsting after knowledge and beauty in this way. Bleakley suggests that the education system itself is much to blame for the lack of passion and excitement: "As it follows the lead of the training culture, Higher Education is about 'earning a living' rather than 'learning a living'." [Ble98, p167]. He suggests that: "we have systematically rationalised away aesthetic in motivation and learning, plucking the heart of beauty from the chest of education" [Ble98, p171]. Given his general mistrust of the "information age", Bleakley might well feel that Computer Science is a major offender in this respect. It is not unreasonable to suppose that a subject in which students are narrowly focused on marketable skills would find it more difficult to provide motivation for the study of other topics.

It may be true that Higher Education itself is promoting such a climate, but it is also the case that students bring their own perspectives. For Computer Science students in particular there seems to be evidence to suggest that students are very much driven by external factors. In the UK, applications to study Computer Science have dropped sharply in the last two years. UCAS figures [UCA] suggest a more than 10 % fall in home student applications from 2002 to 2003 (with a decline in overseas students bringing this down further). Discussion with admissions tutors suggests that applications are down by a further 20% or more for 2004. This large downturn is generally blamed on the declining fortunes of the jobs market. If this is so it seems to indicate that many students in Computer Science are driven as much by employment prospects as by their interest in the subject. It perhaps contrasts with some other subjects in which a direct link to the employment market is not so apparent.

The previous considerations might lead us to suppose that the best way to provide motivation would be to parade as many highly-paid Formal Methods professionals as possible before university and school students. This might well help! This type of extrinsic motivation ("needing to know") is identified by educational researchers such as Race [Rac94] and distinguished from intrinsic motivation ("wanting to know"). Race argues that: "an increased proportion of students do not have an autonomous 'want' to learn, ... and we are not always able to substitute a strong enough 'need' to learn" [Rac98, p47]. Both of these elements can, separately or (better still) together, lead to successful learning. Conversely, a general decrease in intrinsic motivation coupled with a lack of perceived usefulness and "need to know" in a subject is the worst scenario.

How to tackle the problems is a difficult issue. If intrinsic motivation really is decreasing, how can we combat it? If the image of Formal Methods is not convincing, how can we change it? Is Race's notion of substituting "need to know" for "want to know" appropriate or possible? Race's suggestions are aimed at improving teaching methods and support for learning in general - a strategy which encourages students by helping them to learn more effectively. It certainly seems a good general principle to ensure that we are not demotivating students. We should care about all-round good teaching. We might check that any perceptions of a Formal Methods course being harder are not needlessly correct. For example, that the effort required to do well on coursework is not out of line with other courses or that our exam marks averages are not off-puttingly low. For lecturers who resist such "relativist" thinking, these suggestions may be worrying.

An alternative approach would be to abandon the idea of making Formal Methods more popular and to allow it to develop an exclusive nature. The effect might even be to increase interest along the lines of an exclusive club, although currently the club could be viewed as exclusive but membership is not generally sought-after. The suggestion is not as flippant as it might appear. If Formal Methods really are difficult to master and lacking in general appeal, are we wrong to try to engage many students in studying them? Our attempts at making the subject accessible may in any case backfire. Boute [Bou03] warns of the dangers of trying to gloss over the difficulties and make formal techniques more palatable:

> Lightweight formal methods may help illustrating abstract concepts and lowering the threshold for the study of mathematics relevant to software engineering. However, using them without adequate mathematical background or as a substitute for more serious mathematics is dangerously misleading, both in actual applications and in education, because the results will always remain below the expectations and hence possibly even discredit formal methods in general.

The need to integrate Formal Methods into the rest of the curriculum has often been stated as the ideal way forward. Wing [Win00] sets out some ways in which this could be done, allowing concepts to be introduced and developed across many modules with the outcome that students learn Formal Methods without thinking that they are doing anything special or different. This is a lovely idea, but begs a number of questions.

The barriers to progress with this plan are high. Wing notes the difficulty of persuading colleagues to adopt this approach (to the problem of motivating students we add the problem of motivating staff). This really is a huge obstacle.

Boute [Bou03] suggests that the need to re-work courses would be off-putting to colleagues. This is certainly true, but the problems are surely more fundamental. Many (probably most) staff would not believe that Formal Methods should play such a central role in the curriculum. This is more than just a problem: it is a death blow. Further, many pressures on the curriculum and constraints on the syllabus are forced on us by external factors. Large increases in student intake such as those occurring in the UK in recent years make an enormous difference to the student base in terms of ability and expectation. Requirements to attract more students; to decrease the length of programs; to incorporate a range of mandatory skills and subjects teaching; worsening staff-student ratios: these and other factors all affect the position. Obviously, the plan to integrate Formal Methods across the curriculum is an ideal, and small steps made by forging links with other courses could make a difference. But perhaps we should ask how far this can take us.

Here, as often is the case, we are talking about *the* curriculum, but there are of course many curricula involving Computer Science. There are a few theoretically-oriented courses which may already involve a good deal of Formal Methods, and at the other end of the spectrum there are degrees (and other qualifications) which are either more broadly based or are specialised in another area and which cover a bare minimum of Formal Methods (perhaps just enough to satisfy the relevant curriculum guidelines, such as BCS or IEEE). Perhaps we have more of a chance of influencing the former type of program where we already have a foothold. But the question under consideration (as for example by Wing) seems to be the more ambitious one of trying to make Formal Methods an integrated part of the curriculum for all Computer Scientists. In many departments, a "streams" approach is being adopted, in which there is a basic core of subjects, with different options and different routes providing a specialised named degree. It is interesting to consider the effect that this might have. On the one hand, integrating Formal Methods into a core course would reach a wide range of students and could have a large impact. On the other hand, the effect might be to marginalise Formal Methods further, particularly if resistance to Formal Methods keeps them out of the large core courses.

Finally on this point, it might also be an interesting thought-experiment to wonder what would happen if the necessary tools, expertise and will did exist to carry out the plan. It seems highly unlikely that this could happen in isolation to the rest of the world, but if it could, how would students react? How achievable is Wing's idea that computer scientists should "use formal methods without even thinking about it"?

Whilst thinking about the issues involved in motivating the study of Formal Methods, some striking parallels have emerged between this and another rather different area of concern: that of recruiting women on to Computer Science courses. This is obviously a big topic in itself and one that we will not attempt to discuss here, but some of the on-going debates in that area are strangely similar to ours. Recruitment and retention is a problem. One of the major off-putting factors for women is often cited to be the mathematical nature of the subject. Yet there seems to be little real evidence for this. Various suggestions for attracting more students seem similar: the idea of providing realistic examples; the suggestion of linking to other areas of study; the need for good teaching in general. A few initiatives to attract more women to the study of computer science have had success, the most notable being at Carnegie Mellon University [MF02]. However, there is a worrying record of projects set up to improve recruitment of women which have failed to make any difference to the situation. These projects were based on very plausible assumptions about what would motivate women to study computer science; ideas which seemed to be reflected in survey findings. And yet, despite considerable effort on the part of those involved, the initiatives made no difference in terms of recruitment.

Perhaps the similarities should not be pressed too far, but we might introduce a note of caution in our plans. We are eager to attract more students; our ideas seem plausible, but will they have the desired effect? Wing ends her paper by stating: "The main thing is to start doing something." [Win00] We would by no means urge inaction, but would add the need to have clear objectives in mind; to base our plan as far as possible on research and observation; and to monitor the effect of any changes we make. It may even be the case that some of the Social Science research methods used for Educational Research (for example, Action Research [CMM02]), though very different from our usual research methods, might be of use in this respect.

References

[Abr96]   J.-R. Abrial. *The B-Book*. Cambridge University Press, 1996.

[AHMN]   Ángel Herranz and José Moreno-Navarro. Formal extreme (and extremely formal) programming.
           Available at: babel.ls.fi.upm.es/publications/finalcopy-xp03.pdf.

[Ate]   Atelier B. http://www.atelierb.societe.com/.

[Bau02]   Hubert Baumeister. Formal methods and extreme programming. In *Workshop on Evolutionary Formal Software Development*, Copenhagen, Denmark, 2002. Available at: www.pst.informatik.uni-muenchen.de/~baumeist/publications/efsd02.pdf.

[Bec99]   Kent Beck. *Extreme Programming Explained*. Addison-Wesley, 1999.

[Ble98]   Alan Bleakley. Learning as an aesthetic practice: motivation through beauty in Higher Education. In Sally Brown, Steve Armstrong, and Gail Thompson, editors, *Motivating Students*, Staff and Educational Development Series, pages 165–172. Kogan Page, 1998.

[Boe03]   Egon Boerger. Teaching ASMs to practice-oriented students with limited mathematical background. In David Duce et al., editors, *Teaching Formal Methods 2003*, Oxford Brookes University, 2003. Available at: http://wwwcms.brookes.ac.uk/tfm2003/.

[Bou03]   Raymond Boute. Can lightweight formal methods carry the weight? In David Duce et al., editors, *Teaching Formal Methods 2003*, Oxford Brookes University, 2003. Available at: http://wwwcms.brookes.ac.uk/tfm2003/.

[BTo]   Btoolkit. b-Core(UK) Ltd. http://www.b-core.com/.

[CMM02]   Louis Cohen, Lawrence Manion, and Keith Morrison. *Research Methods in Education*. RoutledgeFalmer, 5 edition, 2002.

[D⁺03]   David Duce et al., editors. *Teaching Formal Methods 2003*, Oxford Brookes University, 2003. Available at: http://wwwcms.brookes.ac.uk/tfm2003/.

[Fin03]   Kate Finney. Hello class - let me introduce you to Mr. Six. In David Duce et al., editors, *Teaching Formal Methods 2003*, Oxford Brookes University, 2003. Available at: http://wwwcms.brookes.ac.uk/tfm2003/.

[FME]   Formal methods education resources. http://www.cs.indiana.edu/formal-methods-education/.

[For]   Formal Systems (Europe) Ltd. *Failures Divergence Refinement*. User Manual and Tutorial. Available at: http://www.formal.demon.co.uk/fdr2manual/index.html.

[FvGGM90]   W.H.J. Feijen, A.G.M. van Gasteren, D. Gries, and J. Misra, editors. *Beauty is our business: a birthday salute to Edsger W. Dijkstra*. Springer-Verlag, 1990.

[Gri81]   David Gries. *The Science of Programming*. Springer-Verlag, 1981.

[Hoa85]   C.A.R. Hoare. *Communicating Sequential Processes*. Prentice Hall, 1985.

[Int]   Beauty is our business. http://c2.com/cgi/wiki?BeautyIsOurBusiness.

[Knu69]   Donald E. Knuth. *Fundamental Algorithms*, volume 2. Addison-Wesley, 1969.

[Low96]   G. Lowe. Breaking and fixing the Needham-Schroeder public-key protocol using FDR. In *Proceedings of TACAS*, volume 1055 of *Lecture Notes in Computer Science*. Springer, 1996.

[Low98]   Gavin Lowe. Casper: A compiler for the analysis of security protocols. *Journal of Computer Security*, 6:53–94, 1998.

[MF02]   Jane Margolis and Allan Fisher. *Unlocking the Clubhouse: Women in Computing*. MIT Press, 2002.

[Rac94]   Phil Race. *The Open Learning Handbook*. Kogan Page, 2nd edition, 1994.

[Rac98]   Phil Race. Teaching: creating a thirst for learning? In Sally Brown, Steve Armstrong, and Gail Thompson, editors, *Motivating Students*, Staff and Educational Development Series, pages 47–57. Kogan Page, 1998.

[Sch01]   Steve Schneider. *The B-Method: an introduction*. Cornerstones of computing. Palgrave, 2001.

[UCA]   UCAS. UK Universities and Colleges Admissions Service. http://www.ucas.ac.uk/.

[Win00]   Jeanette Wing. Weaving formal methods into the undergraduate curriculum. In *Proceedings of the 8th International Conference on Algebraic Methodology and Software Technology*, volume 1816 of *Lecture Notes in Computer Science*. Springer, 2000. Available at: www.cs.utexas.edu/users/csed/FM/docs/Wing-abstract.pdf.

Formal Systems, Not Methods

Martin Loomes, Bruce Christianson, and Neil Davey

University of Hertfordshire, Hatfield, Herts AL10 9AB, UK,
m.j.loomes@herts.ac.uk

Abstract. In this paper we will present an approach for teaching formalisms to Computer Science undergraduate students that has been developed over the past 23 years at the University of Hertfordshire (formerly Hatfield Polytechnic). We discuss the background and the evolution of the approach, the theoretical underpinning, the political motivation and some of the pedagogic issues that arise. Examples of the ways in which the generic approach has been specialised for different classes of students are discussed, and some of the implications for other curriculum areas that typically accompany these courses will be briefly mentioned.

1 Background

The approach we take at Hertfordshire to teaching formalisms[1] and their use was novel 23 years ago, and has stood the test of time remarkably well. In 1982, a very deliberate decision was taken to include them in our curriculum and at that time we considered very carefully what we were trying to achieve, and took the decision that we should apply the same rigorous processes to our curriculum design as we encourage for our students in their software design: tinkering with the curriculum is just as much "hacking" as making similar alterations to code. It is important, therefore, that we start the story with an explanation of the ways in which our shared understanding of the curriculum issues, specification, design and implementation began, so that the reader can understand the rationale as well as the result. Of course, condensing 23 years of development into a short paper inevitably means a polished post-rationalisation (like a published proof) rather than the more informative and interesting narrative that shadows the actual processes involved. A much more systematic and detailed discussion of the approach and its implications for whole curriculum issues was published by one of the authors in 1991[10].

1.1 Educating Industrialists

Computer Science at Hatfield Polytechnic started formally in 1964 with our first degree programme. Like many such developments, our department evolved out of a mathematics department, and hence there was always a mathematical component in our degree programmes. This was approached as "applied maths", where

---

[1] We tend to avoid the term *formal methods* for reasons which will become apparent as the paper proceeds: exactly what we mean by *formalisms* will also emerge.

C.N. Dean and R.T. Boute (Eds.): TFM 2004, LNCS 3294, pp. 47–64, 2004.

students were taught a useful toolkit of techniques such as calculus, statistics and algebra, in case they stumbled across a use for them at some later stage.

In 1982, however, we were approached by a local company, STC-IDEC[2] who wanted an education programme developed for experienced software engineers, which would consolidate their many years of experience and provide long-term benefits. The company specifically did *not* want a training programme aimed at meeting short-term training needs in transient methods and techniques. The company had come to this view after embarking on a VDM course, where they realised that the elapsed time needed to understand such material is longer than usually associated with training courses of this nature and also training engineers in the use of such "methods" is problematic unless they will return immediately into an environment where they will utilise the material in a supportive culture. The company was already broadly committed to exploring mathematically-based development methods, based on some past successes, and was prepared to invest in an holistic way in this education programme, rather than relegating such developments to "project specific training" as is often the case. This enlightened view echoed the sentiments expressed by Mills:

"There is a real danger in over using soft topics and survey courses loaded with buzz words to provide near-term job saleability. But without adequate technical foundations people will become dead-ended in mid-career, just when they are expected to solve harder problems as individuals, as members or as managers, of teams." [11, page 1161]

We should stress, however, that we considered "soft topics" and "buzz words" rather more broadly than some others at the time. We interpreted terms such as "formal methods" and specific formalisms, such as "VDM" as soft topics and buzz words in some contexts, just as much as some of the more people-oriented areas typically associated with the term "soft". This theme is developed later in the paper.

Consideration of this issue alerted us to a potential tactical error on the part of educators: attempting to change the curriculum to "meet the needs of industry" without analysis deeper than soft topics and buzz words. When institutions attempt to adapt to changes in demand as quickly as possible, by changing teaching vehicles including programming languages, design methods, architectures and formalisms, they lose the stability usually associated (historically?) with the educational system. As Kozmetsky has observed, however, this may not be the best tactic. What is actually required is that the *student* can adapt, rather than the institution. If we can educate students so that they can adapt quickly in a world of constant change then the institutions can manage to adapt more slowly, thus maintaining their stability [9, page 152]. We therefore saw the challenge as finding a curriculum approach which would not require us to change from VDM to Z to OBJ to CLEAR, Larch, OBJX, CCS, CSP and so

---

[2] The company changed its name several times during the course of the developments, but we will use this one name for simplicity.

on, following "flavours of the month" as they appeared, without good pedagogic reasons.

STC-IDEC had already formulated an initial proposal for the course content, but was prepared to discuss their requirements with us, and also to fully fund development costs for the programme. This latter point was crucial, as it offered the opportunity for the Polytechnic to carry out curriculum design on a scale that would not have been possible otherwise, and also to suggest curriculum approaches in the knowledge that funding would be available for the necessary staff development. This allowed us to recognise and acknowledge the true difficulty of the task, without the complication of attempting to market a product cheaply on the basis that we already had the skills to deliver the curriculum. We did, of course, have the generic knowledge and skills to support teaching such a curriculum, but we were able to interpret these in a completely new way, rather than being forced to undertake purely incremental design. We were also able to form a development team, and to have deep discussions about our curriculum before arbitrary module boundaries were imposed. This should be contrasted with the environment in many institutions attempting to introduce formal methods into their curriculum at a similar time, where one or two evangelistic individuals were seeking to persuade colleagues to embrace the approach with no available resources for real development. Moreover, these individuals were often forced to justify the introduction of formal methods into whatever subject area they happened to be teaching (typically mathematics, programming or systems analysis) and at a variety of levels from introductory undergraduate to specialist postgraduate modules.

The development at Hatfield took another novel approach, when it established three "competing" subgroups within the development team, working on three different approaches to the design[3]:

Group 1 took as its starting point the company's proposal and attempted to develop this into a coherent educational programme that we could deliver.

Group 2 attempted an incremental development based on existing provision, effectively asking what the Polytechnic could offer based on current skills and curriculum structures.

Group 3 took a radical approach, taking a paper by Boute [3] which proposed some fundamental theoretical and formal ideas for the Telecommunications Industry as the point of departure.

This "Boute Group" made some radical curriculum proposals which captured the imagination of the Department, persuading senior managers to adopt the approach in spite of the risks and resource implications. Amongst the specific proposals made were:

- The application of fundamental concepts to produce systematic approaches to problem-solving was more important than *ad hoc* application of specific methods.

---

[3] Once again, a luxury that was only possible because of the nature of the funding.

- Tools and techniques should be studied as arising from this context, not implanted into practice *per se*.
- Many ideas are present at several different levels of activity, and should be viewed in a generic context. For example, "specification", and "proof of correctness" can be applied to any transformation process including program design, language implementation, program coding, system architecture, etc. These concepts and associated tools should be taught once and applied in different settings.
- In general, system designers need to operate in two domains for a given task: a world where the problem resides (populated by application specific objects and concepts including people) and a world where the resulting solution resides (typically including computing objects such as data types, languages etc.). Consideration of these two domains should be reflected explicitly in the curriculum.

It is important to note that this development took a very "theoretical" twist, with the curriculum development group exploring areas such as category theory and abstract algebra in order to refine our ideas of curriculum structure (not just content), but at every stage we were forced to explain and defend our ideas to a group of very well-informed and experienced software engineers. It also resulted in a curriculum that bore no resemblance to any seen before: there were no "programming", "SAD" or " architecture" modules. Indicative of the modules produced are the following:

- Theories and Formalisms
- Types and State
- Communicating Systems
- Performance and Reliability
- Fitness for Purpose

Moreover, it became obvious that teaching this material would require staff to sit in on each other's material, so that the narrative structure would develop corporately within the new framework, and the individual members of staff delivering the curriculum could not seek refuge in conventional ways of teaching the subject. Fortunately, the company was prepared to accept the costs inherent in this approach, and the Department identified so many benefits that it was prepared to support the venture, in spite of the risks involved.

Why was this initiative so important for the development of "formal methods" teaching at Hatfield? The simple answer is that it allowed us the resources and environment to reflect and consider cultural, intellectual, practical and pedagogic issues in an holistic way. We were thus able to build on a shared understanding, with many people able to contribute to discussions. There were, of course, disagreements, but these were grounded in a shared understanding of a broad range of issues. It also gave us considerable confidence: we were not being forced to defend "formal methods" to fellow academics who insisted that they were not relevant in the real world, rather we were being encouraged by very experienced practitioners to consider not just one "method" but the whole approach of using theoretical and formal ideas in practical design settings. A detailed description and evaluation of this curriculum was published in 1986 [7].

1.2 The Undergraduate Curriculum – 1982

Alongside this development, the Department undertook a fundamental review of its undergraduate curriculum. There had always been a mathematics component in the Computer Science curriculum, but this had historically been seen as "applied mathematics", developing skills in techniques that could potentially be useful for Computer Scientists. These skills included statistics as applied to areas such as performance analysis, geometry for graphics and calculus for numerical analysis. Two major failings were observed with this approach. First, students struggled to reach levels of competence where they could really use these techniques safely. Second, students were not really motivated until they started studying the areas where the mathematics was applied, by which time they had forgotten many of the skills and they had to be re-taught. This problem was made worse by the selection of topics that were traditionally judged "entry-level" in a mathematics curriculum, rather than those that relate immediately to Computer Science topics being studied at the time.

The decision was therefore taken to embrace "formalisms" within the degree revisions, but to do so in ways that were more fundamental than "applied maths". Inspired by our work with STC-IDEC we decided to avoid any suggestion that we were teaching applied mathematics and to present formality as a naturally-arising property of computer science. In particular, we did not want to teach "formal methods" because, in our view, a method must be a method for *doing something* – disembodied methods are problematic – and we were wary of restricting formalisms in students' minds to specific activities such as the specification of software.

Our vision was to create an environment where formalisms were used by students in various areas, and students were taught the generic skills and sufficient understanding to support these activities. The key, we believed, was to educate students in such a way that they were able to appreciate high-level processes such as formalisation, abstraction and proof, and also to develop confidence and fluency in symbolic manipulation without binding these skills too tightly to specific notations and application domains. It seemed to us that this re-use was not being exploited in traditional approaches, where, for example, "logic" might be taught and used in programming, computer architecture, software engineering and AI courses, but little effort was made to explain to students exactly what *a logic* meant. Similarly, students encountered various things called *algebras*, but were left to their own devices when trying to generalise from Boolean algebra, relational algebra and algebras for concurrency to some understanding of what constitutes an algebra. One interesting observation we made at the time was that we were addressing some of the fundamental roots of mathematics itself, and even those students with a sound background in mathematics had little experience of such issues. Such topics were usually deemed "advanced" in a mathematics curriculum, and were not normally selected in the applied-mathematics approach.

This was actually a benefit in many ways, as it overcame the problem inherent in the applied mathematics approach where students with weaker backgrounds always felt disadvantaged.

In exploring the feasibility of adopting such an approach, several areas of educational philosophy had to be addressed explicitly, giving rise to heated debates such as:

- Does it really make sense to partition the curriculum in traditional ways? Why do we want small chunks called "courses" or "modules"? Is this simply a convenience for assessment, timetabling, resourcing etc., or are such divisions actually significant for a discipline? Is the knowledge embedded in such structures inherently hierarchical?
- Can we actually teach such general concepts as *algebra* and *logic* without first teaching several specific exemplars of the concepts? Is a top-down approach feasible?

One strategy which helped to resolve some of these areas of contention was the clear separation of the pedagogic model that teaching staff used in developing the curriculum and its delivery (TPM) from the conceptual framework that we were constructing for the students and populating with complex ideas (SPM). For example, there were several areas of the curriculum that arose from a consideration of abstract algebra and category theory, and our approaches to these were informed by deep technical discussions. There was never any suggestion, however, that students needed to appreciate this background in their studies. What we had to do was construct "scaffolding" [18] which was sufficient to support the edifice we were trying to construct, and would not do long-term damage to this structure as it was selectively deconstructed later. What is more, the SPM for formalisation had to fit in to the bigger picture being developed for the whole curriculum: formalisms cannot simply be catapulted into a curriculum in a neutral way unless, of course, they are presented in isolation from the rest of Computer Science (as the applied mathematics had been previously). The significance of notions such as "type", "state", "function", "specification" and "program" cannot simply be left to the students to resolve across modules: they must be teased out explicitly and, where difficult issues arise, the problems addressed properly. That does not mean simply producing a glossary of terms, or agreeing a common syntax, but rather being prepared to admit that a concept such as "inheritance" in OOP is a fairly soft topic that needs really careful treatment if we are to create constructs in our students that will stand the test of time.

2   Developing the SPM

In many ways, the development of a suitable pedagogic framework is central to any curriculum. Unfortunately, this is sometimes overlooked in favour of approaches such as listing all the skills that employers want; asking staff what they want to teach; or "cherry picking" the bits you fancy from other curricula.

Clearly factors such as this must inform and constrain your curriculum design, but in our opinion the intellectual core inherent in the TPM must dominate.

The SPM we identified for our undergraduate developments was primarily rooted in the task of problem-solving in ways that resulted in the writing of software. We recognised that this is only one aspect of Computer Science, but we consciously decided that everything else would flow from this basic idea. Moreover, this would be presented explicitly to students as the core of Computer Science at Hatfield. We also identified two important dimensions to the task which are relevant to this discussion: increasing understanding of the problem (and its solution) and formalising the solution (as we must do if we are to produce a program). Within this simple state space, we can locate formalisation in a variety of ways. For example, for a simple well-understood problem, we might write a formal specification of the problem and use refinement to produce a formal programmed solution. For a very poorly understood problem, with many people involved in the system, we might initially use very informal techniques to improve our understanding, and only formalise as we build prototypes in code. For a safety-critical system, we might use formal methods to increase our understanding, allowing us to carry out proofs and explore emergent properties at various levels as we proceed.

This provided the bare bones of our SPM for the whole curriculum, but we needed to provide more structure to the model to inform our teaching of formalisms. We also needed to overcome several issues surrounding the development of a curriculum that was overtly "formal".

2.1 Soft and Hard Communities

One of the great problems that seemed to hit the Computer Science education community in the 1980s was the pointless and energy-sapping "debates" between the *formalists* and the *soft systems* communities. This seemed largely rooted in ignorance and a lack of willingness to listen and learn: both communities developed "refuges" [1] to avoid potential criticism. Formalists insisted that automation, the next generation of tools, better training or the integration of formalisms would solve many of the problems. Soft systems people argued that people are central to everything, and that this was a good enough excuse for avoiding mathematics. Both communities over-stated their cases, and claimed advantages that were simply not born out by experience[4].

If we wanted a SPM that would be acceptable to all those teaching within our curriculum, clearly we had to address this problem. We could not have the situation where the students were struggling to learn in the midst of a war-zone! The clue to solving this problem came from another curriculum development project underway within the department: a Cognitive Science Degree. It became

---

[4] It should be stressed that much of this debate was carried out by those who had only a limited understanding of the real issues: those developing the formalisms or the soft approaches usually had a very clear understanding of the limitations and challenges.

apparent that cognitive scientists need to address head-on the problems inherent in the formalisation of human issues. There is no suggestion within the Cognitive Science community, however, that this formalisation in any way belittles the people in the process: rather it exposes just how far we have to go to understand the true richness of humanity. The key is the recognition that the process starts with the construction of a *theory* of some aspect of a system.

Something interesting started to happen with the adoption of the term "theory" as a central component of our SCM: both the formalists and the soft systems people immediately started to embrace the ideas as if they had "won" the debate. The word "theory" becomes a powerful integrative factor in our quest to introduce well-founded formalisation. Discussion of the concept of a theory is far beyond the scope of this paper, but suffice it to say that most people accept the range of uses of the term from the very informal ("I have a theory about that . . .") to the formal ("Theory of Relativity"). Within Computer Science, both the Formal and Soft communities had already embraced the term, from its use within algebraic specifications [4] to its use regarding the role of people in the development process [13].

2.2   Theories and Models

One side-effect of this shift towards making theories central artefacts in our curriculum was to identify the need to clarify some of our terminology. In particular, the word "model" is used (and abused) in many ways with subtleties that often escape the novice. When we talk of "the life cycle model", for example, we often fail to identify exactly what this is a model *of*. When an aircraft designer constructs a model of a wing to put in a wind tunnel, what is being modelled in not "the wing" but the designers theory of some particular abstraction of the wing. Using such a model for discussing weight issues rather than airflow, for example, would be an abuse.

Had we remained entirely in the classical software engineering paradigm that was rapidly becoming dominated by the life-cycle, we would have used terms such as "specification" and "design", in typically disembodied ways, and with similar risks of abuse. Specifications, for example, are only subsets of the constraints that will guide the construction of a system - they do not constitute a description of the system itself. By introducing the terms "theory" and "model", we can make explicit the fact that a theory must be a theory of something, discuss the properties that we might reasonably expect of a theory, discuss the ontological status of a theory, and carry out deep analysis that really makes students think carefully about the processes and limitations involved in formalisation.

We can also introduce the concept of a *theory presentation*, as distinct from the theory as held in the mind or distributed amongst a project team. We can explore different ways of making theories explicit such as axiomatic systems, and the ways in which theories are enriched by means such as conservative extensions. We can create word algebras to act as models of our theories, so that explorations of our theories are firmly embedded in the world of models. This creates a clear distinction between theories and models that is not always present when we move from specifications to programs. The constructs of theory extension and enrichment allow us to construct lattices of theories that serve as a basis for processes such as refinement, but also admit interpretations in the human domain.

The notion of a theory presentation now leads us naturally into the world of formal systems. Rather than pre-packaged formal systems being plucked out of thin air and "applied" like Z or CCS, we can now discuss which aspects of the real world we want to formalise and construct theory presentations that are fit for purpose[16]. For example, we can use ZF set theory to present our theories about collections of objects if and only if we are prepared to sign up to all the axioms of both ZF and the underlying logic used to express them. By means of extensions and some syntactic sugaring, we can move on to discuss relations and functions. Ultimately we can move from the theories of our basic building blocks (the computing objects) to those capturing problems we want solved by adding the components to our theory that capture the "specification". Of course, as we accepted some axioms initially, we cannot capture certain issues such as non-monotonic reasoning in our database without some thought. Note that there is no formal difference between the axioms of set theory and those we choose to impose as part of a specification, although there are differences in the heuristics that govern their use. We are not averse to adopting syntax from particular formal methods as a vehicle for our teaching where they are fit for our pedagogic purpose, and so we typically adopt either Z or VDM consistently in a given module, but we are careful not to be drawn into teaching these formalisms as topics of value in their own right.

We can also identify problems in formalisms and change some of our formal systems to address these. For example, we can attempt to specify safety and liveness properties of a communications protocol, only to discover that we need to address different modalities to capture liveness properties. Thus we motivate the study of modal, temporal and non-monotonic logics, but we also expose students to some fundamental issues such as the views we can take of "time" in such analysis and the implications this will have for our formalisms (linear/branching, discrete/continuous). This reinforces the idea that formalisms are man-made, designed to embody some theoretical ideas.

The approach can also be moved into much broader areas. For example, when discussing HCI we can address the issues of which theories are relevant to interface design, and what it means to construct systems when you really don't understand all of the implications of your actions.

We now have the bare bones of a manifesto driving the design of our curriculum for teaching formalisation. Let us recap on the situation so far:

- Develop an SCM that admits formalisation in a well-founded way, admitting its limitations as well as its benefits.
- See formalisation as a concept that influences the whole curriculum, not simply a topic to be inserted.
- Develop a community where formalisation is not threatening or seen as the remit of one small curriculum area.

- Recognise the central role of formal systems, theories and models in "formal methods", and teach these explicitly and generically, rather than expecting the students to generalise from detailed treatment of specific formalisms.
- Don't be afraid to tease out some of the more philosophical issues such as the nature of theories, models and proofs.
- If it is important that students understand something, teach it! If it is unpopular or difficult, find better ways to teach it!
- Motivate students to develop the confidence and ability to learn whatever formalisms a task requires rather than training them to use Z (or CCS, or VDM, or OBJ, or ...).

It is also useful to consider a snapshot of the first year curriculum to illustrate how this manifesto influenced our early developments. The first year was divided into 4 modules: this in itself was counter to the contemporary university structure of 10 modules in the year, and was indicative of our desire to avoid over-partitioning the subject.

Formal Systems introduced the notion of formal languages, syntax, semantics, and deductive apparatus. These were illustrated by a blend of tiny systems (such as the OC system in Figure 1), systems of logic, systems underpinning "formal methods" such as Z, OBJ and CCS, and systems defining programming languages such as lambda calculus and Hoare Logics. Proficiency in specific techniques was not intended. The course also introduced simple model theory and the basic ideas of algebra, including facets such as such as initial and final semantics.

Programming introduced functional programming as a term rewriting system, and explored the ways in which informal descriptions of problems could be formalised and solved (eg using pre and post conditions). Towards the end of the course students moved on to Modula-2, and explored the notion of state.

Problem Solving took a generic approach to discussing how people solve problems for other people and themselves. It started by holistic experiences such as egg-races, and then moved on to consider ways of tackling problems that arise such as group communication, fitness-for-purpose, project management, and notations (including formalisms) for helping in the process. Aspects of the philosophy of science were introduced to promote discussion of issues such as the ways that understanding grows in communities and the notions of refutation of theories

Computer Systems took an approach rooted in the development of abstract machines from simple functions through FSMs and Turing machines (dovetailing with the introduction of Formal Languages) to more sophisticated architectures such as the SECD machine to support Lisp and contemporary "real" architectures.

2.3   Experiences and Implications of This Development

It is important to stress that the decision to embrace formality in this way was a high-risk strategy. Mathematics (in the UK) is not currently a popular

The formal language for the OC system is

$$(O|C)(O|C)(O|C)(O|C)$$

that is, strings of Os and Cs of length 4.In what follows we will often write things like

$$C^3O^1 \quad \text{to denote} \quad CCCO$$

or

$$C^nO^m \quad \text{to denote a string of } n \text{ } C\text{s followed by } m \text{ } O\text{s.}$$

Our formal system has one axiom

AXIOM

$$CCCC$$

and three rules.

C–REDUCTION

$$\frac{C^mO^n}{C^{m-1}O^{n+1}} \quad \text{where } m \geq 0$$

O–INTRODUCTION

$$\frac{C^4}{C^mOC^{3-m}} \quad \text{where } 0 \leq m \leq 3$$

O–REDUCTION

$$\frac{C^mO^nC^{4-m-n}}{C^{m+1}O^{n-1}C^{4-m-n}} \quad \text{where } m + n \leq 4$$

For example,

From   Deduce By Rule
$CCOO$ $COOO$ C–Reduction
$CCOO$ $CCCO$ O–Reduction
$CCCC$ $CCOC$ O–Introduction

Exercise 1. Convince yourself that each rule will only generate strings of the same length as it was given, and hence convince yourself that all theorems of the OC system are of length 4.

Here is a theorem of the OC system.
Show that

$$\vdash COOO$$

Proof

1 $CCCC$ axiom
2 $CCCO$ 1 C–Reduction
2 $CCOO$ 1 C–Reduction
2 $COOO$ 1 C–Reduction

Q.E.D.
Here is a derivation.
Show that

$$OOOC \vdash COOC$$

Derivation

1 $OOOC$ premise
2 $COOC$ 1 O–Reduction

It is important to realise that things we can *derive* are not necessarily theorems.
See if you can find a convincing argument that $COOC$ cannot be a theorem.
Try and perform the following proofs and derivations. For any that you think cannot be done, try and produce convincing arguments.

1. $\vdash CCOO$
2. $CCOO \vdash CCCC$
3. $\vdash CCOO$
4. $CCOO \vdash OCCC$
5. $\vdash COOO$

Fig. 1. The OC System - extracted from HND notes, circa 1985

subject within the school curriculum, and suggesting that our degree was highly mathematical was seen as running counter to many other institutions where mathematics was being systematically removed from the curriculum. Indeed, when these ideas were presented by one of the authors at the Standing Conference for Heads of Maths, Stats and Computing, considerable scepticism was expressed as to whether we could possibly succeed with any but the best students[5]. Of course, our argument was that formalisation is so fundamental to Computer Science that we could not simply remove it without moving to a short-term training regime where we taught transient skills and techniques. It was important that students sign up to this agenda, and so our publicity material and open-day events took great pains to explain the SCM, even if some students consequently chose to go elsewhere.

A few years later, this approach was adopted on various other schemes of study. For example, the Cognitive Science degree was started and contained a single module (making up 40% of the first year) covering all aspects of Computing. The students on this scheme were not expecting Computer Science *per se*, and were certainly not expecting formal logic and mathematics, but by developing theories of relevant areas such as human problem solving, memory and perception, the approach proved very popular and is still largely used today. Of course, the STM needs careful redesign. The inclusion of psychology, linguistics and philosophy offered opportunities for a much deeper treatment of some aspects, whereas the reduced emphasis on the more technical issues necessitated changes in other areas.

We also took the potentially very brave step of adopting the approach on our Higher National Diploma scheme (a 2 year, sub-degree level scheme), where the students on entry have generally much weaker qualifications, suggesting that the more formal material might be very unpopular and difficult to teach. Our decision was, in part, influenced by a desire to ensure that students who performed particularly well on the first year of the HND still had a route for progression onto to the second year of the degree scheme. In the event, the course proved very popular, and well within the abilities of the students[6]. One of the techniques we adopted with this group, which subsequently migrated to other modules, was to develop a number of simple formal systems that seemed abstract but actually had very concrete models. One such system was the OC system shown in Figure 1. This system could be mastered in a few minutes, and the strings were easy to manipulate. One model of this system is a filing cabinet which has drawers in an open or closed state, and has a risk of toppling over, so there are constraints placed on the allowable configurations. The beauty of systems such as these is that issues such as completeness and consistency are quite readily appreciated. They are also capable of design by students, so tasks such as producing a theory

---

[5] One long-standing Head of a Computer Science Department even went so far as to state very loudly that, since he never understood all this discrete maths stuff, why should he expect his students to.

[6] The first year this course ran the pass rate was nearly 100%, even though the level of assessment material was judged by several people to be too hard for these students.

for the next generation of filing cabinet where the bottom drawer acts as a stabiliser can be posed. Indeed, some students surprised lecturers on other modules by answering questions where no formality was intended by designing formal systems to present theories.

One outcome of these developments was to make us consider very carefully the nature of the tasks that we asked students to undertake. It is very tempting with formalisms to focus on activities that sit neatly within the formal system, such as carrying out derivations and proofs. These develop important skills and fluency which are vital if the formalism is to become a useful tool, but they are inward-looking. Some very important higher-order tasks such as developing new formal systems, or discussing the use of formal systems for some particular task, are often overlooked. These require some very sophisticated skills that many students struggle to develop but are precisely those which we value as Computer Scientists: programming is simply one form of formalisation. Thus our approach started to benefit from this cross-fertilisation between modules. Rather than students encountering neatly packaged formalisms but failing to generalise the important concepts, they were starting to carry important ideas such as abstraction across boundaries, often in very challenging ways for the teaching staff.

It was our experience that these sort of activities could be carried out in quite advanced ways with final year students who had spent their third year in industry as the placement component of their degree. They typically had developed an understanding that theories rarely mapped neatly on to customer's problems, and some reflection was needed to bring "theory" and "practice" into contact. For example, in a final year Software Engineering module we set students the task in groups of taking case studies in Z (from Hayes [6]) and presenting them to the rest of the class. We had expected the presentations to focus on how the specifications were written and the use that was made of Z. The students, however, quite rightly stepped outside of the formal systems and considered much wider issues. One particular group noticed that the notion of "Z" as conveyed by generalisation from the case studies, was not just a formal system but also a particular style of use, and an interesting debate ensued over whether every specification that passed through the Z syntax checker was actually Z.

The students also wanted to evaluate the case studies to see whether the use of Z contributed to good design, as discussed in other areas of the curriculum. For example, we noted that the usual style of writing Z (introducing state information early) led to a situation where it was very difficult to achieve a separation of functional and user interface issues. Making trivial changes to an interface, when this style is used, requires changes to the state model. In contrast, if state is not introduced until after all the data transformation operations have been defined, this problem does not arise, but then the specification does not conform to the norms of Z, even though syntactically correct. We subsequently wrote a paper on this [12], and were astounded to find that several people objected to our conclusions on the grounds that we should be using Z the way others did, and not exploring alternatives. This reinforced our desire to avoid teaching "formal methods", which seem to have become cluttered with heuristics and conventions that have not been tested, in favour of teaching formal systems, where the responsibility for use resides with the user. It also led us to explore some of the general claims made for formal systems in more critical ways than hitherto. For example, it is often claimed that the use of formal methods leads to improved reasoning about specifications: after 4 years of experimentation we found this claim hard to substantiate, and there seems to be little improvement of this particular aspect of human performance accompanying formalisation [17]. This leads us to question some approaches to teaching formal methods, where claims such as these are used to motivate their use.

One recent development that we have made to our approach is to think more carefully about the ways in which we can help first year students to explore formalisms, and to experiment with their theories and theory presentations. In addition to using paper-based systems, over the years we have experimented with a variety of simulations for logics, tools for proofs, executable specification tools and other such programs. Individually, many of these are very useful, and have been quite successful in motivating students and helping them to engage with the subject. The problem is, however, that each one of these has a learning cost that often means they become seen as important objects in their own right, rather than as means to an end. Moreover, these systems rarely lead to generic skills that will transfer to the next tool. In particular, many of the interesting aspects of abstraction that we are trying to develop are deeply embedded in the tools, and hence obscured from the student. As a result of this we have gone "back to basics", and introduced symbolic programming alongside the other material, allowing the students to develop their own tools in a very transparent way. We currently use Scheme[8], as it offers the power of Lisp with the added benefit of TeachPacks, so that we can encapsulate some theories for students in robust yet visible and understandable ways. Using this approach, students are encouraged to explore the formalisms by creating executable models throughout. For example, they will implement simple data types such as sets, add relational operators, construct a simple database that meets a specification given as a theory presentation using relations, and so on. They can also run simulations of Turing Machines, and other abstract architectures. There are, of course, far more sophisticated Turing Machine simulators available, with excellent graphical interfaces, but our approach makes very explicit the layers of abstractions in the system.

3   Conclusions

In the course of this paper we have outlined a few of the basic principles that might be considered part of our manifesto for curriculum design in formalisms. Hopefully we managed to do so in such a way that it was obvious we do not want to be considered "formal methods people", but rather as teachers who see real potential in teaching formal systems to Computer Science students and others.

Our objection to the term "formal methods" is not deeply held, but is quite fundamental. We are not quibbling over whether or not artefacts such as Z or CCS constitute "methods", but rather seeking to change the pedagogic emphasis. Methods are often seen as pre-designed and packaged ways of achieving some end. Bjørner, for example, clearly aligns formals methods with " formal specifications and the use of design calculi on such specifications"[2, Page 13]. Whilst we have no objection, and indeed some sympathy, with the teaching of such an approach, we would see this being built on a deeper understanding of formal systems. The danger of admitting formal methods (in Bjørner's sense) into the curriculum is that they are often seen as *the* means by which formalisms are taught, rather than as one example of their use. Moreover, many of the generic skills which, in our view, are the true pedagogic rationale for teaching such "methods" become obscured behind complex syntax and conventional heuristics (such as the use of state in Z). We would argue that the top-down approach to teaching formalisation should be considered by anyone responsible for a Computer Science curriculum.

Such an approach is possible, as we have shown. It is also not limited to students entering higher education with good mathematical qualification, or highly motivated students. We have successfully used the approach on HND and Cognitive Science schemes of study, as well as Computer Science, and achieved excellent pass rates.

We also claim that the approach meets our objective of developing generic skills in our students. These skills include those needed for "formal methods", but are presented in such a way that their applicability to all areas of Computer Science is encouraged. Abstraction, for example, is seen as a process applicable to formal specification, but also to virtually every activity in Computer Science.

One important area addressed by our approach is to challenge the primacy sometimes implied by the various life cycle models on "specification" and "implementation". The use of theories allows us to introduce a number of issues that would not naturally arise if we use a more conventional approach. Ryle noted that possession of a theory is analogous to having the awareness of a set of paths such that you can both use the paths and also explain to others how to navigate using them [15]. Thus we admit *explication* to the process as well as specification. If we introduce formal methods simply as a way of constructing specifications, in a life cycle context, it is easy to overlook their potential for supporting exploration and explication.

We would argue that our approach also encourages students to challenge the use of formal methods in constructive ways, and hence to take responsibility for their use as befits a professional engineer. One interesting illustration of this was encountered when running a Z course for a group of software engineers from a local company. By lunch time on the first day, it became apparent that there was considerable hostility amongst the students, who were cynical, uncooperative, and unwilling to participate in activities. Over lunch we explored the reasons for this, and discovered that the company had decided these experienced engineers needed training in Z so that "they could do their jobs properly", and had "sent them on the course". Many of them suspected they would never use Z, and most of them were deeply sceptical about the merits of formalisation in general. We rapidly changed our approach, and presented to the students the idea that, for the rest of the course, we were going to equip them with enough understanding of formal methods to empower them eloquently and rationally to explain to their managers why such approaches might not work on their projects. By the end of the week the change was dramatic: some students were still highly dubious, but could articulate their reservations in terms of the context in which they constructed theories; others were eager to get back and explore how formalisms might work on their current projects. They might have "learned less" schema calculus than our original syllabus suggested, but the quality of learning was undoubtedly superior in every way.

At undergraduate level, we try to instil in our students the fact that, as professionals, they are responsible for their actions as software developers, including decisions such as the adoption of methods, formal or otherwise. This is not always popular, and we would echo Feyerabend who notes

" . . . it needs only a few well-placed phrases to put the fear of Chaos into the most enlightened audience, and to make them yearn for simple rules and simple dogmas which they can follow without having to reconsider matters at every turn." [5, Page 181].

and indeed for undergraduates

"I do find it a little astonishing to see with what fervour students and other non-initiates cling to stale phrases and decrepit principles as if a situation in which they bear the full responsibility for *every* action and are the original cause for *every* regularity of the mind were quite unbearable to them." [5, Page 182]

These two quotations capture the very essence of many of our beliefs regarding formal methods. There is a serious risk that "formal methods" are regarded by students as ways of avoiding this responsibility. Teachers presenting codified formalisms such as Z may well intend the development of a genuine critical awareness, but students who have invested many hours mastering a complex toolkit often, understandably, believe that the formalism is a method they are free to use without question - something drawn from the realm of truth rather than the embodiment of a set of theoretical ideas that may or may not be appropriate in a given context.

One important issue that we have not developed here but which we would like to leave as homework for the reader is the impact of such an approach on the teaching of the whole design process. There is relatively little deep philosophical analysis regarding software development, or indeed the development of technology in general. There is, however, a vast literature on the philosophy of science, and in particular on the nature and development of theories. Our focus on theories allows access to some of these ideas. We mentioned that our first year students were exposed to these ideas in the Problem Solving module. Some of this material was taught quite explicitly. For example, we introduce ideas such as the ways in which some "truths" become embedded in the hard-core of a research programme, and are accepted uncritically in a scientific community. These ideas can then be interpreted in the context of Computer Science by exploring issues such as the ways in which the selection of a programming paradigm or a formal method influences theories of a system. This, in turn, allows us to challenge such slogans as "a specification should tell you what needs doing, not how to do it". For example, we can question how easy is it to move from a Z specification to a Prolog program, and whether the choice of Z as a formalism influences design decisions.

In conclusion, we should stress that our purpose in writing this paper is not to belittle formal methods in any way, or to be evangelical about their use. Rather it is to present the case that formalisation and the construction of theories are fundamental activities in Computer Science. The generic skills and understanding that these activities require can be taught in a variety of ways, but one way that has stood the test of time for us is to focus on formal systems as a precursor to methods. This brings major benefits of re-use, as students develop high-level skills and can pick up new formalisms, evaluate them and decide whether to invest the time in developing fluency for particular tasks.

References

1. Alexander, C: Notes on the Synthesis of Form, Harvard University Press (1964)
2. Bjørner, D: Pinnacles of software engineering: 25 years of formal methods. Annals of Software Engineering **10** (2000) 11–66
3. Boute, R. T: Some Fundamental Concepts in Computer Science for Telecommunication Engineers. BTM, Antwerp (June, 1980)
4. Burstall, R. M. And Goguen, J.A: Putting theories together to make specifications. Proceedings of the Fifth International Joint Conference on Artificial Intelligence. (1977)
5. Feyerabend P: Against method : outline of an anarchistic theory of knowledge, NLB (1975)
6. Hayes, I.(editor): Specification Case Studies. Prentice-Hall. (1987)
7. Jones, J., Loomes M., Shaw, R: An Education Programme for Practising Software Engineers, Proceedings of Software Engineering 86 (1986)
8. Kent Dybvig, R: The Scheme Programming Language (third edition). The MIT Press. (2003)
9. Kozmetsky, George: The significant role of problem solving in education. In D.T. Tuma and F. Reif, editors, Problem Solving and Education: Issues in Teaching and Research (1980) 151–157 Laurence Erlbaum.
10. Loomes, M. J.: Software Engineering Curriculum Design, University of Surrey PhD Thesis (1991), available from the author m.j.loomes@herts.ac.uk
11. Mills,Harlan D.: Software engineering education. Proceedings of the IEEE. (September, 1980) 1158–1162
12. Mitchell, R., Loomes, M., Howse: Structuring Formal Specifications - A Lesson Relearned, Microprocessors and Microsystems **18(10)** , 593-599, Butterworth-Heine, ISSN 0141-9331 (1994)

13. Naur, Peter: Programming as theory building. Microprocessing and Microprogramming. **15** (1985) 253–261. Invited keynote address at Euromicro 84, Copenhagen, Denmark.
14. Popper, Karl R: Conjectures and Refutations. Routledge and Kegan Paul. (1963)
15. Ryle, G: The concept of mind. Peregrin Books. (1949)
16. Woodcock, Jim.and Loomes, Martin: Software Engineering Mathematics. Pitman. (1988)
17. Vinter, R., Loomes, M.J., Kornbrot, D: Applying Software Metrics to Formal Specification: A Cognitive Approach, , Proceedings of the 5th. International Software Metrics Symposium, IEEE Computer Science Press, pp216-223 (1998)
18. Vygotsky, L.S: The collected works of LS Vygotsky, Volume 1, New York Plenum (1987)

A Practice-Oriented Course on the Principles of Computation, Programming, and System Design and Analysis

Egon Börger

Università di Pisa, Dipartimento di Informatica, I-56125 Pisa, Italy
boerger@di.unipi.it

Abstract. We propose a simple foundation for a practice-oriented undergraduate course that links seamlessly computation theory to principles and methods for high-level computer-based system development and analysis. Starting from the fundamental notion of virtual machine computations, which is phrased for both synchronous and asynchronous systems in terms of Abstract State Machines, the course covers in a uniform way the basics of algorithms (sequential and distributed computations) and formal languages (grammars and automata) as well as the computational content of the major programming paradigms and high-level system design principles. The course constitutes a basis for advanced courses on algorithms and their complexity as well as on rigorous methods for requirements capture and for practical hardware/software design and analysis.

We outline here a successful use one can make of Abstract State Machines (ASMs) as a unifying conceptual ground for a practice-oriented undergraduate course on computation theory which covers classical models of computation—algorithms (undecidability and complexity) and formal languages (grammars and automata of the Chomsky hierarchy)—, but also the principles of programming constructs and of high-level design and analysis of computer-based systems. The fundamental notion of virtual machine computations and the ways to investigate them taught in this course seem to appeal to practice-oriented students and provide a basis for advanced courses on the use of rigorous methods for requirements capture and for the design and the analysis of real-life hardware/software systems, as illustrated in the experience reports [13,15].

In Section 1 we outline the fundamental questions and concepts addressed in the proposed course and introduce the basic notion of Abstract State Machines, a rigorous form of virtual machines which allows one to treat in a uniform way computation theory and system design issues. In Section 2 we explain how to uniformly present the variety of classical formal languages (Chomsky hierarchy grammars and equations for recursive functions) and the corresponding automata, by appropriately instantiating basic ASMs. This naturally leads to a coding-free undecidability proof, on half a page with five lines of proof starting from scratch, for the termination problem of any computation-universal

C.N. Dean and R.T. Boute (Eds.): TFM 2004, LNCS 3294, pp. 65–84, 2004.

language, including any programmming language that satisfies a few natural closure properties, and to a discussion of the Church-Turing thesis, strengthened by ASMs to capture also resource bound considerations. In Section 3 we propose using ASMs to define the computational meaning of the major sequential and concurrent programmming constructs appearing in imperative, object-oriented, functional or logic programs. In Section 4 we indicate how the rigorous-pseudo-code character of ASMs can be exploited to use these machines as conceptual frame for advanced courses on accurate high-level modeling and analysis (validation and verification) of complex real-life computer-based systems.

In this paper we can only give an outline of the themes for the course so that we refer for an elaboration of the technical details to the literature. Except for the undecidability proof, we also restrict our attention on the definitional aspects for which we suggest a novel approach, which allows the lecturer to a) define only once the notion of (mono-agent or synchronous or asynchronous multi-agent virtual machine) computation, which covers all the variations one encounters in the literature, and to b) directly deploy the involved fundamental theoretical concepts for challenging practical problems the working computer scientist has to face in his professional life, covering in a uniform way two things:

- The investigation of the basic concepts from the theory of computation and programming through the well-known classical theorems. The textbook [9] is still a good source for many simple proofs.
- Teaching practical system design principles through building and analysing rigorous high-level models. The AsmBook [30] contains some real-life case studies.

We do not discuss any purely didactical concern or techniques how to teach the course. The AsmBook [30] shows a way how to teach ASMs. It includes a CD with a set of slide decks, in pdf and ppt format, for lecturers of introductory and advanced courses. That material can also be downloaded from the AsmBook website at http://www.di.unipi.it/AsmBook/. As to the level of the course, it depends on the depth chosen. The course fits wherever an introductory course on computability or automata or more generally computation theory is taught. As to the size of the course, it may vary between 20 and 50 hours, depending again on the depth into which the lecturer wishes and can afford to go in treating the proposed arguments.

1   The Basic Questions and Concepts

The proposed course is centered around the following four basic questions any conceptual framework of computation theory and of computer-based system design and analysis has to address.

- **What are the basic virtual machines** needed to perform any kind of computation (universal virtual machine concept), whether stand-alone or in cooperation involving distributed computations?

- *What are the states* (data structures) of such a general-purpose concept of virtual machines? What are the data sharing structures to express the cooperation of these virtual machines?

- **What are the basic programs** (algorithms) for most general virtual machines?

  - *What are the basic control structures* provided by the programs of such machines?
  - *What are the basic communication means* provided by the programs of such machines?
  - *What are the runs,* sequential or distributed, formed by executing instructions for state-transforming or communication steps of such machines?

- **What are the basic properties** of such machines and their programs, like their functionality (required or achieved), their computational power, their memory or time complexity, etc? What are the languages to appropriately express these properties?

- **What are the basic means of analysis** to establish, in terms of experimental validation and of mathematical verification, desired properties for running programs on such machines?

In dealing with these questions we advocate to separate from the very beginning different concerns. This creates in the student a firm *divide-and-conquer* attitude that encourages an approach to system design and analysis which uses systematically the piecemeal introduction of design and verification details (so-called *stepwise refinement* method) and thereby enables the future practitioner to adopt for each development step the appropriate one among the multitude of available definition and proof methods. The three major types of activities we suggest to teach to distinguish are the following ones:

- *Separate design from analysis.* For conceptually simple or small systems as the ones used in classical computation theory, definition and analysis means are often intertwined with advantage, e.g. when a recursive definition of some concept is coupled with recursively defined deduction rules to prove properties for that concept in a calculational manner. Also systems that are tailored to successfully deal with particular classes of to-be-verified programs take advantage from a tight link between means of program development and proof techniques to check program properties; a good example for this is the B-method [2]. However, the complexity of real-life computer-based systems makes it appropriate to generally separate design from analysis. This helps to not restrict the design space or its structuring into components by proof principles which are coupled to the design framework in a fixed a priori defined way, as happens for example with the refinement concept in the B-method.

- *Separate different analysis types and levels.* Such a stratification principle is widely accepted in mathematics. It also applies to system analysis where it can be instantiated in the following way.

- Separate experimental *validation* (system simulation and testing) from mathematical *verification*.
- *Distinguish verification levels* and the characteristic concerns each of it comes with. Each verification layer has an established degree of to-be-provided detail, formulated in an appropriate language. E.g. reasoning for human inspection (design justification by mathematical proofs) requires other features than using rule-based reasoning systems (mechanical design justification). Mathematical proofs may come in the form of proof ideas or proof sketches or as completely carried out detailed proofs. Formalized proofs are based on inference calculi which may be operated by humans or as computerized systems, where one should distinguish interactive systems (theorem proving systems like PVS, HOL, Isabelle, KIV) from automatic tools (model checkers and theorem provers of the Otter type). Another distinction comes through separating static program analysis from a run-time-based analysis of dynamic program properties (so called runtime verification). For each verification level the lecturer finds in the literature case studies, coming from different domains (hardware, programming languags, protocols, embedded systems), showing how to use ASMs to reason about the specification a the given level of abstraction.

1.1 Abstract State Machines

An important reason for starting the course with the notion of Abstract State Machines, whose definition is outlined in this section, is that these machines represent a most general definition of Virtual Machines. This has become clear from over ten years of experience with modelling and analysing outstanding real-life virtual machines and is theoretically underpinned by the ASM thesis, a resource-bound-aware generalization of the thesis of Church and Turing (see the next section). In addition ASMs provide a framework for a theoretically well-founded, coherent and uniform **practical combination of abstract operational descriptions with functional and axiomatic definitions**, thus eventually overcoming an alleged, though unjustified and in fact destructive, dichotomy between declarative and operational design elements which has been advocated for the last thirty years in the literature and in teaching.

Formally, ASMs can be presented as transition systems which transform structures, thus involving two ingredients, namely notions of abstract *state* and of single *computation* step.

Abstract system states are represented by structures, understood the way they appear in Tarski's semantical foundation of classical logic[1], given as domains of objects coming with predicates (attributes) and functions defined on them. If this definition of structures cannot be assumed to be known from an introduction into classical logic, structures can equivalently be viewed as sets of values residing

---

[1] Which is directly related to the object-oriented understanding of classes and their instances.

in abstract memory units, so-called *locations*, which are organized into tables. Here a table is an association of a value to each table entry. Each table entry is a location, consisting of a table (or function) name and an argument. These tables are nothing else than what logicians call the interpretation of a function.

This general concept of structures incorporates truly 'abstract data types', which may be defined in many satisfactory ways, not only by equations or by logical axioms, but also operationally by programs or rules producing dynamic sets of updates of locations, as explained now. In fact ASMs represent a form of "pseudo-code over abstract data", virtual machine programs whose instructions are guarded function updates, structure transforming "rules" of the form[2]

if *Condition* **then** $f(t_1, \ldots, t_n) := t$

Also the auxiliary functions and predicates, which appear in the expressions t_i, t and thus are part of the system states, can be given purely functional or axiomatic or whatever other form of satisfactory definitions. This is supported by a classification of functions into basic and derived. Derived functions are those whose definition in terms of basic functions is fixed and may be given separately, e.g. in some other part ("module" or "class") of the model to be built. An orthogonal classification which supports this combination of declarative and operational features is the distinction between static and dynamic functions. The further classification of dynamic functions with respect to a given (machine executing) agent into controlled (readable and writable), monitored (readable), output (writable) and shared functions supports to distinguish between the roles different 'agents' (e.g. the system and its environment) play in using (providing or updating the values of) dynamic functions. A particularly important class of monitored functions are selection functions, for which also a special notation is provided (see below). Monitored and shared functions also represent a rather general mechanism to specify communication types between different agents, executing each a basic ASM. For details see the AsmBook [30, Ch.2.2.3].

ASM computations are understood as for traditional transition systems, except that the rules of ASMs are executed in parallel[3] so that the students learn from the very beginning to avoid, as long as they are concerned with building a high-level system model, to sequentialize independent actions. The definition of further control structures (like sequential execution or iteration) can be added where needed for a concrete implementation, some standard examples will be discussed in Section 2 in connection with the concept of structured programming. For *asynchronous multi-agent ASMs* it suffices to generalize runs from

---

[2] This definition of machine "instructions" combines the traditional distinction between branching (test) instructions and action instructions (see for example Scott's definition of abstract machine programs in [59]) and avoids, for reasons explained below, to name instructions by labels which support the interruption of the standard sequential instruction execution by branching.

[3] More precisely: to execute one step of an ASM in a given state S determine all the fireable rules in S (s.t. *Condition* is true in S), compute all expressions t_i, t in S occuring in the updates $f(t_1, \ldots, t_n) := t$ of those rules and then perform simultaneously all these location updates.

sequences (linear orders) of transition system moves of just one basic ASM to *partial orders* of moves of multiple agents, each executing a basic ASM, subject to a natural *coherence condition*, see [30, Def.6.1.1].

Non-determinism as incorporated in selection functions has also an explicit standard notation, namely **choose** x **with** ϕ **do** *rule* and

> **choose** x **with** ϕ
>   *rule*

standing for the rule to execute *rule* for one element x, which is arbitrarily chosen among those satisfying the selection criterion ϕ.

Synchronous parallelism, already present in the execution of ASM rules, is extended by a standard notation, namely **forall** x **with** ϕ **do** *rule* and

> **forall** x **with** ϕ
>   *rule*

standing for the execution of *rule* for every element x satisfying the property ϕ.

Control state ASMs, introduced in [10], are an alternative way to define basic ASMs as an extension of finite state machines (FSMs), if for some reason that concept is already known to the students. This comes up to enrich the notion of state and state transition: the *internal states i* become part of general *structures*[4] and the transitions are generalized to guarded synchronous parallel updates of those structures, in addition to updating what is now called more specifically control state i or *mode*. In this perspective, synchronous ASMs are given by sets of locally synchronous and globally asynchronous control state ASMs. To make this generalization of FSMs to control state ASMs transparent, we use the notation $\text{FSM}(i, \textbf{if } cond \textbf{ then } rule, j)$ for the following rule:

> **if** $ctl\_state = i$ **and** $cond$ **then**
>   *rule*
> $ctl\_state := j$

The above working definition refers only to basic intuitions from programmming practice. It suffices for most of the course material discussed below. A formalized definition of the semantics of basic or asynchronous ASMs is obviously needed for detailed proof verifications within the fixed syntax of some logic or to understand special features of implementations of ASMs. Such a definition can be given and is available in textbook form in terms of a first-order-logic-based derivation system in [30, Ch.2].

The use of ASMs on the one side allows one to explain in a uniform way the classical models of computation and the semantics of the basic programming concepts. Furthermore, these very same ASMs can be taught to support describing system behavior by succinct, purely mathematical (read: platform-independent) but intuitive operational models, which the practitioner can use

---

[4] This departs from the unstructured notion of states in the above-mentioned Scott machines, see [59].

for experimentation by running executable versions and for rigorous analaysis. How to present this in a course is what we are going to explain in the following sections.

2   Algorithms: Computability and Undecidability

In this section we outline how in terms of ASMs one can introduce in a uniform manner all the classical models of computation that are most frequently adopted in computation theory courses, namely automata that characterize (generate and accept) languages of the Chomsky hierarchy. We show how simple structured ASMs, defined in terms of sequentialization and iteration of components, can be used to compute the recursive functions (Structured Programmming Theorem). We indicate a coding-free five-lines undecidability proof for the termination problem of programs of any programming language satisfying some natural closure properties and point to a resource-bound-aware generalization of the Church-Turing thesis in terms of ASMs. We have experienced that this core material can be covered in two weeks (6-8 lecture and exercise hours). Details for most of the material and further references can be found in the papers [16,29] and in chapters 7 and 4 of the AsmBook [30].

2.1   Automata and Grammars

We outline here how to uniformly define, in terms of simple ASMs, the classical automata that are related to the grammars forming the Chomsky hierarchy. We concentrate upon deterministic machine versions, from which the non-deterministic counterparts are obtained by governing the *Rules* to select from by a **choose** operator in the form **choose** $R \in Rules$ **in** R.

Finite Automata. Deterministic Mealy and Moore automata can be introduced as control state ASMs, with one *output* function and a monitored *input* function, where every rule has the following form (in the case of Moore automata one has *skip* instead of the output assignment):

FSM(i, **if** $Reading(a)$ **then** OUTPUT(b), j) **where**
$\quad Reading(a) = (in = a)$
$\quad$OUTPUT(b) $= (out := b)$

If one prefers to write programs in the usual tabular form, where one has one entry (i, a, j, b) for every instruction "in state i reading input a, go to state j and print output b", one obtains the following guard-free FSM rule scheme for updating (ctl_state, out), where the parameters *Nxtctl* and *Nxtout* are the two projection functions which define the program table, mapping 'configurations' (i, a) of the current control state and the currently read *in*put to the next control state j and *out*put b.

MEALYFSM(in, out, $Nxtctl$, $Nxtout$) $=$
$\quad ctl\_state := Nxtctl(ctl\_state, in)$
$\quad out := Nxtout(ctl\_state, in)$

We like to discuss important specializations of FSMs through exercises where the students are asked to formalize variations of the above scheme. We give here three simple examples, more can be found in [16]. To formalize an input tape which is scanned piecemeal it suffices to change the monitored function *in* into a shared one which is supposed to be initialized by the environment and is at each step updated by the rule. To obtain *2-way automata* it suffices to include into the instructions also *Moves* (of the position *head*) of a reading device on the input tape *in*—so that *in(head)* represents the currently read part of the input tape *in*—and to add updates of the *head* position.

TwoWayFsm($in, out, Nxtctl, Nxtout, Move, head$) =
    MealyFsm($in(head), out, Nxtctl, Nxtout$)
    $head := head + Move(ctl\_state, in(head))$

In *timed automata* the letter input comes at a real-valued occurrence time which is used in the transitions where clocks record the time difference of the current input with respect to the previous input: $time_\Delta = occurrenceTime(in) - occurrenceTime(previousIn)$. The firing of transitions may be subject to clock constraints[5] and includes clock updates (resetting a clock or adding to it the last input time difference). Thus timed automata can be defined as specialized FSMs with rules of the following form:

Fsm($i,$ **if** $Reading(a)$ **then** $ClockUpdate(Reset), j$)
where
    $Reading(a) = (in = a$ **and** $Constraint(time_\Delta) = true)$
    $ClockUpdate(Reset) =$
        forall $c \in Reset$ **do** $c := 0$
        forall $c \notin Reset$ **do** $c := c + time_\Delta$

Push-Down Automata. In pushdown automata the Mealy automaton 'reading from the input tape' and 'writing to the output tape' is extended to reading from input and/or a *stack* and writing on the *stack*. In the following formulation of the form of PDA-rules, the optional input-reading or stack-reading are enclosed in []; the meaning of the *stack* operations *push, pop* is the usual one.

Fsm($i,$ **if** $Reading(a, b)$ **then** $StackUpdate(w), j$) **where**
    $Reading(a, b) = [in = a]$ **and** $[top(stack) = b]$
    $StackUpdate(w) = \quad stack := push(w, [pop](stack))$

Turing-like Automata. The Turing machine combines readable *in*put and writable *out*put of a two-way FSM into one read/write *tape* memory, identifying *in* and *out* with *tape*. This is a good reason to rename the function *Nxtout* of the TwoWayFsm to *Write*.

---

[5] Typically the constraints are about input to occur within $(<, \leq)$ or after $(>, \geq)$ a given (constant) time interval, leaving some freedom for timing runs, i.e. choosing sequences of $occurrenceTime(in)$ to satisfy the constraints.

TURINGMACHINE(*tape, Nxtctl, Write, Move, head*) =
TWOWAYFSM(*tape, tape*(*head*), *Nxtctl, Write, Move, head*)

Wegner's *interactive Turing machines* [66] in each step can additionally receive some environmental *input* and yield *output* to the environment. So they are an extension of the TURINGMACHINE by an additional *input* parameter of the program table functions *Nxtctl, Write, Move* and by an additional output action[6]. The output action may consist in writing the output on an in-out tape; the input can be a combination of preceding inputs/outputs with the new user input, it also may be a stream vector *input* = (*inp*$_1$, ..., *inp*$_n$) (so-called multiple-stream machines).

TURINGINTERACTIVE(*tape, Nxtctl, Write, Move, head, input*) =
TURINGMACHINE(*tape, Nxtctl*$_{input}$, *Write*$_{input}$, *Move*$_{input}$, *head*)
OUTPUT(*input, ctl_state, tape*(*head*))

Numerous other variations of *Turing-like machines* appear in the literature, e.g. computationally equivalent ones like the k-tape or the n-dimensional Turing machines, the machines of Wang, Minsky, Sheperdson and Sturgis, Scott, Eilenberg, the substitution systems of Thue, Post, Markov, etc., but also weaker machines like the linear bounded Turing machines. Their definitions can be covered by exercises where the students are asked to appropriately instantiate the following scheme of which also the above classical TURINGMACHINE is a specialization. The characteristic feature of every TURINGLIKEMACHINE is that in each step, placed in a certain *pos*ition of its *memory*, it reads this *memory* in the *env*ironment of that *pos*ition (which may be requested to satisfy a certain *Cond*ition) and reacts by updating *mem* and *pos*. Therefore the rules of each TURINGLIKEMACHINE(*mem, pos, env*) are all of the following form:

FSM(*i*, **if** *ReadingCond* **then** Update (*mem*(*env*(*pos*)), *pos*), *j*)
    where *ReadingCond* = *Condition*(*mem*(*env*(*pos*)))

Details of how to instantiate this scheme to the classical machine or substitution systems can be found in [16]. For Chomsky grammars see also Section 3. As example we illustrate how the standard Turing machine is extended to alternating Turing machines, namely by adding new types of control states whose role is to spawn trees for subcomputations, which upon termination are accepted or rejected. The *existential* and *universal* control states play the role of tree roots where subcomputations are spawned; they differ in the way their yield is collected upon termination to either accept or reject the spawned subcomputations. Directly *accept*ing or *reject*ing control states appear at the leaves of such subcomputations. Different subcomputations of an alternating Turing machine, whose program is defined by the given functions *Nxtctl, Write, Move* used by all subcomputations, are distinguished by parameterizing the machine instances by their executing agents *a*, obtaining TURINGMACHINE(*a*) from the standard

---

[6] When introducing additional parameters we write f_p for the function defined by $f_p(x) = f(p, x)$.

TURINGMACHINE by replacing the dynamic functions *ctl_state*, *tape*, *head* with their instances *a.ctl_state* and *a.tape*, *a.head*. For the details of the new submachines see [16].

ALTERNATINGTM(*tape, Nxtctl, Write, Move, head*) =
    if *type*(**self** *.ctl_state*) = *normal* **then**
       TURINGMACHINE(*tape, Nxtctl, Write, Move, head*)(**self**)
    if *type*(**self** *.ctl_state*) ∈ {*existential, universal*} **then**
       ALTTMSPAWN(**self**)
       TMYIELDEXISTENTIAL(**self**)
       TMYIELDUNIVERSAL(**self**)
    if *type*(**self** *.ctl_state*) ∈ {*accept, reject*} **then**
       yield(**self**) := *type*(**self** *.ctl_state*)

We conclude with a short discussion of Petri nets. In their most general understanding they are an instance of multi-agent asynchronous ASMs, namely distributed transition systems transforming objects under given conditions. In Petri's classical instance the objects are marks on *places* ('passive net components' where objects are stored), the *transitions* ('active net components') modify objects by adding and deleting marks on the places. In modern instances (e.g. the predicate/transition nets) places are locations for objects belonging to abstract data types (read: variables taking values of given type, so that a marking becomes a variable interpretation), transitions update variables and extend domains under conditions which are described by arbitrary first-order formulae. Technically speaking, each single transition is modeled by a basic ASM rule of the following form, where pre/post-places are sequences or sets of places which participate in the 'information flow relation' (the local state change) due to the transition and *Cond* is an arbitrary first-order formula.

PETRITRANSITION =
    if *Cond*(*prePlaces*) **then** *Updates*(*postPlaces*)
    where
       Updates(*postPlaces*) = a set of function updates

2.2   Structured ASMs for Recursive Functions

No computation theory course should miss a discussion of the notion of recursion, independently of its realizations in programming languages. This is a place to exploit the elegance of purely functional equational definitions, characterizing primitive recursive and general recursive functions in the Gödel-Herbrand style. We however replace the tedious still widely used programming of the Turing machine to compute recursive functions by the introduction of so-called *turbo ASMs* defined in [29]. These machines solve in a natural way the problem to incorporate into the basic synchronous parallel computation model of basic ASMs the fundamental control structures for sequential execution and iteration (as well as of submachines). This provides a simple proof for Böhm-Jacopini's Structured Programming Theorem and more importantly a programming-language-independent general framework to discuss imperative and functional programming concepts like composition, general recursion and procedure calls, parameterization, naming, encapsulation and hiding, local state, returning values, error handling, etc. We illustrate this by three very simple but characteristic turbo ASMs, namely to compute the composition and the minimalization operator for recursive functions and the classical recursive quicksort algorithm. Every lecturer will make up more examples tailored to his audience and taste. More details can be found in [17,41] or in chapter 4 of the AsmBook [30]. See also the interesting recent comparison of the transition from basic ASMs to turbo ASMs to the transition from FORTRAN/ALGOL58 to ALGOL60 in [53].

For computing recursive functions by turbo ASMs one can follow the standard way to compute them by structured programs for the register machine or Rödding's register operators, see [9, pages 19-23]. The turbo ASMs M we need can be defined, using only the composition operators **seq, while** defined in [29], from basic ASMs whose non-controlled functions are restricted to one (a 0-ary) input function (whose value is fixed by the initial state), one (a 0-ary) output function, and the initial functions of recursion theory as static functions. The 0-ary input function in_M contains the number sequence which is given as the input for the computation of the machine, out_M receives the computed function value as output of M. If functions $g, h_1, \ldots, h_m$ are computed by turbo ASMs $G, H_1, \ldots, H_m$, then their composition f defined by $f(x) = g(h_1(x), \ldots, h_m(x))$ is computed by the following machine $F = \text{FCTCOMPO}$, where we write $out := F(in)$ as abbreviation for $in_F := in$ **seq** F **seq** $out := out_F$, similarly $F(in)$ for $in_F := in$ **seq** F:[7]

$$\text{FCTCOMPO}(G, H_1, \ldots, H_m) =$$
$$\{H_1(in_F), \ldots, H_m(in_F)\} \text{ **seq** } out_F := G(out_{H_1}, \ldots, out_{H_m})$$

The formula for this structured program makes the order explicit in which the subterms in the defining equation for f have to be evaluated. First, the input is passed to the constituent functions h_i to compute their values, whereby the input functions of H_i become controlled functions of F. The parallel composition of the submachines $H_i(in_F)$ reflects that their computations are completely independent from each other, though all of them have to terminate before the next "functional" step is taken, consisting in passing the sequence of out_{H_i} as input to the constituent function g. Finally the value of g on this input is computed and assigned as output to out_F.

In the same way, if f is defined from g by minimalization, i.e. $f(x) = \mu y(g(x, y) = 0)$, and if a turbo ASM G computing g is given, then the following machine $F = \text{MUOPERATOR}$ computes f. The start submachine computes $g(x, rec)$ for the initial recursor value 0, and the iterating machine computes $g(x, rec)$ for increased values of the recursor until for the first time 0 shows up as computed value of g, in which case the reached recursor value is set as output.

---

[7] The set denotes the rules of an ASM which are to be executed in parallel.

$\text{MUOPERATOR}(G) = \{ G(in_F, 0),\ rec := 0 \}\ \textbf{seq}$
$(\textbf{while}\ (out_G \neq 0)\ \{ G(in_F, rec + 1),\ rec := rec + 1 \})\ \textbf{seq}$
$out_F := rec$

The turbo ASM below for Quicksort follows its well-known recursive definition: FIRST partition the *tail* of the list L into the two sublists $tail(L)_{<head(L)}, tail(L)_{\geq head(L)}$ of elements $< head(L)$ respectively $\geq head(L)$ and quicksort these two sublists independently of each other, THEN *concatenate* the results taking *head(L)* between them.

$\text{QUICKSORT}(L) = \textbf{if} |\ L\ | \leq 1\ \textbf{then result}:= L\ \textbf{else}$
   $\textbf{let}$
      $x = \text{QUICKSORT}(tail(L)_{<head(L)})$
      $y = \text{QUICKSORT}(tail(L)_{\geq head(L)})$
   $\textbf{in result}:= concatenate(x, head(L), y)$

The structuring principles of structured programming are directly reflected by the turbo ASM operators **seq** and **while**. Also more sophisticated structuring principles are supported by ASMs. We mention here the decomposition of systems into components [14], the instantiation of parameterized submachines [29] and the organization of classes into an inheritance hierarchy by a subclass (compatibility) relation as formalized for Java and the Java Virtual Machine in [62].

2.3   Undecidability and Church-Turing Thesis

In this section we show the general undecidability proof we use, starting from scratch, using half a page and five lines of proof, for the termination problem of any class of universal programs, as a preparation for the epistemological discussion of the intrinsic boundaries of the notion of virtual machine computation as well as of its wide range (Church-Turing thesis and its generalization by ASMs). **Undecidability.** Consider any programming language L that satisfies the following four closure properties (which are known to suffice to be computationally universal, see for example the above turbo ASMs computing recursive functions)[8]:

- L provides a notion of *sequential execution*, for definiteness say in the form of an operator **seq** such that $P, Q \in L$ implies P **seq** $Q \in L$.
- L provides a notion of program *iteration*, for definiteness say $P \in L$ implies **while** $b = 1\ P \in L$, where b is a program variable with boolean values 0,1.
- L provides a notion of *calling* a program for given input, for definiteness say in the form that $P \in L$ implies **Call** $P(in) \in L$, where *in* is a program input variable.
- L permits program text as input for programs[9].

---

[8] We thank Francesco Romani for having pointed out an oversight in an earlier version of this argument.

[9] This condition is of technical nature: it allows one to avoid the discussion of ways of coding of program text as input for other programs.

We denote for the given L as usual a) by $Halt(p,in)$ that program p started with input in terminates, and b) by 'p computes H' that for every input in, $Halt(p,in)$ and upon termination the output variable, say out, satisfies $out = 1$ if $H(in)$ and $out = 0$ otherwise. We prove by contradiction that there is no L-program h that computes the $Halt$ predicate for L-programs. In fact, otherwise by the above listed closure properties the following program DIAG with input variable in and output variable out would be an L-program (draw the flowchart diagram visualizing the diagonal argument):

$$\text{DIAG} = \textbf{Call } h(in, in) \textbf{ seq } (\textbf{while } out = 1 \textbf{ Call } h(in, in))$$

Due to its definition and to the definition of the $Halt$ing property, this program would satisfy the contradictory property that $Halt(\text{DIAG},\text{DIAG})$ is true if and only if $Halt(\text{DIAG},\text{DIAG})$ is not true.

Church-Turing Thesis. After having shown the above undecidability proof, we link this result to the ASMs for standard machines, algorithms, programming constructs and virtual machine or general system design models to motivate the discussion of what became known as ASM Thesis, stating roughly that for any algorithm (in the intuitive sense of the word) an ASM can be defined which simulates this algorithm with the same number of steps (up to a constant factor). This thesis generalizes the Church-Turing Thesis and provides a chance for the lecturer to attract students who have a mind for epistemological questions and are not afraid of mathematical reasoning. In fact for the case of so-called sequential and synchronous parallel ASMs a proof for the thesis can be given from a small number of postulates, as shown in [46,8] (for the sequential case one may wish to also consult the expositions in [30, Ch.7.2] and [55]).

3   Principles of Programming Languages

The literature offers a rich variety of ASM models the lecturer can choose from for every major programming language paradigm, whether logical, functional, imperative, object-oriented, with or without parallelism. This includes the complete definition (together with a mathematical analysis[10]) of real-life programmming languages and their implementations, like Java [62], C# [21], SDL-2000 [49,45] and the (forthcoming OASIS standard for the) Business Process Execution Language for Web Services BPEL4WS [39,65,38]. It also includes modeling various forms of parallelism and thread handling, for example the ones in Occam [20] or C# [61].

---

[10] The lecturer who speaks to students with interest in verification can expand here as much as he wants. For example, the detailed mathematical analysis of Java/JVM in [62] includes proofs that Java is type-safe, that the compiler is correct and complete and that the bytecode verifier is complete and sound. Also a mechanical verification of such ASM-based mathematical proofs can be presented, see for example the KIV-verification reported in [56] for the ASM-based correctness proof in [27] for the Prolog-to-WAM implementation.

Instead of focussing on a particular language, an alternative is to define an ASM to interpret high-level object-oriented programmming constructs, structured into layered modules of by and large orthogonal language features for an *imperative core* (related to sequential control by while programs, built from statements and expressions over the simple types), *static class features* (realizing procedural abstraction with class initialization and global (module) variables), *object-orientation* (with class instances, instance methods, inheritance), *exception handling, concurrency, delegates* (together with events, properties, indexers, attributes), *unsafe* code with *pointer arithmetic*. In a next step one can then instantiate that interpreter to one for a particular language, as done in [31] to concretely compare Java and C#, distilling their similarities and differences.

As a small illustrative example we extract here from the ASM for the core of Prolog in [26] a basic tree generation and traversal ASM BACKTRACK. This machine yields plenty of modeling and refinement exercises, namely to define by variations of the model the core of ISO Prolog [19] and of its various extensions (e.g. IBM's Protos-L [7,6] and constraint logic programming language CLP(R) [28]), of a functional programming language like Babel [23], of context free and of attribute grammars [50], etc. For details see [16].

The machine dynamically constructs a tree of alternatives and controls its traversal. In control state *mode = ramify*, it creates as many new children nodes to be computation *candidates* for its *currnode* as there are computation *alternatives*, provides them with the necessary *environment* and switches to *selection* mode. In *mode = select*, if at *currnode* there is no more candidate the machine BACKTRACKs, otherwise it lets the control move to TRYNEXTCANDIDATE to get *executed*. The (static or monitored) function *alternatives* determines the solution space depending upon its parameters and possibly the current state. The dynamic function *env* records the information every new node needs to carry out the computation determined by the alternative it is associated with. The macro BACK moves *currnode* one step up in the tree, to *parent(currnode)*, until the *root* is reached where the computation stops. TRYNEXTCANDIDATE moves *currnode* one step down in the tree to the *next* candidate, where *next* is a possibly dynamic choice function which determines the order for trying out the alternatives. Typically the underlying execution machine will update *mode* from *execute* to *ramify*, in case of a successful execution, or to *select* if the execution fails.

BACKTRACK =
  RAMIFY
  SELECT

RAMIFY =
  if $mode = ramify$ **then**
    let $k = |alternatives(Params)|$
    let $o_1, \ldots, o_k = new(NODE)$
      $candidates(currnode) := \{o_1, \ldots, o_k\}$
      forall $1 \leq i \leq k$

$$parent(o_i) := currnode$$
$$env(o_i) := ith(alternatives(Params))$$
$$mode := select$$

SELECT =
  if $mode = select$ then
    if $candidates(currnode) = \emptyset$ then BACK
    else
      TRYNEXTCANDIDATE
      $mode := execute$

BACK =
  if $currnode = root$
  then $mode := Stop$
  else $currnode := parent(currnode)$

TRYNEXTCANDIDATE =
  $currnode := next(candidates(currnode))$
  DELETE$(next(candidates(currnode)),$
    $candidates(currnode))$

The above mentioned exercises consist in finding instantiations of the here not furthermore specified functions *alternatives*, *next* and of the underlying system *env*ironment and execution engine EXECUTE. Instantiating the ASM to one describing tree adjoining grammars generalizes Parikh's analysis of context free languages by 'pumping' of context free trees from *basis trees* (with terminal yield) and *recursion trees* (with terminal yield except for the root variable).

4   High-Level System Design and Analysis

In the very same way we have illustrated in Section 2 ASMs to capture classical models of computation, one can show that they can also be used to model the basic semantical concepts of executable high-level design languages (like UNITY and COLD), of widely used state-based specification languages (e.g. B [2] or SCR [47,48]), of dedicated virtual machines as well as of axiomatic logic-based or stateless modeling systems. The reader can find details in [16].

This naturally leads to continue the course with advanced courses on practical system engineering methods. We have described in [13,15] a program for teaching the ASM system design and analysis method, which over the last decade has been elaborated upon the basis of ASMs as rigorous notion of virtual machine and which within a single, precise yet simple, conceptual framework naturally supports and uniformly links the major activities which occur during the typical software life cycle, namely:

- **Requirements capture** by constructing satisfactory *ground models*, i.e. accurate high-level system blueprints, serving as precise contract and formulated in a language which is understood by all stakeholders (see [11]).

- **Detailed design** by *stepwise refinement*, bridging the gap between specification and code design by piecemeal, systematically documented detailing of abstract models down to executable code (see [12]). This includes refinement steps which lead from a high-level ASM to an executable and thereby mechanically validatable ASM.
- **Validation** of models by their *simulation*, based upon the notion of ASM *run* and supported by numerous tools to execute ASMs (*ASM Workbench* [34], *AsmGofer* [57], C-based *XASM* [3], .NET-executable *AsmL* engine [40]).
- **Verification** of model properties by proof techniques, also tool supported, e.g. by KIV [56] or PVS [36,42] or Stärk's theorem prover [60] or model checkers [67,35,44].
- **Documentation** for *inspection*, *reuse* and *maintenance* by providing, through the intermediate models and their analysis, explicit descriptions of the software structure and of the major design decisions.

The lecturer can choose among a great variety of ASM-based modeling and analysis projects in such different areas as:

- industrial standardization projects: the above mentioned models for the forthcoming OASIS standard for BPEL [65], the ECMA standard for C# [21], the ITU-T standard for SDL-2000 [45], the IEEE standard for the hardware desing language VHDL93 [22], the ISO-Prolog standard [19],
- programmming languages: definition and analysis of the semantics and the implementation for the major real-life programmming languages, e.g. SystemC [54], Java and its implementation on the Java Virtual Machine [62], domain-specific languages used at the Union Bank of Switzerland [52], etc.
- architectural design: verification (e.g. of pipelining schemes [24] or of VHDL-based hardware design at Siemens [58, Ch.2]), architecture/compiler co-exploration [63,64],
- reengineering and design of industrial control systems: software projects at Siemens related to railway [18,25] and mobile telephony network components [33], debugger specification at Microsoft [4],
- protocols: for authentication, cryptography, cache-coherence, routing-layers for distributed mobile ad hoc networks, group-membership etc., focussed on verification,
- verification of compilation schemes and compiler back-ends [27,20,37,62],
- modeling e-commerce [1] and web services [39],
- simulation and testing: fire detection system in coal mines [32], simulation of railway scenarios at Siemens [25], implementation of behavioral interface specifications on the .NET platform and conformance test of COM components at Microsoft [5], compiler testing [51], test case generation [43].

The lecturer may also use instead the AsmBook [30] and the teaching material on the accompanying CD. The book introduces into the ASM method and illustrates it by textbook examples, which are extracted from the above listed real-life case studies and industrial applications.

References

1. S. Abiteboul, V. Vianu, B. Fordham, and Y. Yesha. Relational transducers for electronic commerce. In *Proc. 17th ACM Sympos. Principles of Database Systems (PODS 1998)*, pages 179–187. ACM Press, 1998.
2. J.-R. Abrial. *The B-Book*. Cambridge University Press, Cambridge, 1996.
3. M. Anlauff and P. Kutter. Xasm Open Source. Web pages at http://www.xasm.org/, 2001.
4. M. Barnett, E. Börger, Y. Gurevich, W. Schulte, and M. Veanes. Using Abstract State Machines at Microsoft: A case study. In Y. Gurevich, P. Kutter, M. Odersky, and L. Thiele, editors, *Abstract State Machines: Theory and Applications*, volume 1912 of *Lecture Notes in Computer Science*, pages 367–380. Springer-Verlag, 2000.
5. M. Barnett and W. Schulte. Contracts, components and their runtime verification on the .NET platform. *J. Systems and Software*, Special Issue on Component-Based Software Engineering, 2002, to appear.
6. C. Beierle and E. Börger. Refinement of a typed WAM extension by polymorphic order-sorted types. *Formal Aspects of Computing*, 8(5):539–564, 1996.
7. C. Beierle and E. Börger. Specification and correctness proof of a WAM extension with abstract type constraints. *Formal Aspects of Computing*, 8(4):428–462, 1996.
8. A. Blass and Y. Gurevich. Abstract State Machines capture parallel algorithms. *ACM Trans. Computational Logic*, 2002.
9. E. Börger. *Computability, Complexity, Logic (English translation of "Berechenbarkeit, Komplexität, Logik")*, volume 128 of *Studies in Logic and the Foundations of Mathematics*. North-Holland, 1989.
10. E. Börger. High-level system design and analysis using Abstract State Machines. In D. Hutter, W. Stephan, P. Traverso, and M. Ullmann, editors, *Current Trends in Applied Formal Methods (FM-Trends 98)*, volume 1641 of *Lecture Notes in Computer Science*, pages 1–43. Springer-Verlag, 1999.
11. E. Börger. The ASM ground model method as a foundation of requirements engineering. In N.Dershowitz, editor, *Verification: Theory and Practice*, volume 2772 of *LNCS*, pages 145–160. Springer-Verlag, 2003.
12. E. Börger. The ASM refinement method. *Formal Aspects of Computing*, 15:237–257, 2003.
13. E. Börger. Teaching ASMs to practice-oriented students. In *Teaching Formal Methods Workshop*, pages 5–12. Oxford Brookes University, 2003.
14. E. Börger. Linking architectural and component level system views by abstract state machines. In C. Grimm, editor, *Languages for System Specification and Verification*, CHDL, pages 247–269. Kluwer, 2004.
15. E. Börger. Modeling with Abstract State Machines: A support for accurate system design and analysis. In B. Rumpe and W. Hesse, editors, *Modellierung 2004*, volume P-45 of *GI-Edition Lecture Notes in Informatics*, pages 235–239. Springer-Verlag, 2004.
16. E. Börger. Abstract State Machines: A unifying view of models of computation and of system design frameworks. *Annals of Pure and Applied Logic*, 2004, to appear.
17. E. Börger and T. Bolognesi. Remarks on turbo ASMs for computing functional equations and recursion schemes. In E. Börger, A. Gargantini, and E. Riccobene, editors, *Abstract State Machines 2003 – Advances in Theory and Applications*, volume 2589 of *Lecture Notes in Computer Science*, pages 218–228. Springer-Verlag, 2003.

18. E. Börger, H. Busch, J. Cuellar, P. Päppinghaus, E. Tiden, and I. Wildgruber. Konzept einer hierarchischen Erweiterung von EURIS. Siemens ZFE T SE 1 Internal Report BBCPTW91-1 (pp. 1–43), Summer 1996.

19. E. Börger and K. Dässler. Prolog: DIN papers for discussion. ISO/IEC JTCI SC22 WG17 Prolog Standardization Document 58, National Physical Laboratory, Middlesex, England, 1990.

20. E. Börger and I. Durdanović. Correctness of compiling Occam to Transputer code. *Computer Journal*, 39(1):52–92, 1996.

21. E. Börger, G. Fruja, V. Gervasi, and R. Stärk. A high-level modular definition of the semantics of C#. *Theoretical Computer Science*, 2004.

22. E. Börger, U. Glässer, and W. Müller. The semantics of behavioral VHDL'93 descriptions. In *EURO-DAC'94. European Design Automation Conference with EURO-VHDL'94*, pages 500–505, Los Alamitos, California, 1994. IEEE Computer Society Press.

23. E. Börger, F. J. López-Fraguas, and M. Rodríguez-Artalejo. A model for mathematical analysis of functional logic programs and their implementations. In B. Pehrson and I. Simon, editors, *IFIP 13th World Computer Congress*, volume I: Technology/Foundations, pages 410–415, Elsevier, Amsterdam, 1994.

24. E. Börger and S. Mazzanti. A practical method for rigorously controllable hardware design. In J. P. Bowen, M. B. Hinchey, and D. Till, editors, *ZUM'97: The Z Formal Specification Notation*, volume 1212 of *Lecture Notes in Computer Science*, pages 151–187. Springer-Verlag, 1997.

25. E. Börger, P. Päppinghaus, and J. Schmid. Report on a practical application of ASMs in software design. In Y. Gurevich, P. Kutter, M. Odersky, and L. Thiele, editors, *Abstract State Machines: Theory and Applications*, volume 1912 of *Lecture Notes in Computer Science*, pages 361–366. Springer-Verlag, 2000.

26. E. Börger and D. Rosenzweig. A mathematical definition of full Prolog. *Science of Computer Programming*, 24:249–286, 1995.

27. E. Börger and D. Rosenzweig. The WAM – definition and compiler correctness. In C. Beierle and L. Plümer, editors, *Logic Programming: Formal Methods and Practical Applications*, volume 11 of *Studies in Computer Science and Artificial Intelligence*, chapter 2, pages 20–90. North-Holland, 1995.

28. E. Börger and R. Salamone. CLAM specification for provably correct compilation of CLP(ℛ) programs. In E. Börger, editor, *Specification and Validation Methods*, pages 97–130. Oxford University Press, 1995.

29. E. Börger and J. Schmid. Composition and submachine concepts for sequential ASMs. In P. Clote and H. Schwichtenberg, editors, *Computer Science Logic (Proceedings of CSL 2000)*, volume 1862 of *Lecture Notes in Computer Science*, pages 41–60. Springer-Verlag, 2000.

30. E. Börger and R. F. Stärk. *Abstract State Machines. A Method for High-Level System Design and Analysis*. Springer, 2003.

31. E. Börger and R. F. Stärk. Exploiting abstraction for specification reuse. The Java/C# case study. In M. Bonsangue, editor, *Proc. FMCO'03*, Lecture Notes in Computer Science. Springer, 2004.

32. W. Burgard, A. B. Cremers, D. Fox, M. Heidelbach, A. M. Kappel, and S. Lüttringhaus-Kappel. Knowledge-enhanced CO-monitoring in coal mines. In *Proc. Int. Conf. on Industrial and Engineering Applications of Artificial Intelligence and Expert Systems (IEA-AIE)*, pages 511–521, Fukuoka, Japan, 4–7 June 1996. .

33. G. D. Castillo and P. Päppinghaus. Designing software for internet telephony: experiences in an industrial development process. In A. Blass, E. Börger, and Y. Gurevich, editors, *Theory and Applications of Abstract State Machines*, Schloss Dagstuhl, Int. Conf. and Research Center for Computer Science, 2002.

34. G. Del Castillo. *The ASM Workbench. A Tool Environment for Computer-Aided Analysis and Validation of Abstract State Machine Models.* PhD thesis, Universität Paderborn, Germany, 2001.

35. G. Del Castillo and K. Winter. Model checking support for the ASM high-level language. In S. Graf and M. Schwartzbach, editors, *Proc. 6th Int. Conf. TACAS 2000*, volume 1785 of *Lecture Notes in Computer Science*, pages 331–346. Springer-Verlag, 2000.

36. A. Dold. A formal representation of Abstract State Machines using PVS. Verifix Technical Report Ulm/6.2, Universität Ulm, Germany, July 1998.

37. A. Dold, T. Gaul, V. Vialard, and W. Zimmermann. ASM-based mechanized verification of compiler back-ends. In U. Glässer and P. Schmitt, editors, *Proc. 5th Int. Workshop on Abstract State Machines*, pages 50–67. Magdeburg University, 1998.

38. D. Fahland. Ein Ansatz einer Formalen Semantik der Business Process Execution Language for Web Services mit Abstract State Machines. Master's thesis, Humboldt-Universität zu Berlin, June 2004.

39. R. Farahbod, U. Glässer, and M. Vajihollahi. Specification and validation of the business process execution language for web services. In W. Zimmermann and B. Thalheim, editors, *Abstract Sate Machines 2004*, volume 3052 of *Lecture Notes in Computer Science*, pages 78–94. Springer-Verlag, 2004.

40. Foundations of Software Engineering Group, Microsoft Research. AsmL. Web pages at http://research.microsoft.com/foundations/AsmL/, 2001.

41. N. G. Fruja and R. F. Stärk. The hidden computation steps of turbo Abstract State Machines. In E. Börger, A. Gargantini, and E. Riccobene, editors, *Abstract State Machines 2003–Advances in Theory and Applications*, volume 2589 of *Lecture Notes in Computer Science*, pages 244–262. Springer-Verlag, 2003.

42. A. Gargantini and E. Riccobene. Encoding Abstract State Machines in PVS. In Y. Gurevich, P. Kutter, M. Odersky, and L. Thiele, editors, *Abstract State Machines: Theory and Applications*, volume 1912 of *Lecture Notes in Computer Science*, pages 303–322. Springer-Verlag, 2000.

43. A. Gargantini and E. Riccobene. Using Spin to generate tests from ASM specifications. In E. Börger, A. Gargantini, and E. Riccobene, editors, *Abstract State Machines 2003–Advances in Theory and Applications*, volume 2589 of *Lecture Notes in Computer Science*, pages 263–277. Springer-Verlag, 2003.

44. A. Gawanmeh, S. Tahar, and K. Winter. Interfacing ASMs with the MDG tool. In E. Börger, A. Gargantini, and E. Riccobene, editors, *Abstract State Machines 2003–Advances in Theory and Applications*, volume 2589 of *Lecture Notes in Computer Science*, pages 278–292. Springer-Verlag, 2003.

45. U. Glässer, R. Gotzhein, and A. Prinz. Formal semantics of SDL-2000: Status and perspectives. *Computer Networks*, 42(3):343–358, June 2003.

46. Y. Gurevich. Sequential Abstract State Machines capture sequential algorithms. *ACM Trans. Computational Logic*, 1(1):77–111, July 2000.

47. C. Heitmeyer. Using SCR methods to capture, document, and verify computer system requirements. In E. Börger, B. Hörger, D. L. Parnas, and D. Rombach, editors, *Requirements Capture, Documentation, and Validation*. Dagstuhl Seminar No. 99241, Schloss Dagstuhl, Int. Conf. and Research Center for Computer Science, 1999.

48. C. Heitmeyer. Software cost reduction. In J. J. Marciniak, editor, *Enc. of Software Engineering.* 2nd edition, 2002.
49. ITU-T. SDL formal semantics definition. ITU-T Recommendation Z.100 Annex F, International Telecommunication Union, November 2000.
50. D. E. Johnson and L. S. Moss. Grammar formalisms viewed as Evolving Algebras. *Linguistics and Philosophy,* 17:537–560, 1994.
51. A. Kalinov, A. Kossatchev, A. Petrenko, M. Posypkin, and V. Shishkov. Using ASM specifications for compiler testing. In E. Börger, A. Gargantini, and E. Riccobene, editors, *Abstract State Machines 2003–Advances in Theory and Applications,* volume 2589 of *Lecture Notes in Computer Science,* page 415. Springer-Verlag, 2003.
52. P. Kutter, D. Schweizer, and L. Thiele. Integrating domain specific language design in the software life cycle. In *Proc. Int. Workshop on Current Trends in Applied Formal Methods,* volume 1641 of *Lecture Notes in Computer Science,* pages 196–212. Springer-Verlag, 1998.
53. H. Langmaack. An ALGLO-view on TURBO ASM. In W. Zimmermann and B. Thalheim, editors, *Abstract Sate Machines 2004,* volume 3052 of *Lecture Notes in Computer Science,* pages 20–37. Springer-Verlag, 2004.
54. W. Mueller, J. Ruf, and W. Rosenstiel. An ASM-based semantics of systemC simulation. In W. Mueller, J. Ruf, and W. Rosenstiel, editors, *SystemC - Methodologies and Applications,* pages 97–126. Kluwer Academic Publishers, 2003.
55. W. Reisig. On Gurevich's theorem on sequential algorithms. *Acta Informatica,* 39(5):273–305, 2003.
56. G. Schellhorn and W. Ahrendt. Reasoning about Abstract State Machines: The WAM case study. *J. Universal Computer Science,* 3(4):377–413, 1997.
57. J. Schmid. Executing ASM specifications with AsmGofer. Web pages at `http://www.tydo.de/AsmGofer`.
58. J. Schmid. *Refinement and Implementation Techniques for Abstract State Machines.* PhD thesis, University of Ulm, Germany, 2002.
59. D. Scott. Definitional suggestions for automata theory. *J. Computer and System Sciences,* 1:187–212, 1967.
60. R. F. Stärk. Formal verification of the C# thread model. Department of Computer Science, ETH Zürich, 2004.
61. R. F. Stärk and E. Börger. An ASM specification of C# threads and the .NET memory model. In W. Zimmermann and B. Thalheim, editors, *Abstract State Machines 2004,* volume 3052 of *Lecture Notes in Computer Science,* pages 38–60. Springer-Verlag, 2004.
62. R. F. Stärk, J. Schmid, and E. Börger. *Java and the Java Virtual Machine: Definition, Verification, Validation.* Springer-Verlag, 2001.
63. J. Teich. Project Buildabong at University of Paderborn. `http://www-date.upb.de/RESEARCH/BUILDABONG/buildabong.html`, 2001.
64. J. Teich, R. Weper, D. Fischer, and S. Trinkert. A joint architecture/compiler design environment for ASIPs. In *Proc. Int. Conf. on Compilers, Architectures and Synthesis for Embedded Systems (CASES2000),* pages 26–33, San Jose, CA, USA, November 2000. ACM Press.
65. M. Vajihollahi. High level specification and validation of the business process execution language for web services. Master's thesis, School of Computing Science at Simon Fraser University, March 2004.
66. P. Wegner. Why interaction is more powerful than algorithms. *Commun. ACM,* 40:80–91, 1997.
67. K. Winter. Model checking for Abstract State Machines. *J. Universal Computer Science,* 3(5):689–701, 1997.

Teaching How to Derive Correct Concurrent Programs from State-Based Specifications and Code Patterns*

Manuel Carro, Julio Mariño, Ángel Herranz, and Juan José Moreno-Navarro

Facultad de Informática
Universidad Politécnica de Madrid
28660 Boadilla del Monte, Madrid, SPAIN
{mcarro,jmarino,aherranz,jjmoreno}@fi.upm.es

Abstract. The fun of teaching and learning concurrent programming is sometimes darkened by the difficulty in getting concurrent programs to work right. In
line with other programming subjects in our department, we advocate the use of
formal specifications to state clearly how a concurrent program must behave, to
reason about this behavior, and to be able to produce code from specifications
in a semi-automatic fashion. We argue that a mild form of specification not
only makes it possible to get programs running easier, but it also introduces
students to a quite systematic way of approaching programming: reading and
understanding specifications is seen as an unavoidable step in the programming
process, as they are really the only place where the expected conduct of the
system is described. By using formal techniques in these cases, where they are
undoubtedly appropriate, we introduce formality without the need to resort to
justifications with artificial or overly complicated examples.

Keywords: Concurrent Programming, Formal Specification, Code Generation,
Safety, Liveness, Ada.

1 Introduction

At the Universidad Politécnica de Madrid (UPM), the intents of introducing rigorous
development methods into mainstream Computer Science takes place in two fronts. In
the research front, several groups work in the application of logic to the development of
safe software through the design and implementation of multiparadigm programming
languages such as Ciao [9] or Curry [6], or environments for the development of industrial software around formal specifications, such as SLAM [10]. But we have also a
strong commitment on the *academic* front. In 1996, with the introduction of the current
curriculum, programming courses were completely redesigned and formal specifications
made an early appearance at the first year — *understanding* the problem at hand and
devising a solution was given the same importance as the sheer fact of *coding* it.

---

* This research was partly supported by the Spanish MCYT project TIC2002-0055 and by EU
projects FET IST-2001-33123 and FET IST-2001-38059.

C.N. Dean and R.T. Boute (Eds.): TFM 2004, LNCS 3294, pp. 85–106, 2004.

Teaching Programming and the Use of Formal Methods. Classic approaches to programming courses in computing curricula tend to be *language centered*: learning is to some extent driven by the features available in some (often imperative) programming language (Ada, C, C++, Java...), and programming techniques follow from them. The typical argument is that students get a better motivation by having a *hands-on* experience as soon as possible. While this is true to some extent, there are also some problems. As the number of imperative constructions in many programming languages is large, they are usually presented in an informal manner and the corresponding classroom examples are just designed to practice the last piece of syntax. In most cases, students do not need to know all the idioms provided by a given programming language, and their use tends to obscure, rather than to illuminate, the principles behind algorithms, data, and program structures.

In this model, formal methods appear just as an *a posteriori* evaluation tool. Students have problems trying to interleave the program development process with these techniques, which are perceived as complicate, boring and useless. For instance, formal verification is introduced when the student is able to develop complex problems (e.g. a phone agenda), but it is used for almost toy examples (e.g. at most a QuickSort is verified). This is clearly disappointing.

We advocate an approach to the teaching of programming where a rigorous process is used from the very beginning as a design and development tool. But students will perceive these techniques as *useful*, and not as a necessary evil, only if a systematic way of developing programs is provided. The starting point is *problem specification*. A formal specification language is introduced in the first year. This language uses pre/post-condition pairs for describing the relationship between the input and output of every operation, using a language heavily based on first-order logic. We distinguish between *raw* specifications (with a distant connection to implementation) and *solved* specifications, refined in such a way that some generic method can be used to obtain a prototypical code from them. Most of the specification in the concurrent programming course can be considered in *solved form*, as an algorithm can be easily read in them.

Types are also introduced from the very beginning, as we consider modeling an essential activity of software development.[1] A basic toolkit and the ability to introduce new types suited to specific problems are also built into the specification language. In the second year the specification notation is extended to abstract data types and classes in order to cover the programming-in-the-large phase. Finally, in the third year the notation is further extended with annotations for concurrency.

We have been using a functional language (Haskell) as first target language, which allows our students to get familiar with programming and rigorous development more rapidly — and having more fun. Nevertheless, the use of a functional language is not compulsory, as the way to obtain imperative code from solutions is almost as easy as in the declarative case. In fact, at the end of the first semester imperative programming is introduced and Ada 95 [19] is used in most of the following courses.

All these ideas have been applied at our department over the last seven years, with satisfying results:

---

[1] By the way, something usually ignored even in textbooks where formal methods are used.

- Students attack problems from a systematic point of view, leaving *eureka* steps as a last resort.
- Students understand and acknowledge the role of a rigorous, careful methodology in the programming process.
- The average of marks is better, which (modulo interferences inherent to the teaching and examination process) makes it reasonable to think that more students are able to develop computer programs with a satisfactory degree of correctness.
- The knowledge of students seems to be more solid, as per the opinion of our colleagues from other subjects (Software Engineering, Databases, Artificial Intelligence, etc.).

Organization of the Paper. Next section discusses issues specific to teaching concurrency in the CS curriculum and how formal methods can be an improvement. Section 3 introduces the notation used to specify shared resources in an architecture-independent way. Section 4 (resp. 5) deals with the derivation of correct concurrent programs for the shared-memory (resp. message-passing) setting, starting from a shared resource specification. Section 6 discusses some related work in this area, and finally Sect. 7 summarizes successful aspects of our experience and points out shortcomings and possible improvements of this approach.

2   Teaching Concurrent Programming

Concurrent programming is not a prevalent topic in undergraduate curricula [7]. When it appears in a curriculum, it is usually approached from the perspective of teaching concurrency concepts and mechanisms, and seldom from the problem-solving perspective. Very often, known solutions for known problems are described, but not how solutions for new problems can be devised, which is left to the intuition of the students. This is aggravated by the inclusion of concurrency as part of subjects whose core belongs to operating systems and/or architecture,[2] and then concurrent programming has to serve the aims of the main subject. Sadly, this neglects the role of concurrency as a key aspect for the overall quality of almost every serious piece of software today – not just systems software – addressing issues such as usability, efficiency, dependability, etc.

For our students, concurrent programming is both an opportunity of having more fun – programs are suddenly interactive, and a new dimension appears: *time* – but also a challenging activity, as reasoning on the correctness (both partial and total) of a concurrent program may be rather involved. Discovering that previous ideas on how to debug a program are of little help when your application deadlocks or shows an unpredictable (and irreproducible) or unexpected behavior comes as a shock.

These difficulties make this subject an ideal vehicle for convincing students of the benefits of using methods which emphasize rigor in the development of high integrity software. In fact, years before 1996, concurrent programming was already the more logic-biased of our courses, and some kind of logic tables were used to aid the development of

---

[2] Even the Computing Curricula 2001 for Computer Science [16] includes concurrency into the operating systems area.

code for monitors. It took several years, however, to evolve these tables into a language for the specification of shared resources, separate the static and dynamic components of concurrent systems, and devise a development methodology.

There is a wealth of teaching material on concurrent languages and concepts that many authors have developed for years, and improving it is not an easy task. Therefore we do use introductory documentation on basic concepts [2,1] and on systems and language extensions. We try to make students aware of this material by devoting a sizable amount of time (the concurrent programming course spans over a semester) to going over it and classifying different language proposals in a taxonomy, while giving hints on how to adapt the development method we teach to languages other than Ada 95.[3] When dealing with, e.g., semaphores, this gives also precious insights about how compilers generate code for high-level concurrency proposals, but without the burden of having to deal with the whole compilation process.

After the introduction of these standard contents – properties and risks of concurrent programs (mutual exclusion, absence of deadlock, fairness, etc.); classic synchronization and communication mechanisms (from semaphores to monitors and CSP) – our students learn a development methodology that can be summarized in the following six stages:

1. Process identification.
2. Identification of inter-process interactions.
3. Defining the control flow of processes.
4. Process interaction definition.
5. Implementation/refinement of process interaction.
6. Analysis of the solution's properties (correctness, security and liveness).

Obviously, this is an iterative process. The main idea is that steps 1 to 5 should produce a *partially correct* solution, i.e. code that meets the safety requirements of the problem. Moreover, this code is generated in a semi-automatic way from the definition of interactions (stage no. 4.) Further iterations of stages 5 and 6 should only be used to enforce liveness and priority properties, or to improve the system's performance.

The other key idea is that the process is highly independent of the language and architecture used. This is clearly true of stages 1–4 and, for stage 5, specific code generation schemes (in our case for Ada 95) are provided, giving support to both shared-memory mechanisms (protected objects [19, Sect. 9.4]) and message-passing ones (rendez-vous [19, Sect. 9.7]). Some reasons for using Ada 95 as the development environment are: most programming courses in our University run with Ada so students do not need to learn a new language, Ada is not a toy language so serious programs can be implemented, Ada has mature built-in concurrency constructs (Ada Tasking Model) well suited to the code synthesis schemes, Ada is a very well designed programming language with high level abstraction mechanisms, and there are free tools available for several platforms.

Stage 1 (process identification) is done via an informal (but systematic) analysis of the interactions of the application, and abstract state machines are used in stage 6. We have left these issues out of the scope of this paper.

---

[3] Or CC-Modula [15], a variant of Modula developed in-house which featured semaphores, monitors, message passing, and conditional regions, and which was used for several years before Ada 95 was adopted.

CADT Resource Name
  OPERATIONS
    ACTION Op_1: *Resource_Type[io]* $\times$ *Type$_1$[i]* $\times \ldots \times$ *Type$_n$[o]*
    ACTION Op_2: *Resource_Type[io]* $\times$ *Type$_1$[i]* $\times \ldots \times$ *Type$_n$[o]*
     $\vdots$

SEMANTICS
  DOMAIN:
   TYPE: *Resource_Type* $= \ldots$
   INVARIANT: $\forall r \in Resource\_Type \bullet I(r)$

  INITIAL(r): *A formula on r specifying initial values for the resource*
  PRE: $P(a_1, \ldots, a_n)$
  CPRE: *This is an explanation of what the concurrency precondition means*
  CPRE: $C(r, a_1, \ldots, a_n)$
   Op$_1$(r, a$_1$, ..., a$_n$)
  POST: *This is an explanation of what the postcondition means*
  POST: $Q(r, a_1, \ldots, a_n)$
   $\vdots$

Fig. 1. Resource specification: a minimal template

One definite advantage of our approach is that it offers a general framework for analyzing problems where concurrency is mandatory, and a method to detect processes and resources (i.e., to wrap up the architecture of the system) and to specify and implement the system. Teaching design patterns in a language-independent fashion is also easier, since there is a language with which these can be expressed. To the best of our knowledge, the path we follow is novel in an undergraduate curriculum.

3 Notation and Logic Toolkit

We will now introduce shortly the formalism we use. This is necessary as it has been devised for the subjects taught at (and teaching style of) our institution. Although the core ideas are basically a simplification of well-known formal methods, such as VDM [14], some special constructions (regarding, e.g., concurrency) have been added. Following the classification in [20], our resource specifications are state-based, and this state is accessed only through a set of public operations. A template of a resource specification is shown in Fig. 1.

The development methodology we advocate relies strongly on the assumption that the system to design and implement can be expressed as a collection of processes which interact through shared resources (see Fig. 2) called **CADT** (for **C**oncurrent **A**bstract **D**ata **T**ype) in our notation. Introducing concurrency as an evolution of data types presents it as a generalization of data abstractions where emphasis is put on the interaction with the environment instead of on their internal organization and algorithms. As we will see

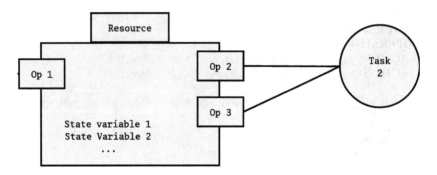

Fig. 2. Typical architecture of a concurrent program

later, it does not matter whether the final implementation is based on shared or distributed memory, as we have developed code generation schemes for both paradigms.

Unlike other approaches, our specification language does not aim at capturing the behavior of the processes, which are instead coded directly in the final programming language (or can even be derived using the methodology for sequential algorithms taught in other courses, which is out of the scope for this paper). In what follows we will give a brief account of the main characteristics of the specification language, leaving out some parts not needed for our purposes in this paper.

We will use as running example the specification and implementation of a multibuffer, in which processes can store and retrieve items from an encapsulated queue in series of k elements, instead of just one by one. This example is simple to state, but at the same time it makes it possible to review quite a few different points: synchronization which depends on the input parameters, liveness properties which depend both on the interleaving of calls and on their runtime arguments, and different schedules based on priority requirements. The lack of need of a partial exclusion protocol, like the one in the readers/writers problems, is the only relevant missing characteristic.

We want to point out that the method we teach can easily go beyond this example to small prototypes of train barriers, video broadcast systems, robot interaction in industries, computer-controlled auctions, and a wide range of other non trivial cases, which we use as homework assignment and exam problems. See pointers to them at the end of Sect. 7. We consider that the average difficulty of these problems is high for an undergraduate course, and they certainly surpass that of the typical (but not less relevant) producers and consumers.

The specification language is strongly based on first-order logic, which is taught to most CS students at some point. Using it avoids introducing additional formalisms, reinforces the use of logic(s), often subject to misconceptions or poorly taught, and supports their role within computer science and related fields at several levels, from hardware design to program analysis and development [3].

3.1 Public Interface: Actions and Their Signatures

The **OPERATIONS** section defines the names and signatures of the public operations. Additionally, the input/output qualification of every argument can be optionally stated by marking them as i (input, immutable), o (output), or io; see the example below. We will show in Sect. 3.3 how changes to the arguments are expressed.

Unlike other approaches to specifying resources (e.g., [8]), the state is not directly available to the body of the specification, but it must be a formal parameter of every operation. We adopt the convention that this parameter is the leftmost one, and it has always input/output mode.[4]

Example: Operation names and signatures in the multibuffer

CADT MultiBuffer

OPERATIONS
ACTION Put: *Multi_Buffer[io]* × *Item_Seq[i]*
ACTION Get: *Multi_Buffer[io]* × *Item_Seq[o]* × $\mathbb{N}[i]$

Note that **Put** does not receive the number of items to be stored — we assume that we want to deposit the whole sequence held in the second parameter. **Get**, on the other hand, receives the number of items to retrieve, but it could as well have received a sequence of the appropriate length.

3.2 Domain: Types and Invariants

We chose to have a relatively rich set of initial types which help in modeling different situations. This makes it possible to have short and understandable specifications, to factor out well-known issues related to data structures, and to focus on concurrency matters. We will now describe very briefly the available types and how invariants are written.

Basic, Algebraic and Complex Types. Basic types include booleans ($\mathbb{B}$), naturals ($\mathbb{N}$), integers ($\mathbb{Z}$), and real numbers ($\mathbb{R}$). We include also algebraic types to define enumeration, subranges, products, unions, and constructors. There is also syntax for sequences, sets, finite mappings, and to assign names to fields of algebraic constructors and components of product types. The availability of complex types helps to have specifications which are more readable and closer to what many programmers are used to. Note that many computer languages do not have builtin types for all of the above. Implementing them is a matter of another subject which escapes the present piece of work.[5]

We will here describe sequences very briefly, as they will be used in the rest of the paper. Sequences are a superset of lists and one-dimensional arrays. They represent

---

[4] We want to remark that this is not a key requirement. Adapting the specification to allow operations to refer to resource-wide variables does not affect greatly its syntax and semantics. We prefer, however, to keep it in a non object-oriented state for coherence with other subjects taught before at our school.

[5] But libraries are, of course, acceptable.

finite (but with no fixed length) indexed collections of elements. Assuming s_1 and s_2 are sequences and i, j are integers, operations on sequences include finding their length (Length(s_1)), accessing the i-th element ($s_1(i)$), accessing a subsequence ($s_1(i..j)$) and concatenating two sequences (s_1+s_2). Sequences are written with their elements between angle brackets, the empty sequence being $\langle\rangle$. A sequence of elements of type T is declared as Sequence(T).

Invariants. The invariant is a formula which constrains the range of a type, aiming both at having only meaningful values and at specifying which states the resource must **not** evolve into: since the invariant does not have a notion of history, it can be used to state at most safety properties. The resource specification, and the processes accessing it, must ensure that banned states cannot be reached. For example, a type definition of a strictly increasing sequence follows:

TYPE: *Increasing* = Sequence($\mathbb{N}$)
INVARIANT: $\forall s \in Increasing \bullet$
$\qquad (l = \mathsf{Length}(s) \wedge (l < 2 \vee \forall k, 1 \le k \le l - 1 \bullet s(k) < s(k+1)))$

In the multibuffer example, a possible type definition is the following:

Example: Type definition for the multibuffer

TYPE: *Multi_Buffer* = Sequence(*Data*)
$\qquad$ *Item_Seq* = *Multi_Buffer*
INVARIANT: $\forall b \in Multi\_Buffer \bullet \mathsf{Length}(b) \le MAX$

Note that the aim of the invariant here is just to set an upper limit to the size of the multibuffer. We have used the same data structure both for the multibuffer itself and for the parameters which store the data to be read and written. Since *Item_Seq* is of type *Multi_Buffer*, it is subject to the same constraints.

3.3   Specifying the Effect of Operations

Preconditions and postconditions are used to describe the changes operations make to the resource state, and when these operations can proceed. Both are first-order formulas which involve the resource and the arguments of the operations. For clarity reasons, we accept also natural language descriptions to back up (but not to replace) the logical ones.

Synchronization. We assume that resource operations proceed in mutual exclusion, but ensuring this is left to the final implementation, and is fairly easy to do in most languages (and automatic in Ada 95).

Condition synchronization is taken care of by means of concurrency preconditions (**CPRE**), which are evaluated against the state the resource has at the time of performing the (re)evaluation. A call whose **CPRE** is evaluated to *false* will block until a change in the resource makes it *true*, i.e., when some other process modifies the resource in the adequate direction. Since our design method assumes that the resource is the only means of inter-process communication, call parameters cannot be shared among processes (they should go into the resource in that case). This implies that their value can be changed only by the process *owning* them, and they cannot be updated while the call is suspended. A **CPRE** must therefore involve **always** the resource. From all calls to operations whose **CPRE**s evaluate to *true*, only one is allowed to proceed. We do not assume any fixed selection procedure — not even fairness.

CPREs are intended to express safety conditions. Liveness properties might be dealt with at this level by adding state variables to the resource and enriching the preconditions. However, in most cases this makes specifications harder to read and hides safety properties. Besides, programming languages often have their own idioms to deal with liveness. Therefore, and as part of the methodology we teach, studying liveness properties is delayed until code with provable safety properties has been generated. This study is made more intuitive (but not less formal) with the help of a graph representing the states of the resource. From an educational point of view this is in line with a top-down development which aims at achieving correctness first.

Sequential preconditions (**PRE**) can be added to the operations. These are not aimed at producing code; rather, they are required to hold for the operation to be called safely, and ensuring this is responsibility of the caller. Naturally, **PRE**s should not reference the state of the resource, or races in its evaluation can appear. Having this distinction at the level of the specification language makes it clear which conditions stem from synchronization considerations, and which are necessary for data structure coherence.

Example: Condition synchronization in the multibuffer example

PRE: $quant \leq \mathsf{Length}(seq)$

CPRE: $\mathsf{Length}(mbuffer) \geq quant$

Get(mbuffer, seq, quant)

POST: ...

CPRE: $\mathsf{Length}(mbuffer + seq) \leq MAX$

Put(mbuffer, seq)

POST: ...

In this example, the synchronization uses the size of the multibuffer and the amount of data to be transferred. The **Get** operation uses the parameter *quant* to know how many items are to be withdrawn, and the **Put** operation uses the length of the sequence holding the data. Synchronization boils down to making sure that there are enough empty places/items in the multibuffer — calls to **Put/Get** would suspend otherwise. Additionally, the sequence passed to **Get** as parameter must be large enough to hold the required number of items; this is expressed by the **PRE** condition. Failure to meet that property can certainly cause malfunction.

Updating Resources and Arguments. Changes in the resource and in the actual call arguments are specified using per-operation postconditions (**POST**) which relate the state of the resource (and of the output variables) before and after the call. When **POST**s are executed, the **PRE** and **CPRE** of the operation and the invariant are assumed to hold.

Values before and after the operation are decorated with the superscripts "in" and "out", respectively.[6]

Example: State update in the multibuffer

We add the lacking postconditions to the previous piece of code:

CPRE: ...   **CPRE:** ...

   Get(mbuffer, seq, quant)   **Put(mbuffer, seq)**

POST: $mbuffer^{in} =$ **POST:** $mbuffer^{out} =$

   $seq^{out}(1..quant)+mbuffer^{out}$ $mbuffer^{in}+seq^{in}$

Since we had required that the length of the retrieved sequence be large enough to hold the number of items required, we just fill in a prefix of that sequence.

3.4   Process Code

The skeletons of two minimal processes (a consumer and a producer) which access the multibuffer using the shared variable M are shown below. The Data variables are assumed to be local to each process. When teaching we adopt directly the Ada 95 object style for task and protected object invocation. This slight syntax change does not surprise students at all.

Example: Skeletons of processes accessing the multibuffer

```
loop                              loop
   Get(Mb, Data);                    -- <Produce some Data>
   -- <Do something with Data>       Put(Mb, Data);
end loop;                         end loop;
```

3.5   Other Goodies

The initial value of a resource can be expressed using a first-order formula. Specifying desirable concurrency or a necessary sequentiality among calls to resource operations is also possible. This is useful to perform a stepwise refinement towards a resource which does not require partial exclusion, or whose preconditions and postconditions can be fine tuned so that they do not perform unnecessary checks/suspensions.

4   Deriving Ada 95 Protected Objects

Concurrent programming based on shared memory is done via the *protected objects* mechanism of Ada 95. A protected object in Ada 95 is a kind of module (*package*, in Ada lingo) that guarantees mutual exclusion of public operations (*entries*, left column of Fig. 3). Protected objects can have also private entries which can be invoked only from inside the code of the same object. We will term them *delayed operations* because we will use them to split a public operation into several stages in order to suspend the caller

```
protected type Protected_Type is          protected body Protected_Type is
  entry Public_Op_1 (parameters);           entry Public_Op_1 (parameters)
    ...                                         when condition is
private                                         begin
  <Constant and variable declarations>            ...
  <(resource state)>                          end Public_Op_1;
  entry Private_Op_1 (parameters);              ...
    ...                                       entry Private_Op_1 (parameters)
  <Constant and variable declarations>          when  condition is
  <(additional resource state)>                 begin
                                                  ...
    ...                                       end Private_Op_1;
end Protected_Type;                             ...
                                            end Protected_Type;
```

Fig. 3. Scheme of an Ada 95 protected object

task under some synchronization circumstances. They are shown in the right column of the code in Fig. 3.

Boolean conditions associated to every entry are called *guards* and are used to implement conditional synchronization. They are said to be *open* when they evaluate to *true*, and *closed* otherwise. Once a protected type has been defined and implemented, protected objects (instances of the protected type) can be declared, and operations on objects are invoked using an object oriented syntax:

PO_1, PO_2 : Protected_Type;
PO_1.Public_Op_i (actual parameters);

4.1 Dynamic Behavior of Protected Objects

This is a partial description of the behavior of a protected object when it has been invoked. The reader is referred to any of the several good books on Ada (e.g., [4,5]) for more precise details on protected objects and Ada 95 tasks.

When an operation is invoked on a protected object, the caller task must acquire exclusive read/write access first, suspending until any task with a lock on the object relinquishes it. Execution can proceed if the corresponding guard is open; the caller task is otherwise added to an *entry queue* and suspended until it is selected (or cancelled). Mutual exclusion (as it was required by the **CADT**s) is ensured by the protected object itself. This relieves the student from repeating once and again the same code pattern to achieve mutual exclusion, and leaves more time to focus on more complex concurrency matters.

Although conditional synchronization can often be directly left to the guards of each (public) entry, Ada 95 states (based on efficiency considerations) that guards can not refer to formal parameters of the operations, which is a clear handicap when **CPRE**s depend on them, as in the case of the multibuffer.

---

[6] Although this requirement is sometimes overlooked when the mode declaration in the signature is enough to disambiguate expressions.

```
entry Op_X (parameters)
when  CPRE is
   -- CPRE does not depend on parameters
begin -- CPRE holds here (just checked)
   -- PRE can be tested here
   <Op_X implementation>
   -- POST should hold here; it can be checked
end Op_X;
```

Fig. 4. Independence of the input data

Several approaches to overcome this limitation are found in the Ada literature [4], ranging from having multiple protected objects (when possible) to performing polling on the variables shared by the **CPRE** and the entry head. We, however, opt for a less "clever trick" type of approach which is applicable to any case.[7] This, in our opinion, furnishes the student with a (perhaps not very shiny) armor to fend off problems with, and which makes the implementation in itself not challenging at all. This leaves more time to focus on, e.g., design matters, which we have found to be one of the weaker points of our students.

4.2 Code Schemes for Condition Synchronization

In a first, general approach (see Sect. 4.4 for more interesting cases), each public operation in the resource is mapped onto a public entry of a protected object and, possibly, on one or more private entries. Distinguishing those cases is key to achieve a correct code; however, a syntactic analysis of the resource specification provides a safe approximation.

Synchronization Independent of Input Data. When the **CPRE** does not depend on the formal parameters of the operation (in a simplistic approach: when it does not involve them), the translation is straightforward, as shown in Fig. 4. Note that this is a very common case, found in many classical concurrency problems.

Note that in Fig. 4 runtime checking is added to the code. Although students are expected to be able to understand a specification well enough so as to generate correct code for postconditions and preconditions, we strongly advice to include these extra checks. They are usually easy to write — easier than crafting an entry body which implements constructively the postcondition — and they provide an additional support that the code is indeed correct. In a *production* stage (e.g., when the homework is handed in) these checks may be removed.

Remember also that **CADT**s do not allow to specify *side-effects*, i.e. change of state outside the resource or the actual parameters. According to our methodology, these should be placed in the processes' code.

Synchronization Dependent on Input Data: Input Driven Approach. When the **CPRE** uses formal parameters of the operation, the method we apply to overcome the

---

[7] The witty apprentice can always find in the design process a source of mind challenges.

limitations of Ada 95 resorts to using a more involved implementation which saves the state of the input parameters onto an enlarged object state, or which maps this state onto a larger program code. Both techniques use delayed entries.

In the latter case, new delayed entries (one for each of the instances of the **CPRE** obtained by instantiating the shared variables with all the values in their domain) are introduced. Let Φ be the formula corresponding to some **CPRE**, and let us suppose that Φ depends on the entry parameter $a_1 : D$ where $D = \{x_{11}, \ldots, x_{1n_1}\}$. The versions of Φ induced by the values of a_1 are:

$$\Phi[a_1 := x_{11}] \quad \ldots \quad \Phi[a_1 := x_{1n_1}]$$

where $\Phi[a_1 := x_{1i}]$ denotes Φ after substituting a_1 for x_{1i}. The process can be repeated if Φ depends on other parameters $a_2, \ldots, a_k$ (but we will assume that $k = 1$ and we will not use subscripts to name the variables). The resulting scheme is shown in Fig. 5. An advantage of this approach is that parameters do not need to be copied, and that the type D does not matter — it can therefore be applied, in principle, to any program (when D is finite). On the other hand, if $|D|$ is large, the number of delayed entries becomes impractical to be written manually.

```
entry Op_X (a,b)                          entry Delyd_Op_X_x_i (a,b)
-- CPRE depends on parameter a            -- Private delayed entry for Op_X
when True is                              when CPRE[a := x_i] is
begin                                     -- CPRE completely coded in the guard
   case a is                              begin
      when x_1 => requeue Delyd_Op_X_x_1;    -- CPRE holds
      ...                                     <Op_X assuming a = x_i>
      when x_n => requeue Delyd_Op_X_x_n;    -- POST holds
   end case;                                  <Runtime assertions to check POST>
end Op_X;                                 end Delyd_Op_X_x_i;
...
```

Fig. 5. General scheme for parameter-dependent preconditions

Ada 95 has a code replication mechanism, termed *entry families* [19, Sec. 9.5.2 and 9.5.3] which makes it possible to write code parametric on scalar types (see the example in Sect. 4.3). While this solution works around replication problems in many cases, it has also some drawbacks: it cannot be applied to the case of complex or non-scalar types (e.g., floats), and using it when $|D|$ is very large may lead to low performance. We therefore recommend using it with care. Possible solutions to this problem are to abstract large domains, when possible, into a coarser data type (which needs some art and craft), or resort to solutions based on the *Task Driven Approach*, explained next.

Synchronization Depends on Input Data: Task Driven Approach. A solution to avoid a large number of replicated delayed entries is to move the indexing method from the types of the variables to the domain of tasks accessing the resource. In general, the number of tasks that may access the resource is smaller than the number of versions

```
entry Op_X (Caller : PID, a, b)
-- CPRE depends on a. Only
-- one call with the same Caller
when True is
begin
    -- Save parameter in CPRE
    -- into vectors A_Copy
    A_Copy(Caller):=a;
    requeue Delayed_Op_X(Caller);
end Op_X;
```

```
entry Delayed_Op_X(Caller : PID) (a, b)
-- This is a private entry
when CPRE[a := A_Copy(Caller)] is
-- CPRE is completely coded
begin   -- CPRE holds
    <Op_X assuming a = A_Copy(Caller)>
    -- POST holds
    <Runtime assertions to check POST>
end Delayed_Op_X;
```

Fig. 6. Scheme for the *Task Driven* approach (using entry families)

```
entry Op_X (a, b)
-- CPRE depends on a
when not Closed_X is
begin
    -- Copy parameters
    A_Copy := a;
    Closed_X := True;
    requeue Delayed_Op_X;
end Op_X;
. . .
```

```
entry Delayed_Op_X (a, b)
-- This is a private entry
when CPRE[a := A_Copy] is
-- CPRE is completely coded
begin
    -- CPRE holds
    <Op_X assuming a = A_Copy>
    Closed_X := False;
    -- POST holds
    <Runtime assertions to check POST>
end Delayed_Op_X;
```

Fig. 7. Scheme for the *One-at-a-time* approach

generated by the input driven approach, and in practice it is usually bound by some reasonable figure — and the resource can also simply put an upper limit on the number of requests that can be stored, pending to be reevaluated.

The method consists of introducing a delayed entry per possible process and adding a new parameter to identify that process. With this approach, at most one process will be queued in each delayed entry, and the parameters involved in the **CPRE** can be saved to the (augmented) resource state, indexed by the task identifier, and checked internally. If we let PID be the type of task identifiers, the scheme we are proposing appears in Fig. 6.

Synchronization Depends on Input Data: One-at-a-time. Other techniques can be applied in order to reduce entry replication: for example, selecting a per-call identifier from a finite set in the code fragment between the public and the delayed entries, and assigning it to the call. The guard of the external entry will be closed iff all identifiers are in use. When this set is reduced to a single element, the resulting code is simple: arrays are not needed to save input parameters, and entry families are not necessary either (Fig. 7). Yet, it is able to cope with a wide variety of situations. As entries would not serve calls until the current suspended one has been finished, we have termed this scheme the "One-at-a-time" approach. While it restricts concurrency in the resource, the policy it implements is enough to ensure liveness in many a case.

4.3   Code for the Multibuffer Example

We will show here a direct derivation of the resource into protected objects using family entries indexed by the buffer size, as suggested previously. The specification of the resource is simple enough as to be mapped straightforwardly onto Ada 95 data structures. We want to note that this is often the case during the course, and algorithms and data structures have never been an issue in our experience. Also, in order to appreciate clearly concurrency issues, data have not been completely represented — we show only the length of the sequences of data.

Example: Multibuffer as a protected type

```ada
protected type MultiBuffer is
  entry Get (Items: in Quant_Range);
  entry Put (Items: in Quant_Range);
private
  Item_Counter: Buffer_Quantity := 0;
  entry Get_Fam(Quant_Range) (Items : in Quant_Range);
  entry Put_Fam(Quant_Range) (Items : in Quant_Range);
end MultiBuffer;

protected body MultiBuffer is
  entry Get (Items : in Quant_Range) when True is begin
    requeue Get_Fam(Items);
  end Get;
  entry Put (Items : in Quant_Range) when True is begin
    requeue Put_Fam(Items);
  end Put;
  entry Get_Fam (for Q in Quant_Range)
             (Items : in Quant_Range)
  when Q <= Item_Counter is begin
    Item_Counter := Item_Counter - Q;
  end Get_Fam;
  entry Put_Fam (for Q in Quant_Range)
             (Items : in Quant_Range)
  when Q <= Buffer_Size - Item_Counter is begin
    Item_Counter := Item_Counter + Q;
  end Put_Fam;
end MultiBuffer;
```

4.4   Complex Behavior and Fine Synchronization

In some situations it is impossible to implement a resource by using a straightforward translation, because mutual exclusion is inappropriate for some problems, or because a more fine grained control is necessary in order to implement *ad-hoc* scheduling patterns aimed at ensuring liveness properties.

Partial Exclusion. A simple design pattern is enough to cope with partial exclusion: the resource to be programmed has to include operations to signal when execution enters and exits the *partial exclusion zone*, similarly to the classical *Readers and Writers* problem. The resulting resource features full mutual exclusion, and can be treated as we have seen so far. The tasks must follow a protocol similar to:

```
Resource_Manager : Protected_Object;
...
Resource_Manager.Init_Op_X (actual parameters);
<Actual operation on the resource>
Resource_Manager.Finish_Op_X (actual parameters);
```

The scheme is identical to that used to implement mutual exclusion with semaphores, and it is subject to the same weaknesses — protocol violation would cause havoc. Therefore we do require that these operations are wrapped inside procedures (maybe into a package of their own) which ensures that the protocol is abode by.

Finer Control on Suspensions and Resumptions. Sometimes a fine-grain control is needed to decide exactly when suspended calls are to be resumed (because of, e.g., liveness conditions or performance considerations). Without entering in implementation details, in our experience, students used to end up mixing safety and liveness conditions before specifications were used extensively. Now, we expect for them to produce always safe code first, which as we have seen is easy to derive from the specification, and then to proceed to refine it in order to meet with efficiency/liveness conditions. In general, the code is transformed from guards such as

```
          when Safeness_Condition is ...
```

to guards like

```
          when (Safeness_Condition) and (Liveness_Condition) is ...
```

which will not violate safety, but in which the set of open guards is reduced. If only one guard is active at a time, the effect is precisely that of an explicit wakeup, which mimics the behavior of signals in semaphores or condition variables in the monitors — and which needs the same implementation techniques.

5   Deriving Message Passing Systems with Rendez-Vous

Rendez-Vous was the mechanism originally proposed for process communication and synchronization in Ada. It can be seen as a mixture of ideas from CSP and RPC. Expressiveness and semantics are those of an *alt* construct in CSP – synchronous communication; alternative, non-deterministic reception – but the syntax is more concise, resembling that of a remote procedure call.

These procedures are called *entries* (like in protected objects) and every input parameter hides a send from the client to the server, and every output parameter is a message back from the server to the client. This notation allows to express client-server solutions in a very elegant manner but, unfortunately, is not expressive enough to capture certain requirements, which motivated the introduction of protected objects and the *requeue* mechanism in Ada 95. Our approach here is to complement the rendez-vous mechanism with a sporadic use of a home-made implementation of channels and explicit message passing in order to overcome these limitations, thus obtaining a coherent method for distributed-memory concurrent applications in Ada.

```
task type Server_Type is
  entry Operation1 (parameters);
  ...
end Server_Type;
```

Fig. 8. Declaration of public services of
a task

```
task body Server_Type is
  <Declaration of additional variables>
  <Initialization of the server state>
begin
  <Remaining initialization>
  loop
    select
      when CPRE1 =>
        accept Op1 (parameters) do
        ...
        end;
        <Sentences outside the rendez-vous>
      or
      ...
```

```
select
  when condition =>
    accept Op1 (parameters) do
    ...
    end;
    <Sentences outside the rendez-vous>
  or
  ...
end select
```

Fig. 9. Select loop in the body of a task   **Fig. 10.** Main loop for a server

Due to space limitations, and also to emphasize the pedagogical issues rather than
the technical ones, our treatment of this part will be more schematic.[8]

Using the rendez-vous mechanism, the shared resource will be the property of a server
process which will declare a number of public services to the client processes (Fig. 8).
According to our method, these services will correspond, ideally, to the operations in
the interface of a **CADT**. Client processes may invoke these operations using a syntax
similar to that of protected objects. The code inside the server task is often a loop in
which the alternative reception of requests takes place via the *select* construct (Fig. 9).

The semantics of the *select* is similar to that of the *alt* construct in CSP/Occam.
Entries whose guards are evaluated to *false* are discarded. The remaining *accept* clauses
are the services available, at this moment, to the clients. As in the original CSP proposal
and similarly to protected objects, guards can only refer to the inner state of the server,
never to formal parameters of the *accept* clause.

Code Generation Schemes. As in the protected object case, the simplest situation is a
CADT where none of the **CPRE**s depend on input parameters. In this case the resource
server will have an entry for each **CADT** operation and a main loop where services
satisfying the **CPRE** will be made available to clients (Fig. 10).

If some **CPRE** depends on input parameters a two-stage blocking scheme – rather
similar to that used with protected objects – will be used: there will be an *accept* clause
in the *select* with the guard set to *true* which will be used to send the data needed to
evaluate the **CPRE**, followed by a suspension of the client task until the **CPRE** holds
so that the request is ready to be served. The evaluation of the pending **CPRE**s can take
place outside the *select* loop (Fig. 11).

---

[8] At *http://babel.ls.fi.upm.es/publications/publications.html?keyword=concurrent*, the interested
reader can find a full explanation including the rendez-vous code for the multibuffer example
and the realization of channels.

```
task body Server_Type is
  <Declaration/initialization of the server's inner state>
begin
  <Remaining initialization>
  loop
    select
      when True =>
        accept OperationX (input parameters + reply channels) do
          <Store request>
        end;
      or
        . . .
    end select
    while <there are pending requests to serve> loop
      <Extract (ReplyChannel, RequestData)>
      <Perform operation>
      ReplyChannel.Send(reply/ack);
    end loop;
  end loop
end Server_Type;
```

Fig. 11. Server loop for **CPRE**s dependent on input parameters

This two-stage blocking can be implemented via explicit message passing using a generic package *Channel* that provides a type for simple synchronous channels with *Send* and *Receive* operations. It is, thus, an explicit channel naming scheme, not present natively in Ada, but implemented using, in our case, protected objects. The client can be blocked by making it wait for a message from the server. The client task will therefore perform a call to the *entry* followed by an unconditional reception:

```
CReply : InstanceOfChannel.Channel_P;
. . .
Server_Type.OperationX (..., CReply);
CReply.Receive (reply/ack);
. . .
```

The answer from the server may be used to transmit output parameters of the **CADT** operation – when they exist – or just a mere acknowledgment. Observe that sending a reference to the reply channel allows the server to uniquely identify the client.[9] This is a clear counterpart of the process identifier strategy mentioned in Sect. 4.2.

Of course, mixed schemes, where some operations are synchronized on the guard and others use the two-stage blocking, are allowed.

Explicit Signalling Using Channels. The scheme presented above provides also a more straightforward and elegant mechanism for programming explicit wakeups than the one used with protected objects. Depending on

a) the data structures used to store pending requests, and
b) the selection criteria used to traverse them

---

[9] Which is rather usual in the client/server philosophy, e.g. by sending an IP:port address of the client to a web server.

different versions of a (partially correct) solution can be obtained fulfilling different liveness criteria.

Wakeups implemented via explicit sends from the server resemble more faithfully the ideas originally present in the *Signal* of old-time semaphores or the *Continue* in classic monitors. Remember that explicit wakeups could only be *simulated* when using protected objects by forcing all guards but one to be false. Explicit wakeups bring the following advantages:

A more elegant code. One problem with the protected objects code was that enforcing liveness/priority properties would often force to strengthen the entry guards, which, on one hand, led to losing the straight connection with the **CPRE**s and, on the other, would increase the risk of lacking concurrency or even deadlock. With the scheme introduced above, the liveness/priority logic is moved outside the *select* and the guards remain intact.

Lower risk of starvation. Another problem with explicit wakeups in protected objects (and also in monitors) is that waking up a set of waiting processes had to be done via a *cascade* of wake-ups, where each task finishing execution of an entry must establish the necessary conditions to wake up the following task, and so on. The logic implied by this mechanism is very error-prone, easily leading tasks to starvation if the cascade breaks.

With the server scheme, the loop following the *select* must ensure that the server will not enter the *select* while there are pending requests that could be served. This avoids the risk of new requests getting in the middle of the old ones, thus greatly reducing the risk of starvation.

6   Related Work

To the best of our knowledge, there is not much work published on teaching concurrent programming as a self-contained subject — let alone teaching concurrent programming with the support of formal methods.

A pilot test reported in [7] supports the hypothesis that teaching concurrency to lower-level undergraduates increases significantly the ability to solve concurrency problems, and that concurrency concepts can be effectively learned at this level. Our own experience makes us agree with this view. Besides, we think that the use of a formal notation and the application of a rigorous development process helps in clarifying concepts with independence from the final implementation language and it really paves the way to having correct programs, even at undergraduate levels.

Undergraduate concurrency courses in the context of programming are also advocated in [13]. However, the approach of that paper is more biased toward parallelism than ours. We see parallelism as somewhat orthogonal to concurrency, and we tend to focus on interaction and expressiveness rather than on independence and performance.

Other pieces of work try to teach concurrency with the help of tools and environments which can simulate a variety of situations (see [17] and its references). This is indeed helpful to highlight peculiarities of concurrent programs, but from our point of view it does not help to directly improve problem-solving skills. That is what we aim at with a more formal approach.

```
lecsescs                                                                                                          _ □ ✕
                              Scroll using the arrow keys inside the output windows
Lector  1 lee          Lector  2 lee          Lector  3 lee          escribir               escribir               Escritor  3 escribe
Lector  1 termina      Lector  2 termina      Lector  3 termina      Escritor  1 escribe    Escritor  2 escribe    Escritor  3 termina
Lector  1 quiere leer  Lector  2 quiere leer  Lector  3 quiere leer  Escritor  1 termina    Escritor  2 termina    Escritor  3 quiere    ₽
Lector  1 lee          Lector  2 lee          Lector  3 lee          Escritor  1 quiere    ₽Escritor  2 quiere    ₽escribir
Lector  1 termina      Lector  2 termina      Lector  3 termina      escribir               escribir               Escritor  3 escribe
Lector  1 quiere leer  Lector  2 quiere leer  Lector  3 quiere leer  Escritor  1 escribe    Escritor  2 escribe    Escritor  3 termina
Lector  1 lee          Lector  2 lee          Lector  3 lee          Escritor  1 termina    Escritor  2 termina    Escritor  3 quiere    ₽
Lector  1 termina      Lector  2 termina      Lector  3 termina      Escritor  1 quiere    ₽Escritor  2 quiere    ₽escribir
Lector  1 quiere leer  Lector  2 quiere leer  Lector  3 quiere leer  escribir               escribir               Escritor  3 escribe


  Suspend    Enter      Suspend    Enter      Suspend    Enter      Suspend    Enter      Suspend    Enter      Suspend    Enter
```

Fig. 12. Input / output of a *Readers / Writers* execution

In line with [21], we think that concurrent programming is of utmost importance. That piece of work also mentions the relationship concurrency / ADTs, but from a point of view different from ours: while our **CADT**s are concurrency-aware right from the beginning, that work seems to aim more at hiding concurrency than at exposing it.

Concurrency has also been animated with educational purposes, as in [11], which depicts dependencies among processes and semaphores. While we have not developed animations for Ada multitasking, we have built an Ada library which provides a subset of Ada.Text_IO, and which generates dynamically and user-transparently per-task input/output areas (Fig. 12). This is similar in spirit and motivations to [18], but with less system-oriented information, more user-transparent, and completely interactive (it runs in real time, in step with the main application).

7   Conclusion

Our students are taught concurrent programming according to the methodology herein presented. The subject is at undergraduate level, and delivered in the third year, after students have gone through several programming subjects in which a certain deal of specifications has been used. This makes the idea of reading and understanding a formal language not too strange for them.

We think that this is a success story: albeit the design of the concurrent system is by far the hardest task, when this is done students are able to develop almost mechanically Ada code for projects of fair complexity and with a high confidence on their reliability. Safety properties are guaranteed to hold, while liveness properties, when needed, have certainly to be developed with some care and on a case by case basis. We believe that being aware of the importance of keeping these properties is certainly a better investment than becoming an expert in, say, POSIX threads. These kind of abilities can be acquired later with comparatively little effort.

Due to space limitations, we have not detailed the last stages of the methodology which involve reasoning about the dynamic behaviour of resources and processes. This is done with the help of *labelled transition systems*. **CADT**s are still useful in this stage, as transitions are identified with invocations of **CADT** operations and states with (abstractions of) the state of the shared resources in the system. In other words, liveness issues can also be dealt with in an architecture-independent way.

Besides the translation schemes provided here, we have also developed, in previous stages of the curricula, similar translations for languages based on monitors [12] and on CSP. We have a similar translation scheme for Java, although probably not as clean as the ones we have presented here.

Courseware Pointers. Although the bulk of the information is in Spanish, we invite the reader to have a look at the web pages of our Concurrent Programming course at Universidad Politécnica de Madrid: `http://lml.ls.fi.upm.es/pc/`. Lecture notes, examples, homework assignments and test problems can be found at the subdirectories `apuntes`, `ejemplos`, `Anteriores/Examenes`, and `Anteriores/Practicas`.

References

1. G.R. Andrews and F.B. Schneider. Concepts and notations for concurrent programming. In N. Gehani and A.D. McGettrick, editors, *Concurrent Programming*. Addison-Wesley, 1989.
2. Greg Andrews. *Concurrent Programming: Principles and Practice*. Benjamin/Cummings, 1991.
3. Maurice Bruynooghe and Kung-Kiu Lau, editors. *Program Development in Computational Logic: A Decade of Research Advances in Logic-Based Program Development*, volume 3049 of *Lecture Notes in Computer Science*. Springer, 2004.
4. Alan Burns and Andy Wellings. *Concurrency in Ada*. Cambridge University Press, 1998.
5. Norman H. Cohen. *Ada as a Second Language*. McGraw-Hill, 1995.
6. M. Hanus (ed.), H. Kuchen, and J.J. Moreno-Navarro et al. Curry: An integrated functional logic language. Technical report, RWTH Aachen, 2000.
7. Michael B. Feldman and Bruce D. Bachus. Concurrent programming can be introduced into the lower-level undergraduate curriculum. In *Proceedings of the 2nd conference on Integrating technology into computer science education*, pages 77–79. ACM Press, 1997.
8. Narain H. Gehani. Capsules: a shared memory access mechanism for Concurrent C/C++. *IEEE Transactions on Parallel and Distributed Systems*, 4(7):795–811, 1993.
9. M. Hermenegildo, F. Bueno, D. Cabeza, M. Carro, M. García de la Banda, P. López García, and G. Puebla. The Ciao Multi-Dialect Compiler and System: An Experimentation Workbench for Future (C)LP Systems. In *Parallelism and Implementation of Logic and Constraint Logic Programming*, pages 65–85. Nova Science, Commack, NY, USA, April 1999.
10. A. Herranz and J. J. Moreno. On the design of an object-oriented formal notation. In *Fourth Workshop on Rigorous Object Oriented Methods, ROOM 4*. King's College, London, March 2002.
11. C. William Higginbotham and Ralph Morelli. A system for teaching concurrent programming. In *Proceedings of the twenty-second SIGCSE technical symposium on Computer science education*, pages 309–316. ACM Press, 1991.
12. C.A.R. Hoare. Monitors, an operating system structuring concept. *Communications of the ACM*, 17(10):549–557, October 1974.
13. David Jackson. A Mini-Course on Concurrency. In *Twenty-second SIGCSE Technical Symposium on Computer Science Education*, pages 92–96. ACM Press, 1991.
14. Cliff B. Jones. *Systematic Software Development Using VDM*. Prentice-Hall, Upper Saddle River, NJ 07458, USA, 1995.
15. R. Morales-Fernandez and J.J. Moreno-Navarro. CC-Modula: A Modula-2 Tool to Teach Concurrent Programming. In *ACM SIGCSE Bulletin*, volume 21, pages 19–25. ACM Press, September 1989.

16. The Joint Task Force on Computing Curricula IEEE-CS/ACM. Computing Curricula 2001. http://www.computer.org/education/cc2001/.
17. Yakov Persky and Mordechai Ben-Ari. Re-engineering a concurrency simulator. In *Proceedings of the 6th annual conference on the teaching of computing and the 3rd annual conference on Integrating technology into computer science education*, pages 185–188. ACM Press, 1998.
18. Steven Robbins. Using remote logging for teaching concurrency. In *Procs. of the 34th SIGCSE Technical Symposium on Comp. Sci. Education*, pages 177–181. ACM Press, 2003.
19. T.S. Taft, R.A. Duff, R.L. Brukardt, and E.Ploedereder, editors. *Consolidated Ada Reference Manual. Language and Standard Libraries International Standard ISO/IEC 8652/1995(E) with Technical Corrigendum 1*. Springer Verlag, 2001.
20. Axel van Lamsweerde. Formal Specification: a Roadmap. In A. Finkelstein, editor, *The Future of Software Engineering*, pages 147–159. ACM Press, 2000.
21. Dorian P. Yeager. Teaching concurrency in the programming languages course. In *Proceedings of the twenty-second SIGCSE technical symposium on Computer science education*, pages 155–161. ACM Press, 1991.

Specification-Driven Design with Eiffel and Agents for Teaching Lightweight Formal Methods

Richard F. Paige[1] and Jonathan S. Ostroff[2]

[1] Department of Computer Science, University of York, UK.
paige@cs.york.ac.uk
[2] Department of Computer Science, York University, Canada.
jonathan@cs.yorku.ca

Abstract. We report on our experiences in teaching lightweight formal methods with Eiffel. In particular, we discuss how we introduce formal methods via Eiffel's design-by-contract and *agent* technologies, and how we integrate these techniques with test-driven development, in an approach called *specification-driven design*. This approach demonstrates how formal methods techniques fit with industrial software engineering practice.

1 Introduction

For a number of years we have been teaching formal methods (FMs) in a variety of different ways, including traditional program verification (via weakest preconditions as well as refinement calculi), to Computer Science and Engineering undergraduates with a range of backgrounds. Our focus in the past few years, though, has been on teaching formal methods as an integrated part of software engineering. Specifically, we want to teach FMs in such a way so that students – especially those who are maths-phobic – do not get the impression that they are an eccentric, specialised technology. Instead, we want students to obtain the view that they are part of the software engineer's toolkit, and are supported by mainstream, industrially applicable tools.

The approach that we have taken, developed over a number of years of experiment and careful consideration, is based upon the use of Eiffel [11]. Eiffel is an important and substantial language for teaching formal methods, for a number of reasons:

– It is both a specification and programming language and as such is compatible with the ideas of refinement [15].
– It is one of the best object-oriented languages available, in terms of its generality and expressiveness, its support for building reliable systems, static type checking, reusable libraries, and ease of use.
– It has industrially proven tools that support checking of specifications against code, while also providing important features such as incremental compilation, debugging, and GUI construction.

The first point is a critical one for teaching FM. It is not well-known that Eiffel can be easily used as a formal specification language, and that tools can be used to check the correctness of Eiffel specifications. The specification elements of the language go as far as

C.N. Dean and R.T. Boute (Eds.): TFM 2004, LNCS 3294, pp. 107–123, 2004.
© Springer-Verlag Berlin Heidelberg 2004

supporting quantifiers in boolean expressions, via Eiffel's agent technology (discussed in the sequel). The ability to use Eiffel both as a specification and programming language allows broader us of the language over one or more courses that emphasise different elements, such as GUI design, real-time and embedded systems programming, etc.

There are of course substantial challenges to teaching Eiffel as a lightweight formal method. In particular, students are sometimes hesitant to learn Eiffel, because it is not perceived as a mainstream OO language – i.e., they want to learn Java or C++. As well, students sometimes think that Eiffel tools are inferior to tools for, e.g., Java, and that Eiffel libraries are less comprehensive and expressive than similar ones for C++ and Java. The second point is one that can best be addressed by experience with Eiffel tools and libraries; after some experience the students tend to change their assessment in favour of Eiffel. The first point can be addressed by teaching Eiffel in a software engineering context, and by emphasising that a programming language is not specifically being taught. To this end, we introduce Eiffel and its FM techniques in a very specific way, which we discuss shortly.

In this paper, we describe our experiences and approach to teaching lightweight FM with Eiffel. We start with an overview of Eiffel, dwelling on its support for formal specification, and describe its agent technology briefly. We then describe three important definitions: specifications, requirements, and programs – and explain why it is critical to ensure that students know these before starting to program. The definitions are critical to understanding when teaching and using a wide-spectrum language such as Eiffel. We then describe our approach to teaching with Eiffel, including how we introduce agents to students, and how we integrate Eiffel techniques with software engineering practices such as testing. This approach, termed *specification-driven design*, encompasses elements from Extreme Programming and formal methods, and is highly suited (though not strictly dependent) on teaching with Eiffel. We then briefly outline how a typical course using this approach could be structured, and conclude with some observations.

2   Eiffel, Design-by-Contract, and Agents

Eiffel is an object-oriented programming language and method [12]; it provides constructs typical of the object-oriented paradigm, including classes, objects, inheritance, associations, composite ("expanded") types, generic (parameterised) types, polymorphism and dynamic binding, and automatic memory management. It has a comprehensive set of libraries – including data structures, GUI widgets, and database management system bindings – and the language is integrated with .NET.

A short example of an Eiffel class is shown in Fig. 1. The class *CITIZEN* inherits from *PERSON* (thus defining a subtyping relationship). It provides several attributes, e.g., *spouse, children* which are of reference type (in other words, *spouse* refers to an object of type *CITIZEN*); these features are publicly accessible (i.e., are exported to *ANY* client). Attributes are by default of reference type; a reference attribute either points at an object on the heap, or is *Void*. The class provides one expanded attribute, *blood_type*. Expanded attributes are also known as composite attributes; they are not references, and memory is allocated for expanded attributes when memory is allocated for the enclosing object.

The remaining features of the class are routines, i.e., functions (like *single*, which returns *true* iff the citizen has no spouse) and procedures (like *divorce*, which changes the state of the object). These routines may have preconditions (**require** clauses) and postconditions (**ensure** clauses), but no implementations. Finally, the class has an invariant, specifying properties that must be true of all objects of the class at stable points in time, i.e., before any valid client call on the object. While we have used predicate logic in specifying the invariant of *CITIZEN*, it should be observed that Eiffel does not support this exact syntax. It does possess a notion of *agent* that can be used to simulate quantifiers like the ones used in the example; we discuss this in Section 2.2, and show how to rewrite the quantifiers given in Fig. 1 using agents there.

```
class CITIZEN inherit PERSON
feature {ANY}

   spouse: CITIZEN
   children, parents: SET[CITIZEN]
   blood_type: expanded BLOOD_TYPE

   single: BOOLEAN is
     do Result := (spouse=Void)
     ensure Result = (spouse=Void)
     end

feature {BIG_GOVERNMENT}

   marry is ...
   have_child is ...
   divorce is
     require not single
     do ...
     ensure single and (old spouse).single
     end

invariant
   single or spouse.spouse = Current;
   parents.count <= 2;
   for_all c member_of children it_holds
     c.parents.has(Current)
end -- CITIZEN
```

Fig. 1. Eiffel class interface

Other facilities offered by Eiffel, but not demonstrated here, include generic (parameterised) types, dynamic dispatch, multiple inheritance, and static typing. We refer the reader to [11] for full details on these and other features.

In teaching Eiffel, we give thorough coverage to the language, and consider all aspects of it, including agents, multiple inheritance (and its challenges), and covariant redefinition. We introduce language design principles that are supported or enforced by Eiffel, such as the query/command separation principle (which states that functional routines should be side-effect free). The discipline that these principles provide is generally appreciated and applied by the students in their projects and assignments.

2.1 Design-by-Contract

Design-by-Contract (DbC) is a mathematical description technique for engineering software systems with significant requirements for reliability and robustness. DbC is typically integrated with a programming language, providing formal annotations for interfaces of components and services. It differs from well-known formal methods such as B and Z in its cost: it can be selectively applied to those parts of the system associated with the highest risk; it integrates mathematical descriptions with code, ensuring consistency; and it is designed to be supported by tools that are comfortable and familiar to developers, e.g., compilers, debuggers, static checkers, and testing frameworks.

DbC recommends annotating classes with preconditions, postconditions, and class invariants. This was illustrated in the Eiffel example in Fig. 1. These assertions imply contracts that bind callers of class services with implementers of said services: callers guarantee to satisfy preconditions, while implementers guarantee to satisfy postconditions. This convention guarantees that conditions which may affect the correct operation of a class are checked only once. In Eiffel, these assertions are built in to the programming language, and the assorted Eiffel compilers and IDEs (e.g., ISE EStudio and GNU SmartEiffel) provide tools for managing and debugging assertions.

The benefits of using contracts and DbC are as follows.

– Contracts provide precise mathematical specifications of software and its services.
– Many views of the software can be automatically extracted. One view (automatically extracted) is the *contract view* that provides the client with the precise interface specifications. For example, a routine can only be invoked if the client satisfies the routine precondition.
– With assertion checking turned on, the contracts are checked every time the code is executed, and contract violations are immediately flagged. This test for consistency between code and specifications comes for free as opposed to the 3-fold cost mentioned earlier.
– Classes and components are self-documenting: the contracts are the documentation. There is no way that the documentation and code can become inconsistent, because the contracts are included within the code – the code would not execute if there are inconsistencies.
– Contracts provide design rules for maintaining and modifying the behaviour of components, cf., behavioural subtyping.
– Contracts provide a basis for formal verification. We discuss this further in the sequel when we suggest how Eiffel can form the basis for a formal verification course.

Contracts may of course be incorrect or incomplete, and thus need to be supplemented with a rigorous testing process. A key point to note then is that an Eiffel program annotated with assertions can result in errors due to incorrectly implemented functionality, or violation of contracts. As well, some conditions are extremely difficult to express using executable contracts – the paper [13] considers examples.

2.2   Agents

Agents in Eiffel are objects that represent operations. Agents can be passed to different software elements, which can use the object to execute the operation *whenever* they want. Agents thus provide a way of separating the definition of an operation from its execution. They also are a way of combining high-level functions (operations acting on other operations) with static typing in Eiffel. This should be contrasted with similar techniques, e.g., reflection in Java, which allows similar functionality at the cost of loss of static type checking.

Here is a simple example of an agent, using Eiffel's GUI library EiffelVision. Suppose you want to add the routine *eval_state* to the list of event handlers that will be executed when a mouse click occurs on the widget *my_button*. To carry this out, the following Eiffel statement would be executed.

$$my\_button.click\_actions.extend(\textbf{agent }\ eval\_state)$$

The operation being added to the button is indicated by the **agent** keyword. The keyword distinguishes an operation call to *eval_state* from a binding of the operation to the button. In general, the argument to *extend* can be any agent expression. An agent expression will include an operation plus any context that the operation may need (e.g., arguments). The ability to supply context with an agent expression is essential. Suppose that you want to integrate the three-argument function

$$h(a : T1; \ x : REAL; \ b : T2) : REAL$$

over its second argument in the domain $[0, 1]$. Given a suitable integration scheme *integrator* the following agent call will suffice.

$$integrator.integral(\textbf{agent }\ h(u, ?, v), 0.0, 1.0)$$

The question mark ? indicates an open argument (similar to a wild card, representing an element taken from the collection) that is provided by iterating through the range arguments provided.

To support agents in Eiffel, it is necessary to introduce a number of classes, including ones to represent $FUNCTION$ and $PROCEDURE$ operations, $PREDICATE$ operations, and arguments. These meta-level classes provide introspection facilities.

Predicate agents are of significant use; they feature heavily in how we introduce formal methods to students, and how we carry out testing. Predicate agents apply boolean-valued operations to collections. For example:

$$intlist.for\_all(\textbf{agent }\ is\_positive(?)) \tag{1}$$
$$intlist.exists(\textbf{agent }\ perfect\_cube(?)) \tag{2}$$

The first example applies the boolean-valued function *is_positive* to elements of the integer list *intlist*, and conjoins together the result. Equation (2) applies the boolean-valued function *perfect_cube* to elements of the integer list *intlist* and disjoins the result. The question mark indicates an open argument that is provided by the list interator. Using this approach, we could rewrite the third clause in the invariant of class *CITIZEN* in Fig. 1 as follows.

```
children.for_all((c:CITIZEN):BOOLEAN
  do
    Result := c.parents.has(Current)
  end)
```

The above example illustrates anonymous operations (i.e., the argument passed to the iterator `for_all`). c, the bound variable, is an element taken from the collection *children*, to which the body of the anonymous operation (contained within the inner `do..end` block) is applied. Operations bound in agent expressions may make reference to attributes and routines of objects, since when the operation is finally invoked, the operation will have been bound to a target object.

3   Specifications and Requirements

The terms "requirements" and "specifications" are ambiguous, and often used interchangeably in the literature. The traditional understanding of requirements is that they say *what* the system will do and not *how*. Students learning formal methods – and other software engineering techniques – often struggle with the distinction between requirements and specifications. This is particularly the case when they are using a wide-spectrum language like Eiffel or B. It is important that they understand the distinction in order to make it easier to validate systems against requirements, to clarify whether they are modelling the physical world or the system itself, and to simplify system designs. We thus spend a small amount of time – aproximately half a lecture – making the definitions more precise, following [9,16], though with a slight change in nomenclature.

The computer under description (consisting of software and/or hardware) is called the *System*, and it operates in an *Environment*. There are some *phenomena* (states, signals, events and entities) that the System and the Environment do not share, but there are also some phenomena that they do share – these are called the *shared phenomena* as illustrated by the intersection of the two ellipses in Fig. 2, which uses a banking system as an example.

In a banking system, the bank and its customers are not interested in hashtables or sort routines. The bank is interested in customer satisfaction, and that customers can request withdrawals or make deposits. An example of a requirement, written in temporal logic, is

$$[R1] \qquad \Box(x < balance \land withdrawal\_request(c, x) \rightarrow$$
$$\Diamond(withdraw(c, x) \land teller\_gives(c, dollar - bill)))$$

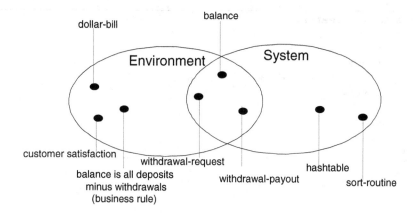

Fig. 2. The World: *System* and *Environment*

i.e., a withdrawal request of an amount x for customer c must lead to a withdrawal payout by the teller to the customer in *dollar-bill*s, provided that the requested amount does not exceed the current *balance*. The phenomenon *dollar-bill* is actual money in the bank teller's till (and is therefore not a System phenomenon), while *balance* is a shared phenomenon. All the requirement phenomena are a subset of the of the Environment ($REQ \subset Environment$). Additional physical constraints or business rules (the application domain knowledge) will also need to be described.

The *balance* is a shared phenomenon in $Environment \cap System$. It represents the debt owed by the bank to the customer. It may also occur as code in the System (e.g. see [S1] in Fig. 3).

Programs, in contrast to requirements, are concerned solely with the System phenomena. Programs may need to implement the requirements by using internal data structures and algorithms such as hash-tables and sort routines to do the job. All such program phenomena are a subset of the System.

The gap between requirements and programs is bridged by *specifications*. Specifications are concerned solely with the shared phenomena. Specifications are neither requirements nor programs. Specifications are unsatisfactory programs as they may not be executable. They are unsatisfactory requirements because requirements are not limited only to the coastline where the Environment and the System meet. But, specifications are useful as we transition from requirements to programs that will satisfy the requirements as specifications allow us to describe the black-box behaviour of the code at the observable input-output interface. For example, in order to satisfy requirement [R1], we might have a specification [S2] that specifies the behaviour of class $ACCOUNT$ as shown in Fig. 3. The specification in the figure is the contract view; hence, all the phenomena described in the figure are shared.

In the absence of implementation detail, the specification is not executable, but it can be compiled and automatically checked for type errors and the like by the compiler. Once implementation detail is provided, then the implemented code is automatically checked against the specification (i.e., the specifications now become "executable").

```
class ACCOUNT feature
    balance: INTEGER
    withdrawal(amount:REAL)
        require
            0 < amount and amount <= balance
        ensure
            balance = old balance - amount
    invariant
        balance >= 0
    end
```

Fig. 3. Specification [S2]

The perspective shown in Fig. 2 avoids the problem of implementation bias (when stating requirements) because no statements are made about the internals of the proposed System. Requirements and specifications are not descriptions of the state of the System, but rather a description of the state of the Environment. A specification might be compromised by a poor choice of designated phenomena or invalid domain knowledge, but it cannot overconstrain the implementation [16].

Eiffel, of course, can be used for capturing requirements, writing specifications, and implementation. The distinctions often escape students, especially early in their first software engineering course. We thus go over numerous case studies where we make the distinctions clear, and challenge them on this issue when they present reports, or participate in in-class discussions. We find that emphasising the distinctions as discussed above shows marked improvement in the clarity of assignment and project reports as the course proceeds.

4 Teaching Formal Methods with Eiffel

We have been teaching lightweight formal methods with Eiffel to third year Computer Science and Computer Engineering students for around six years now. Our approach has evolved over time, from simply using the Eiffel programming language to teach object-oriented techniques, to a whole-view approach for teaching software engineering, wherein formal techniques play a substantial role.

The course that we teach is one semester, and is project-focused, i.e., students (typically working in teams of 2-4) engineer working systems, based on requirements provided by the instructor. A substantial amount of instructor effort goes into the preparation of a comprehensive software engineering project that involves design (using UML or BON diagrams), implementation, testing, and documentation; we discuss this further later.

Students taking the course will already have some experience with object-oriented programming in Java. The typical student will have previously taken three one-semester courses that make use of Java as a programming language for introductory computer science, algorithms, and data structures. The students will also have taken two one-semester courses in logic and discrete mathematics and will have some experience with propositional and predicate logic, though their experience with using mathematics in programming (e.g., in introductory Computer Science courses that teach basic pre/postconditions and loop invariants) typically shows hesitancy in using these techniques in building systems.

After the usual preliminaries on software quality and engineering processes, the course leaps into a case study, designed to illustrate fundamentals of Eiffel and two typical approaches to building systems: plan-driven (in terms of modelling languages such as UML and BON) and test-driven. The case study proceeds by giving some informal requirements for a simple banking system. Use cases and scenarios are sketched very briefly, and from these a set of candidate classes is determined. The students are then posed the question: where should design commence?

This question is aimed at getting students to thinking about *acceptance tests* and testing in general. For the next stage is to introduce test-driven development [3] as (a) a general development technique, and (b) a way to introduce contracts (pre- and postconditions) and agents (for predicates) in a lightweight and indirect way. Our experience is that students who are less inclined towards mathematical techniques are more amenable to their study, use, and description if they are couched in terms of accepted engineering tasks, particularly testing, with which they have some experience. (We provide the students with an Eiffel testing framework, ETester, which supports unit tests and test suites, and also provides infrastructure for distinguishing between failures of the system versus failures in contracts. This is discussed elsewhere [10]. ETester has a similar design to JUnit for Java, but is targeted at languages that support contracts, where it is important during testing to distinguish failures in contracts from failures in code.)

Writing tests introduces the students to Eiffel's agent technology (used in ETester for automating testing) while at the same time serving to introduce them to the concept of writing formal specifications. Tests are a "backdoor" mechanism for introducing formal specifications and the usefulness of contracts. This is a critical point, which we now discuss.

4.1 Tests and Contracts Are Both Formal Specifications

The test-driven development (TDD) process described by Beck [3] is as follows.

1. Write a little test which may not work initially (especially if code hasn't been written for a class).
2. Make the test work quickly, focusing on doing the simplest thing that works.
3. Refactor the design to eliminate duplication and improve the style and architecture in terms of reusability and maintainability.

Unit tests (from TDD) and contracts (DbC) are both forms of specifications associated with shared phenomena of the System and the Environment. Unit tests can also be used to do regression testing at the end of coding, but in TDD, unit tests are seen as formal specifications that drive the design [1, p38 and p51].

Unit tests are normally used to check small chunks of a design. JUnit and E-Tester are useful tools for writing unit tests. However, these tools can also be used to write tests that verify higher level behaviours such as system-level tests involving the shared

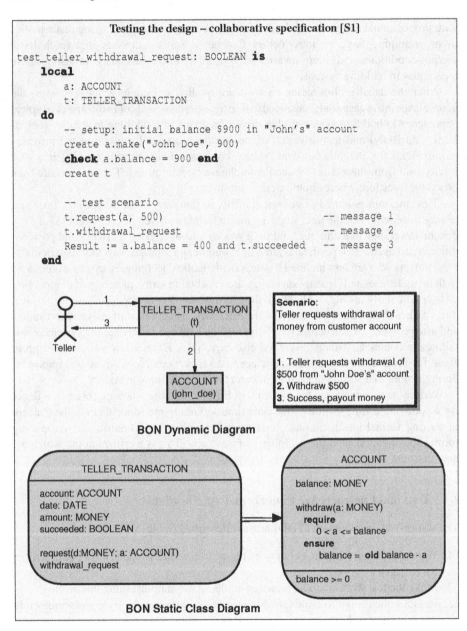

Fig. 4. Test and Design of a simple banking system

phenomena (Fig. 2). Such tests could verify parts of the collaborative behaviour of the kind mentioned in the small banking example involving requirement [R1]. We shall call these higher level tests *collaborative specifications*.

Collaborative specifications are related to UML interaction descriptions such as sequence or collaboration diagrams, and BON dynamic diagrams, especially where these diagrams describe a use case. The diagrams show a number of example objects and the messages that are passed between these objects within the use case. Such interaction diagrams provide an intuitive and visual way of describing (partial-order) executions of the system at the input-output interface, and therefore capture apsects of customer requirements useful in integration and acceptance tests.

Unfortunately, UML's interaction diagrams do not yet have a fully agreed-upon semantics, although various fomalizations have been proposed (but with conflicting semantic assumptions about the underlying communication system).

An equivalent to the interaction diagrams is the BON *dynamic diagram*. The BON dynamic and class diagrams for a simple banking system are shown in Fig. 4. These two diagrams describe the design of the system. At the top of Fig. 4 is a test that checks the dynamic diagram [14]. This test is an example of a collaborative specification (called [S1] in the figure). We note that [S1] is close to the temporal logic requirement [R1] described earlier in this section. It omits *dollar-bills* but otherwise mirrors all other phenomena described by [R1].

When we run the test [S1], we also exercise the detailed *contractual specification* [S2] for *ACCOUNT* shown in Fig. 3. [S2] is repeated in the class diagram of Fig. 4.

The advantage of a test-based collaborative specification such as [S1] over the dynamic diagram (and the UML interaction diagrams) is that it is a formal artifact written in the same progamming language as the design. It can be compiled, type-checked and executed. If it fails, then there is a problem in the design, and if it succeeds then the expected behaviour is in place, at least for this execution. Finally, if the test succeeds then contracts such as those outlined in the design class diagram of Fig. 4 are also verified.

The key point to note with this approach is that it emphasises the use of different kinds of *formal specifications*, and that these specifications are introduced via testing. There is substantial value to introducing (particularly maths-phobic) students to formal specifications that can be executed, as they can get immediate feedback as to their quality and can immediately see their value in catching mistakes and clarifying assumptions.

The other point to note is that different syntaxes can be used for writing formal specifications. On one hand, they can be written using precise boolean logic, in terms of pre- and postconditions and class invariants. Or they can be written as executable unit tests or test suites. Or they can be written as dynamic diagrams. These are all useful syntaxes to know and apply.

4.1.1 Collaborative vs. Contractual Specifications.

Test-based collaborative specifications are incomplete, especially in contrast to the details that can be supplied by formal specifications in the form of contracts. Consider the following unit test.

```
test_integers_sorted:BOOLEAN is
    local
        sa1,sa2: SORTABLE_ARRAY[INTEGER]
    do
        sa1 := <<4, 1, 3>>
        sa2 := <<1, 3, 4>>
        sa1.sort
        Result := equal(sa1, sa2)
    end
```

in which we create an unsorted array sa1, execute routine sort, and then assert that the array is equal to the expected sorted array sa2. The unit test specifies that array <<4, 1, 3>> must be sorted. But what about tests for all the other (possibly infinite) arrays of integers. Furthermore, the test does not check arrays of REAL, or arrays of PERSON (say by age). After all, the class SORTABLE_ARRAY[G] has a generic parameter G. Also, it is hard to describe preconditions with unit tests. For example, we might want the sort routine to work only in case there is at least one non-void element in the array.

By contrast, the contract-annotated specification in Fig. 5 is a precise and detailed specification of the sorted array (the *count* attribute used in the figure is inherited from *ARRAY*). The quantifiers have been specified in Eiffel using the *agent* construct, as students would be required to do.

```
class SORTABLE_ARRAY [G -> COMPARABLE] inherit
  ARRAY[G]
feature
  sort is
    require
        count_positive: count > 0
        elements_not_void:
          Current.for_all((i:INTEGER): BOOLEAN
            do
              Result := (lower <= i <= upper) implies item(i) /= Void
            end)
    do
      ...

    ensure
      sorted:
        Current.for_all((i:INTEGER): BOOLEAN)
          do
            Result := (lower <= i <= upper) implies item(i) <= item(i+1)
          end)
        count_unchanged: count = old count
    end
end
```

Fig. 5. Contractual Specification

The generic parameter G of class SORTABLE_ARRAY is constrained to inherit from COMPARABLE. This allows us to compare any two elements in the array, e.g the expresion item(i) <= item(i+1) is legal whether the array holds instances of integers or poeple, provided the instances are from classes that inherit from COMPARABLE.

Routine sort is specified via preconditions and postconditions. The preconditions state that there must be at least one non-void element to sort. The unit test did not specify this, nor is it generally simple for unit tests to specify preconditions.

The postcondition states that the array must be sorted and is unchanged. This postcondition specifies this property for all possible arrays, holding elements of any type (integers, people, etc.). Again, only an infinite number of unit tests could capture this property.

However, while contract-based specifications are detailed and complete, they have disadvantages and limitations. Consider class $STACK[G]$ with routines given by $push(x : G)$ and pop. While contracts can fully specify the effects of of $push$ and pop taken individually, the contracts cannot *directly* describe the last-in-first-out (LIFO) property of stacks which asserts that

$$\forall s : STACK, x : G \bullet pop(push(x, s)) = s \qquad (3)$$

Of course, given the complete contracts and an appropriate refinement calculus [15], the LIFO property can be expressed in the calculus as

$$push(x); \ pop \rightarrow skip \qquad (4)$$

so that the LIFO behaviour indirectly *emerges* from the contractual specifications. The calculus can also be used to calculate if the implementation indeed satisfies the LIFO property. However, neither the description nor the calculation can be directly expressed as contracts.

By contrast, the emergent LIFO behaviour is easy to describe using collaborative specifications.

4.2 SDD

The approach that we teach students, which integrates elements of TDD and design-by-contract, is called *specification-driven design*; a full description of this approach is in [13]. It is an agile method tailored for Eiffel. It is perhaps surprising that agile techniques can be integrated successfully with formal methods. It is less surprising when one considers the commonalities between TDD and DbC.

- Both tests and contracts are formal specifications, each with their own limitations and advantages.
- Both TDD and DbC seek to transform requirements to compilable (high level) programming constructs as soon as possible. In TDD, tests describe designs. In DbC, contracts (and BON or UML diagrams) describe designs.
- Both TDD and DbC are automated (and hence easy-to-use) lightweight verification methods. Neither are complete, but both have simple-to-use tool support.
- Both are incremental development methods that intertwine analysis, design, coding and testing.
- Both TDD and DbC strive to obtain quality first for each unit of functionality, before proceeding to the next unit; this in effect aims to implement the Osmond Curve [2].

These commonalities indicate that we can combine TDD and DbC in a beneficial fashion. Boehm and Turner have argued in detail [6, p148] that (a) neither agile nor plan-driven methods provide a silver bullet; (b) each method has home ground where one clearly dominates the other; (c) future trends indicate that both will be needed; (d) it is better to build your method up than to tailor it down. Two case studies of actual

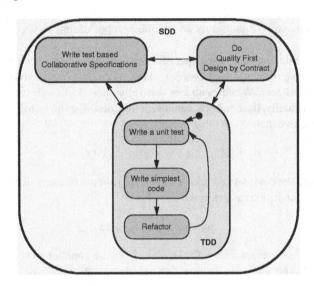

Fig. 6. SDD – Specification Driven Design

projects indicate how a balance can be achieved between agile and plan-driven method. The authors also detail the empirical evidence of how the costs and benefits of each method can be, and have been measured.

Conclusion (d) states that it is better to start small and elaborate one's development method over time. Boehm and Turner point out that plan-driven methodologies have a tradition of developing all-inclusive processes. Experts can can tailor the methodology down to fit a particular situation. However, non-experts tend to play it safe and use the whole thing often at considerable and unnecessary expense. Agilists offer a better approach of starting with minimal sets of practices, adding extras which can be justified by cost-benefits. This is extremely important for teaching: students may be turned off by presenting a large, complex methodology (or a large set of practices or principles), especially when they are first introduced to large-scale software engineering ideas.

In this spirit, the statechart of Fig. 6 describes *specification-driven design*. SDD is not complete but it does represent a core practices of a balanced method.

As described in Fig. 6, SDD does not dictate where to start – it is the developer's choice based on the context. However, whatever the starting point, the emphasis is on translating customer requirements to compilable and executable specifications, designs and tests. It might initially be possible to write a high level collaborative specification, or perhaps the developer wants to sketch out some class diagrams and contractual specifications.

Designs may need to be tested, or small chunks of design could be developed by TDD. In TDD mode, a developer might get stuck in an "infinite refactoring loop", indicating that more than an incremental design change is called for. The current chunk of design may need to be documented. This might be the right time to switch to DbC mode. In DbC mode, a developer might be stuck in the infamous "analysis paralysis", or the design may need to be tested and verified against the requirement. The trigger conditions on the statechart edges are thus not exhaustive.

Our experience in teaching with this approach is that captures the interest of students immediately, particularly because of the emphasis on executable specifications. Students see the value of formal specifications when they are couched in terms of testing. But at the same time, when testing is an emphasised part of development, they quickly see that tests as a form of specification are incomplete, and one needs to go further – and use contracts. We discuss our observations more in the next section.

4.3 Verification: Going Further

In current teaching with Eiffel we emphasise formal specification and lightweight verification and validation via testing. There is of course a desire to teach software engineering specialists more advanced techniques, in particular tool-supported formal verification, e.g., as with the B-Tool or with theorem provers like PVS. It is desirable to be able to teach verification using the same framework that students used for specification, design, and testing, so as to make use of students' existing expertise with notation and tools.

It is possible to teaching formal program verification using Eiffel. To this end, we have formulated the Eiffel Refinement Calculus, ERC. The full details are presented in [15]. ERC uses Eiffel as both a specification and programming language; Eiffel specifications consist of classes with contracts. A subset of the programming language – including reference types – is formalised using Hehner's predicative theory of programming [8], and verification rules are presented that show how to prove that a program satisfies a specification. The rules can be used for both after-the-fact verification, and for refinement. The rules are novel in that they apply directly to a subset of Eiffel, and allow introduction of object-oriented concepts such as method calls in refinement steps; translation to a non-OO language is not required.

More advanced projects can be defined to build on ERC, e.g., better tool support, case studies, addition of further constructs from Eiffel to the calculus (such as the novel **like** construct which introduces substantial challenges), and improving data refinement theories. This would be most suitable for an advanced post-graduate course on formal methods.

5   Some Observations and Conclusions

We now summarise some of our observations in teaching specification-driven design in Eiffel.

1. *The learning curve with SDD is initially very steep.* The students have a great deal of material to assimilate and apply in a short period of time: they must get to grips with Eiffel and TDD; they must learn elements of UML/BON for modelling; and they must learn how to write tests and to test effectively. Requirements for evaluation and teaching mean that students are given an assignment shortly after the start of term and need to submit their solutions within 3-4 weeks.
   The curve is somewhat lessened by the previous experience students have had with object-oriented programming and, to a smaller extent, writing up programming

assignments. To lessen the curve further, the course starts with a detailed case study showing the development process and how to use the Eiffel IDE, E-Tester framework, how to write test cases, etc. Students also work in pairs (one of the practices of Extreme Programming) on their assignments, and can work in slightly large teams on their projects.

2. *Student feedback is that the course is challenging,* but not because of the level of mathematics required or applied. It is challenging because of the scale of design projects that the students must work on (previously they have worked only on small projects), the amount of information that must be learned and understood over the course of approximately 12 weeks, and the level of rigour required in assignment and project write-ups. The fact that the knowledge accrued in the course is to be applied in future software engineering courses is considered very helpful.

3. *Students learn the formal method gradually.* Their initial use of the formal method is by writing collaborative specifications, i.e., BON dynamic diagrams and test cases. This also introduces them to Eiffel's agent syntax. They quickly realise the value of pre- and postconditions for capturing collaborative specifications that are awkward, complicated, or inexpressible. Their use of preconditions invariably starts at a very simple level, e.g., that arguments to methods are non-*Void*; postconditions are not used much initially. Postconditions are applied more broadly once appreciation for the complexity of collaborative specifications is gained. There is a feedback loop here – once complex unit tests start to occur during assignments and projects, there is more of an appreciation for the expressiveness of postconditions. And once complex postconditions appear, there is more of a reliance on the use of unit tests.

4. *Collaborative specifications are a better way to introduce agents* than some of the alternatives, particularly as a way of introducing predicate quantifiers into contracts. There is resistance from many of the students to using quantifiers in contracts when they are not shown motivation via testing.

5. *Eiffel is underappreciated at first.* There is backlash against it from some students at first, in the sense that they desire to learn a more 'commercially relevant' language, e.g., C++ or Java. We deal with this in several ways: by introducing them to simple GUI techniques in Eiffel in the course of the initial case study; by presenting information on the industrial use of Eiffel; and by carrying out comparisons with competing technologies throughout the course. As well, the students have previous experience with Java and are generally aware of its limitations and abilities. When starting with Eiffel, the students find its support for generic classes and contracts very helpful.

We should not underplay the substantial time and effort that the instructor must put into making the course a success. Setting up suitable assignments and projects for this course is challenging, and requires much effort, especially in producing quality solutions. It is also difficult to obtain high-quality teaching assistants and laboratory demonstrators familiar with Eiffel and agile techniques. It is of course possible to teach such a course using Java (or C++) based technologies (e.g., by using a contract framework and testing framework for such a language), and we have done so, but in our experience the tools that support contracts in these languages are typically weaker than Eiffel's tools. While the iContract preprocessor for Java provides much the same functionality as Eiffel's contract mechanism, it does not have Eiffel's integrated tool support, e.g., a built-in debugger for tracing contract failures. As well, the fact that iContract is a preprocessor makes it more cumbersome to use for editing contracts, testing them, and keeping the code consistent with the contracts.

We have taught this course using both ISE EiffelStudio (a commercial tool) and GNU SmartEiffel, on a variety of development platforms. We have generally found it easier to make use of EiffelStudio, in part because of its complete integrated development environment (including debugger) and more comprehensive set of libraries. The SmartEiffel compiler and toolset is powerful and generally straightforward to use, but the lack of integrated debugging facilities is a weakness at this stage.

The general feedback that we have received on the course is predominantly positive: the course is perceived as challenging, hard work, practical, and insightful. A few students remain unconvinced by Eiffel as an industrially applicable language; some have been completely convinced and are now using Eiffel in industrial development [7]. Most have commented that they now think they have a better understanding of the principles of software engineering, object-oriented design, formal methods, and formal specification, which is in the end a good measure of success.

References

1. S. Ambler. Extreme Testing. *Software Development*, 11(5), June 2003.
2. S. Ambler. Agility for Executives. *Software Development*, September 2003.
3. K. Beck. *Test-driven Development: by example*, Addison-Wesley, 2003.
4. K. Beck, A. Cockburn, R. Jeffries, and J. Highsmith. Agile Manifesto www.agilemanifesto.org/history.html. 2001.
5. D. Berry. Formal methods: the very idea – some thoughts about why they work when they work. *Science of Computer Programming*, 42(1), 2002.
6. B.W. Boehm and R. Turner. *Balancing Agility and Discipline: a guide for the perplexed*, Addison-Wesley, 2003.
7. H. Cater. Strategic Command 2, web site at www.battlefront.com, last accessed June 2004.
8. E.C.R. Hehner. *A Practical Theory of Programming* (Second Edition), Prentice-Hall, 2003.
9. M. Jackson. *Software Requirements and Specifications*, ACM Press, 1995.
10. J.S. Ostroff, R.F. Paige, D. Makalsky, and P.J Brooke. *ETester: an Agent-Based Testing Framework for Eiffel*, submitted June 2004.
11. B. Meyer. *Eiffel: the Language* (Second Edition), Prentice-Hall, 1992.
12. B. Meyer. *Object-Oriented Software Construction (Second Edition)*, Prentice-Hall, 1997.
13. J.S. Ostroff, D. Makalsky, and R.F. Paige. Agile Specification-Driven Design. In *Proc. Extreme Programming 2004*, LNCS, Springer-Verlag, June 2004.
14. R.F. Paige, J.S. Ostroff, and P.J. Brooke. A Test-Based Agile Approach to Checking the Consistency of Class and Collaboration Diagrams. In *Proc. UK Software Testing Workshop*, University of York, September 2003.
15. R.F. Paige and J.S. Ostroff. ERC: an Object-Oriented Refinement Calculus for Eiffel. *Formal Aspects of Computing* 16(1):51-79, Springer-Verlag, April 2004.
16. P. Zave and M. Jackson. Four dark corners of requirements engineering. *ACM Transactions on Software Engineering and Methodology*, 6(1), 1997.

Integrating Formal Specification and Software Verification and Validation

Roger Duke, Tim Miller*, and Paul Strooper

School of Information Technology and Electrical Engineering
The University of Queensland, Brisbane, Qld. 4072, Australia
`{rduke,timothym,pstroop}@itee.uq.edu.au`

Abstract. It is not surprising that students are unconvinced about the benefits of formal methods if we do not show them how these methods can be integrated with other activities in the software lifecycle. In this paper, we describe an approach to integrating formal specification with more traditional verification and validation techniques in a course that teaches formal specification and specification-based testing. This is accomplished through a series of assignments on a single software component that involves specifying the component in Object-Z, validating that specification using inspection and a specification animation tool, and then testing an implementation of the specification using test cases derived from the formal specification.

1 Introduction

There are a number of courses at The University of Queensland that cover formal methods, such as formal specification and refinement. Past feedback on these courses indicate that while some students find this material interesting and stimulating, they often fail to recognise the relevance of these courses. We believe that part of the reason for this is that the material in these courses is not well integrated into the rest of the curriculum. There are two aspects to this problem:

1. the formal methods are taught in isolation, without showing how they relate to other processes or products in the software lifecycle;
2. courses that are not focused on formal methods do not refer to these methods at all, not even as a possible alternative to the methods and tools that are used in these courses.

Moreover, examples chosen in formal methods courses, especially courses on formal specification, are not always software-based, further compounding the problem.

In this paper, we address the first problem above, by discussing the integration of formal specification with more traditional verification and validation

---

* Tim Miller's current address: Department of Computer Science, The University of Liverpool, Liverpool, L69 7ZF, UK, email: tim@csc.liv.ac.uk

C.N. Dean and R.T. Boute (Eds.): TFM 2004, LNCS 3294, pp. 124–139, 2004.

(V&V) techniques in a single course. The course, COMP4600: *Software Specification and Testing*, is a fourth-year course that aims to develop the students' ability to formally specify systems using the object-oriented specification language Object-Z [3], and then to use that formal specification as a basis for testing the implementation. COMP4600 has been taught for a number of years, but the parts on formal specification and specification-based testing have been taught and assessed separately in previous years. We felt the link between the two parts could and should be made much stronger. In 2003, we moved a step in that direction by using a single example as part of a series of assessment items.

In particular, as a first task, the students were asked to specify a software component in Object-Z. As a second task, the students were then asked to validate the specification using a combination of inspection and the Possum animation tool [7,8]. Finally, as a third task, the students were asked to apply the Test Template Framework [18] to the validated specification to derive test cases and expected outputs, and to implement these test cases in a test driver to test a Java implementation (which we supplied) of the specification.

This approach has the benefits that it shows students both how formal methods can support other software processes (V&V in this case) and how traditional techniques (software testing) can be applied to formal specifications (to validate the specification). The approach we have taken is lightweight in that we do not teach or ask students to use more rigorous approaches to V&V such as theorem proving. Despite this, the manual effort involved in the specification-based testing part of the assignments is such that, given the restriction on students' available time and effort, it can only be applied to the smaller examples from the specification part of the course. While this is unfortunate, we believe that in any case it is a reality of many of the current state-of-the-art formal methods tools.

Related work is reviewed in Section 2. Section 3 provides a brief overview of COMP4600 and Section 4 then details the assessment tasks for the students. This section also summarises how well the students did on the assessment tasks. Student and our own feedback is discussed in Section 5 and Section 6 contains concluding remarks.

2   Related Work

A number of authors have commented on the lack of integration of formal methods with other parts of the software engineering curriculum [4,5,9,14,17,19,12, 6]. Of these, we discuss two proposals for specific approaches to the integration in one or more courses in more detail below.

The motivation and overall approach for the work reported by Utting and Reeves [19] is similar to ours. They describe a course on formal methods that is based on a pragmatic approach that emphasises testing. The course is more general than COMP4600, in that it encompasses risk and hazard analysis; reading and writing formal specifications in Z; validation of specifications using inspection, testing, and animation; and the relationship between formal specifications and code. The paper describes two assignments that are similar to our assessment tasks:

– The first covers specification animation using the Z/Eves theorem prover [15], validation of the specification by defining test cases, and test set generation from the specification using the Test Template Framework [18].
– The second covers adding assertions to an implementation of the specification that was part of the first assignment and implementing another class from a separate specification and adding assertions to it.

The course has other assignments as well, but these are not discussed in [19] because they do not relate to testing or assertions.

The main difference between the above assessment tasks and the assessment tasks in COMP4600 is that we require the students to write the original specification themselves and then to validate their own specification. This is a more realistic use of an animation tool, but can lead to problems since some student assignments will have a significant number of errors in both syntax and semantics. These problems are compounded by the fact that the animation tool we use does not provide the most informative error messages, which means that students sometimes struggle to get going with the animator. In the 2004 offering of the course, these problems were somewhat alleviated by recommending the use of the Sum type checker before the students attempt to animate their specification and by providing a practical handout for the students to help them with the type checker and the animator.

Another difference is that we carry the specification-based testing part of the assessment through further in that the students have to implement a test driver that is based on the test cases derived from the formal specification. However, on the other hand, we do not ask students to implement a class from a specification and we do not deal with how assertions can be derived from formal specifications.

A more radical approach to the integration of formal methods is presented by Garlan [4]. He describes the Master of Software Engineering Program at Carnegie Melon University, in which formal methods are integrated into four of the five core courses in the curriculum. In these courses, the formal methods are treated in parallel with other, informal approaches and techniques. As a result, they have found that students apply some of the formal techniques in the Studio work, even though this is not an explicit requirement of the Studio. Moreover, Garlan reports that "students have chosen to apply formal methods in different, but appropriate ways."

3   Course Overview

The overall aim of COMP4600 is for students to gain an understanding of object-oriented formal specification, and the use of formal specifications in testing. They are expected to develop practical skills in formal specification and testing.

COMP4600 is normally taken by third or fourth-year students in the Bachelor of IT or the BE(Software) programs. However, it is also cross-listed as

COMP7600, a postgraduate course taken by postgraduate diploma and course-work masters students. In 2003, 48 students were enrolled in COMP4600 and 9 students in COMP7600. This number was significantly higher than usual (for example, 19 students are enrolled in both courses in 2004), which is most likely due to the fact that the course was not offered in 2002. Other than the course codes, COMP4600 and COMP7600 are identical, and we will refer to it as the single course COMP4600.

COMP4600 focuses on formal object-oriented specification and processes, and specification-based testing. The specification section in the first half of the course reviews the logic and set-theoretic bases used throughout specification and refinement. The object-oriented specification language Object-Z [3], an extension of the Z specification language, is covered in detail including several medium-scale case studies.

The specification-based testing section covered in the second half of the course uses formal specifications as a starting point for deriving test cases and oracles. In this section of the course, testing the formal specifications themselves and testing implementations of the specifications is explored.

Each student taking COMP4600 is required to have previously completed the course COMP3601: *Software Specification*, intended to "introduce students to a formal notation for specifying software systems and to the use of proof to validate such specifications"[1]. The B specification language [16] is used as a teaching aid in that course.

In addition, the students would have had the opportunity to complete two other optional courses covering material relevant to COMP4600. The first is COMP3600: *Reasoning about Software*, intended to "develop skills in both specifying programs and reasoning about the correctness of programs, with the aim of being able to derive correct programs from specifications".

The second is COMP4601: *Rigorous Software Development*, intended to "provide students with experience with rigorous development of software from specifications (refinement); mechanised support for program development; program and refinement semantics; and integrating refinement into software engineering methodology". The B specification language and B-Toolkit [16] are used as teaching aids in this course.

In the 2003 offering of COMP4600, the assessment consisted of:

- Six worksheets, each worth 4%, with only the five best marks counted toward a student's final grade. Students had a week to complete each worksheet. The aim of the worksheets was to explore the basic concepts introduced in the lectures. The first four worksheets were associated with the specification part of the course; the last two with the testing part.
- Four assignments, with the first two both worth 10% and the last two both worth 20%. The students were given 3 or 4 weeks to complete each assignment. The assignments aimed at extending the students understanding by asking the students to work on a substantial problem involving a deeper

---

[1] Taken from the course profile. For more details visit the School web site at http://www.itee.uq.edu.au

appreciation of the concepts. The first two assignments involved creating
Object-Z specifications; the last two dealt with testing issues.
- A written exam, worth 20%, at the end of the semester. This exam was
concerned only with the Object-Z specification part and involved no testing.

4   Relevant Assessment Tasks

Three items of assessment were particularly relevant to the issues being explored
in this paper: the third worksheet and the last two assignments.

4.1   Worksheet 3 – Specification

For the third worksheet, students were asked to complete a specification of an
undirected graph. To ensure that the specification would "match" with the implementation that we wanted the students to test in later assignments, we provided
the students with a skeleton of the specification, containing the state variables
and the signatures of the methods in the class (see Figure 1). As King [10] points
out, this has the added benefits of reducing the confusion by students about the
requirements of the assignment and reduces the overall marking time. The task
as set out on the worksheet was as follows:

Complete the Object-Z specification of the Graph class shown on the next page
(Figure 1). The Graph class maintains a set of nodes and can be used to generate
a path between two nodes, if one exists. Let

$$[Node]$$

denote the set of all possible nodes. An edge is an (undirected) link between two
distinct nodes. Hence

$$Edge == \{n_1, n_2 : Node \mid n_1 \neq n_2 \bullet \{n_1, n_2\}\}$$

defines the set Edge of all possible edges.

Marks were awarded to the students for using the correct syntax and for
having a semantically correct solution. Although specification "quality" as such
was not graded, students did have marks deducted if their predicates were ex-
ceptionally convoluted. A sample solution can be found in Appendix A. After
marking, each worksheet was returned to the student, who was asked to keep it
for use in the later assignments.

4.2   Assignment 3 – Specification Validation

For Assignment 3, students were asked to apply inspection and specification testing to their solution to Worksheet 3 (the graph specification) in order to validate
that their solution was correct. However, the students had to first translate their
specification from Object-Z to Sum [1], a modular extension to Z, because there

```
┌─ Graph ─────────────────────────────────────────────────────────
│  ┌──────────────────────────────┐  ┌─ INIT ──────────────────────┐
│  │ nodes : ℙ Node               │  │ insert predicate to         │
│  │ edges : ℙ Edge               │  │ capture the initial state   │
│  │ ─────────────────────        │  │                             │
│  │ insert predicate to capture  │  └─────────────────────────────┘
│  │ the invariant relationship   │
│  │ between a graph's nodes      │
│  │ and edges                    │
│  └──────────────────────────────┘
│
│  ┌─ addNode ────────────────────┐  ┌─ removeNode ────────────────┐
│  │ Δ(nodes)                     │  │ Δ(nodes)                    │
│  │ n? : Node                    │  │ n? : Node                   │
│  │ ─────────────────────        │  │ ─────────────────────       │
│  │ insert predicate to capture  │  │ insert predicate to capture │
│  │ the addition of any node n?  │  │ removal of any node n? from │
│  │ to the graph; if n? is already  │ the graph; n? must not be   │
│  │ a node of the graph, the graph │ in any edge of the graph; if │
│  │ is unchanged                 │  │ n? is not a node of the graph, │
│  │                              │  │ the graph is unchanged      │
│  └──────────────────────────────┘  └─────────────────────────────┘
│
│  ┌─ addEdge ────────────────────┐  ┌─ removeEdge ────────────────┐
│  │ Δ(edges)                     │  │ Δ(edges)                    │
│  │ e? : Edge                    │  │ e? : Edge                   │
│  │ ─────────────────────        │  │ ─────────────────────       │
│  │ insert predicate to capture  │  │ insert predicate to capture │
│  │ the addition of any edge e?  │  │ the removal of any edge e?  │
│  │ to the graph; e? must link   │  │ from the graph; if e? is not │
│  │ existing nodes of the graph; │  │ an edge of the graph, the   │
│  │ if e? is already an edge of  │  │ graph is unchanged          │
│  │ the graph, the graph is      │  └─────────────────────────────┘
│  │ unchanged                    │
│  └──────────────────────────────┘
│
│  ┌─ findPath ───────────────────────────────────────────────────┐
│  │ n₁?, n₂? : Node                                              │
│  │ p! : seq Node                                                │
│  │ ─────────────────────────────────────────────────           │
│  │ insert predicate to capture the requirement that n₁? and n₂? │
│  │ are distinct nodes of the graph and p! is a sequence of nodes │
│  │ defining a cycle-free path between n₁? and n₂?; a pre-condition │
│  │ of the operation is that such a path exists                  │
│  └──────────────────────────────────────────────────────────────┘
└──────────────────────────────────────────────────────────────────
```

Fig. 1. Skeleton of the *Graph* class

are currently no good animators available for Object-Z. This is a straightforward step, because there was no creation of objects in the specifications of the graph, and as a result an Object-Z specification and Sum specification would look similar.

The major difference is that Sum has *explicit preconditions*, which we asked students to specify. The students were asked to ensure that the preconditions of the operations and the state invariant were correct. The students were also asked to consider four properties of their specification [13], and had to show that either these properties were satisfied or that they were not satisfied, but that the specification was still correct (this is possible for the second and fourth properties below). The four properties are:

1. **Weak precondition**: For every pre-state and input, if an operation's precondition is true, then there must exist a post-state and outputs (if the operation has outputs) that satisfy the postcondition. Unlike Z and Object-Z, Sum has explicit preconditions, and in Sum, if this property is not satisfied, then this is an error in the specification.
2. **Strong precondition:** If there exists a post-state and outputs for a prestate and inputs, then the precondition must hold for the pre-state and inputs. A violation of this property does not necessarily imply an error, but it is worth checking the property because in some cases it does indicate an error in the specification [13].
3. **Strong state invariant**: For every operation, if the precondition and postcondition (not including the state invariant) of that operation allow it to reach a particular state, that state must satisfy the state invariant. In Sum, if this property is not satisfied, then this is an error in the specification.
4. **Weak state invariant:** For every state that satisfies the state invariant, it must be reachable via the operations in the specification. A violation of this property does not necessarily imply an error [13].

Students were encouraged to use animation to test for these properties using a simplified approach from [13].

The students were required to complete 3 tasks for this assignment. These tasks, from the assignment sheet, were as follows:

1. *Translate your Object-Z to Sum. To assist you with this task, we have created a skeleton Sum specification of the Graph class in the file* Graph.sum *on the student network. In the process of translation, you may incorporate any feedback you received on your specification. Any other substantial changes to your specification should be documented and justified in a separate text file (see submission requirements below).*
2. *Using Possum and any other tools/techniques available to you, remove all errors and inconsistencies from your Sum specification. For each change you make, carefully describe the change itself, why you made the change, and how you discovered the need for a change. A sample format you could use for this is shown in the text file* notes.txt *on the student network.*
3. *Write a Possum script that tests the final Sum specification. Briefly document the test cases you use in your script and why you chose them in the file* notes.txt

In addition, you must document which operations, if any, in your final specification still have a weak or strong precondition. You must also state whether or not the specification has a weak/strong state invariant and justify your answers. The file notes.txt *again contains skeleton sections for this part of the assignment.*

The students were asked to submit 4 documents:

1. Graph1.sum: the Sum specification obtained by translating their Object-Z specification from Worksheet 3.
2. Graph2.sum: their final version of the Sum specification.
3. Graph.scr: a Possum script that tests Graph2.sum.
4. notes.txt: a file that contains a description of any changes made to the original Object-Z specification to translate it to Sum, errors/inconsistencies found in the Sum specification and how they were fixed, a brief description of the test cases in the Possum script, and a discussion of weak/strong preconditions and state invariant.

Students were able to achieve a maximum of 20 marks for this assignment. The marks breakdown was as follows:

- 2 marks for the initial Sum specification in Graph1.sum: an appropriate translation of initial Object-Z specification (with changes justified in notes.txt). The Sum specification may contain errors or inconsistencies.
- 4 marks for the updated Sum specification in Graph2.sum: a correct and appropriate Sum specification that meets the requirements of the *Graph* class.
- 4 marks for the list of changes described in notes.txt: a clearly documented list of changes that is easy to read and understand.
- 4 marks for a description of the Sum test cases in notes.txt: a thorough, well-structured and reasonable set of test cases that are described concisely.
- 4 marks for a Possum script in Graph.scr: an accurate implementation of test cases described in the notes.txt file that can all be executed in Possum.
- 2 marks for a discussion of weak/strong preconditions and state invariant in notes.txt: a correct and convincing discussion.

4.3   Assignment 4 – Specification-Based Testing

For Assignment 4, students were asked to apply a specification-based testing framework called the *Test Template Framework* (TTF) [18] to the graph specification. The students then had to derive a *Finite State Machine* (FSM) from the test cases that they selected using the TTF following the method described in [2]. Finally, they were required to implement a test driver to test a Java implementation using either the test cases or the finite state machine as a basis.

The TTF is a generic framework for applying specification-based testing strategies for partitioning the input space of an operation. Test case selection begins with the operation's *valid input space*, which is the inputs and pre-state values for which the precondition holds. This input space is partitioned into *templates*, using a test case selection strategy that is selected by the tester, such as *cause-effect analysis*. Each of the templates (partitions) is represented as a child of the input space using a tree structure. The child partitions can then be further partitioned, and this continues until no further partitioning is possible or the tester feels that further partitioning will not lead to additional valuable test cases. This results in a tree, called a *Test Template Hierarchy*, and the leaf templates of this tree are instantiated to form test inputs. An *Oracle Template* is calculated for each input by using the specification.

The students were required to complete 3 tasks for this assignment. These tasks, from the assignment sheet, were as follows:

1. *Show the detailed application of the Test Template Framework and derive instance and oracle templates for three of the operations from the Graph class. You must apply the TTF to one of addNode and removeNode, to one of addEdge and removeEdge, and to findPath.*
2. *Following the method described in the lectures, develop a state machine to test the operations of the Graph class and their interaction. You should base the state machine on the Test Template Hierarchies developed for the first part of the assignment. For the operations that you did not cover in the first part, you should include a brief description (no justification is needed) of the Test Templates that you use as a starting point for your state machine.*
3. *Implement a test driver to test a Java implementation of the Object-Z specification. We will provide a Java implementation in the file* **Graph.java** *on the student network. You should base the implementation of your test driver on the testing information (either the Test Template Hierarchies or the state machine) developed for the first and second part of this assignment.*

   For this part of the assignment, you should explain how your test driver works and how it relates to the Test Template Hierarchies and/or the state machine you derived. You should also discuss any difficulties you encountered, and any shortcomings in the test driver or in the method you used to derive the test driver. You should include a printout of the code for the test driver as an appendix to your report.

   You must also submit an electronic copy of all the code (and any other files needed to run your test driver, such as Makefiles) electronically.

Students were able to achieve a maximum of 24 marks for this assignment. The marks breakdown was as follows:

- 2 marks for overall presentation: easy to read and understand.
- 6 marks for the Test Cases: evidence of systematic development, coverage of specification, justification for strategies.
- 4 marks for the Finite State Machine: evidence of systematic development, reasonable initial test templates, explanation of process used.
- 6 marks for the description of the Test Driver: evidence of systematic development, use of TTHs/state machine, discussion of method and driver.
- 6 marks for the Test Driver Implementation: clear and concise driver that executes correctly.

4.4   The Students' Performance

The marks awarded for the worksheet were quite high, with the average mark being 3.1/4 (77%). This is not surprising considering that from a specification point of view, the graph is not challenging, and in fact, the students had already been asked to complete worksheets that could be considered more difficult than this. However, we decided to keep the specification simple so that the following assignments were not too challenging for the students.

Even though the marks were high, some students struggled with the *findPath* operation. For the purpose of this research, we analysed the students *findPath* operations and placed them into one of four categories. Out of the 46 students who submitted the assessment, 11 had no solution for *findPath*, or their solution had little academic merit, 9 demonstrated some understanding of the material, but the answer was only partially correct, 15 demonstrated good understanding and provided an answer that was mostly correct, and 11 submitted either a correct answer, or an answer with one or two minor problems.

We found from submissions and from discussions with students that although students already had experience using B, some still seem to struggle with the abstract level of specification. One example of this is a question from a student asking one of the teaching staff how to specify while-loops using Object-Z. When the staff member explained that there are indeed no loop constructs in Object-Z, the student asked how one could possibly solve this problem without them. By the end of this course, the students had improved considerably in their ability to reason at the specification level.

The marks awarded for Assignment 3 (specification validation) were also high, with an average mark of 15.8/20 (79%). Students seem to like the idea of testing specifications, most probably due to the fact that they had experience in several previous courses with software testing, and were therefore comfortable with specification testing. However, they did appear to struggle with the overhead of learning how to use the animator.

Students were much less comfortable with the final part of Assignment 3, which asked them to discuss why they thought the precondition and state invariant were suitable for their specification. While some students provided detailed proofs with their discussion, others were much less convincing, stating things such as "The precondition is correct", when in some cases their test cases clearly demonstrated that it was not, or "The precondition is weak", while offering no discussion as to why it was not corrected, or why they thought it was weak.

Again, we analysed the students answers to the final part of the assignment. Out of the 51 students who submitted this assignment, we found that 31 had a solution that was incorrect, and did not demonstrate an understanding of the properties; 5 solutions were mostly correct, but their argument for why was unconvincing, indicating that they may have been lucky and guessed the correct answers; 8 were incorrect, but demonstrated that they understood the material and simply made a fatal error; and 7 submitted a correct and convincing solution, possibly with one or two minor problems.

This indicates that perhaps the students are comfortable thinking about example behaviours of the specification, but not so with more general reasoning about all possible behaviours of a specification.

The marks for Assignment 4 were slightly lower, with an average mark of 14.7/24 (61%). It appears that the students did not have any trouble grasping the concept of the TTF, but some did have trouble selecting test cases using the framework. For example, even for the *findPath* operation, a higher-than-expected percentage of students focussed only on testing the number of nodes and edges in the graph, with no consideration of the length of the paths or the number of possible paths between nodes.

Most students struggled with the generation of a finite state machine from their TTH. The approach for deriving the state machine is to extract the states from all of the leaf templates of the TTH, partition them into disjoint templates (removing duplicates), with each of these partitions becoming a state in the state machine. Then, transitions are drawn between two nodes if there is a possible transition between them. Most students seem to over-simplify this. For example, although a lot of students did select cases for *findPath* that tested different length paths and more than one possible path between two nodes, when they came to partitioning the templates they seemed to ignore these and focused only on the number of nodes and edges in the graph (similar in the end to those students who did not initially select test cases for these). Even then, most of the students who did include these test cases left many overlaps in their states, or fudged the simplification to leave much fewer states than there should have been.

One influencing factor of this final assignment that should be noted is that most of the students were busy with the final preparation for a full-day exposition for their honours project, and it seemed to the teaching staff that some students chose to minimise the amount of time spent on the final assignment to concentrate on the exposition preparation instead.

5   Feedback

5.1   Student Feedback

Students were asked to supply anonymous feedback about the course through feedback sheets distributed at the final class. Here is a representative sample of the comments we received in response to the question *"What are the strengths of this course?"*:

"...one of my favourite courses.."
"...material presented in a relatively well-structured way..."
"...interesting topic, material is interesting..."
"...Object-Z was worthwhile learning..."
"...the spec section of the course was interesting, but I found the testing section much harder..."
"...while course wasn't 'making testing fun', it gave me ideas how to make testing easier and more straightforward; writing test cases isn't boring, but figuring out

what test cases should be is boring and difficult; this course has helped me in that respect..."
"...the assessment structure was good..."

Here is a representative sample of the comments we received in response to the question "*What improvements would you suggest in this course?*":

"...I still have trouble with strong/weak preconditions..."
"...this would be an excellent course if better integrated into the BE(Software) program; B was useless and Object-Z was excellent; Sum wasn't bad either..."
"...the Object-Z material is really interesting, but the assessments and assignments don't really use large amounts of the material..."
"...make the specification part more structured..."
"...possibly reduce the scope of the testing bit so that areas can be considered in more detail, especially TTF..."
"...scrap Possum or significantly improve it; it is a nice concept, but quite unstable; if used in future it should be improved in stability and error diagnosis..."
"...demos of the testing software we had to use and also detailed explanations would have helped..."
"...more references for the test template material, especially with more examples..."
"...the assignments for testing were too complicated since we had to implement things - it would be better to have non-implementation assignments or at least focus more on the software in the lectures..."

The overall impression is that the students struggled with the animator and generally found the formal specification part easier. While we agree that the animator is not very robust, we believe it is one of the better animation tools currently available. In the 2004 offering of the course, the students were also encouraged to use the Sum type checker before attempting to animate their specifications and a practical handout was prepared to help them going with the type checker and the animator. Although we have only anecdotal evidence, it appears that these measures have helped alleviate this problems to a certain extent.

The students also struggled with the assignment requirements for specification-based testing, and in particular were unsure when to stop testing; of course, there is no easy answer to this.

The students commented, not just in the final survey quoted above but also in informal discussion during the course, that the specification examples were simple compared with the testing. The problem here is that we needed to set relatively simple problems to specify, or else the validation and specification-based testing would have been too complicated. Compounding this was the fact that we tended to grade the formal specifications simply on correctness rather than "quality". In fact, the quality of students' specification was often dubious and marks for this part of the course would have been more in line with the testing part if quality was a grading consideration.

5.2 Discussion

It is instructive to compare the feedback we received from students taking this course compared with feedback from formal methods courses we have taught previously. A typical comment from students of our previous courses was "...quite enjoyed the course but doubt it will be useful in the real world...". For this current course, the integration of testing with formal specification has made both techniques more relevant and practical. That is not to say all the students were totally convinced of this, but most students were prepared to accept that formal methods cannot be simply dismissed as impractical and may well have a place in the software lifecycle.

An issue that several students raised was that the formal specification assessment for the course was relatively easier than the testing assessment. We tried to address this in the 2004 offering of the course by ensuring that the formal specification assessment fully covers some of the more abstract aspect of Object-Z, e.g. polymorphism and object containment [3]. In addition, the assessment marking scheme was extended to include not only logical correctness, but also specification style and quality.

A problem that still remains, however, is that the formal specification used for testing needs to be relatively straightforward. There are two main reasons for this. First, a specification of a real-world software problem would be too difficult for the students to handle, given that they are limited both by the time available and their background experience. Second, although great strides have been taken recently in the quality and effectiveness of modeling and specification-based testing tools, they are still not easy to learn or use.

One area that students did not really comment on (perhaps surprisingly), is the use of two formal notations (Object-Z and Sum) in a single course. Perhaps this is because they felt that the additional overhead in learning a second notation (Sum) was offset by having tools available to help them analyse their specifications. Of course, it also helps that Object-Z and Sum specifications are very similar for simple specifications such as the ones dealt with in the specification-based testing part of the course.

6 Concluding Remarks

In this paper, we have described three assessment tasks in a course on formal specification and specification-based testing that include a range of activities related to the formal specification of a single software component. The tasks include the specification of the component in Object-Z, validation of that specification using inspection and the Possum animator, and then the testing of an implementation using test cases derived from the Object-Z specification. We believe that by linking the formal specification with other parts of the software lifecycle, the students will be able to get a better appreciation of how and where formal methods fit in and how they can be used to support other activities in the software lifecycle. Informal student feedback so far confirms this belief.

In conclusion, it is interesting to review how the teaching of formal methods at the University of Queensland has changed over the past 10 years. Back in 1995, the Z specification language was taught as part of a first-year formal methods undergraduate course. Although this course was generally well-received, as the techniques introduced there were not well-integrated into other aspects of the curriculum students often doubted the benefits of a formal approach. These days, the first-year syllabus is devoted almost entirely to programming and related practical techniques and there is no first-year course specialising in formal methods as such. Formal methods do not appear until third year with the courses COMP3601: *Software Specification* and possibly also COMP3600: *Reasoning about Software*. COMP4600 follows on from these courses.

Currently the course offerings are undergoing review and rationalisation; from next year (2005), the courses COMP3600 and COMP4601: *Rigorous Software Development* will be merged with COMP4600. This new course will have COMP3601 as a prerequisite. With such limited exposure to formal methods it becomes even more crucial that the methods are seen to be relevant in the broader software lifecycle. At present COMP4600 uses Object-Z as the underlying specification language. The reasons for this are partly pragmatic and partly historical. With the changes proposed for next year it will be necessary to widen the coverage of COMP4600 and somewhat narrow its depth, so we will have to re-think our strategy and may revert to Z/B and associated tools; the students will have already met these languages and tools in COMP3601.

The other part of the problem discussed in the Introduction, the integration of formal methods in other parts of the curriculum, is harder to address. A good example of such integration is given by Magee and Kramer [11]. Their textbook is used in the course COMP3402: *Concurrent and Real-Time Systems* and its approach of "model, analyse, implement" works well for both students and lecturer. The formal language adopted by Magee and Kramer is Finite State Processes (FSP), a variant of CSP. Students see the direct practical benefit of incorporating formality into the overall process. Our general aim is to encourage this approach in other software engineering courses as well.

Acknowledgements. We thank Graeme Smith for his comments on an earlier version of this paper.

References

1. A. Bloesch, E. Kazmierczak, P. Kearney, J. Staples, O. Traynor, and M. Utting. A formal reasoning environment for Sum - a Z based specification language. Technical Report 95-02, Software Verification Research Centre, 1995.
2. David Carrington, Ian MacColl, Jason McDonald, Leesa Murray, and Paul Strooper. From Object-Z specifications to ClassBench test suites. *Journal on Software Testing, Verification and Reliability*, 10(2):111–137, 2000.
3. R. Duke and G. Rose. *Formal Object-Oriented Specification Using Object-Z*. MacMillan Press Limited, London, 2000.

4. David Garlan. Making formal methods education effective for professional software engineers. *Information and Software Technology*, 37(3–4):261–268, 1995.
5. D. Gries. The need for education in useful formal logic. *IEEE Computer*, 29(4):29–30, 1996.
6. Henri Habrias and Sebastien Faucou. Some reflections on the teaching of formal methods. In *Teaching Formal Methods: Practice and Experience*, 2003. http://wwwcms.brookes.ac.uk/tfm2003.
7. Daniel Hazel, Paul Strooper, and Owen Traynor. Possum: An animator for the sum specification language. In *Proceedings Asia-Pacific Software Engineering Conference and International Computer Science Conference*, pages 42–51. IEEE Computer Society, 1997.
8. Daniel Hazel, Paul Strooper, and Owen Traynor. Requirements engineering and verification using specification animation. In *Proceedings 13th IEEE International Conference on Automated Software Engineering*, pages 302–305. IEEE Computer Society, 1998.
9. M.G. Hinchey and J.P. Bowen. To formalize or not to formalize. *IEEE Computer*, 29(4):18–19, 1996.
10. Steven King. The assessment of students on FM courses: A position paper. In *Teaching Formal Methods: Practice and Experience*, 2003. http://wwwcms.brookes.ac.uk/tfm2003.
11. J. Magee and J. Kramer. *Concurrency: State Models and Java Programs*. Wiley, 1999.
12. Savi Maharaj. Formal methods teaching at the University of Stirling. In *Teaching Formal Methods: Practice and Experience*, 2003. http://wwwcms.brookes.ac.uk/tfm2003.
13. T. Miller and P. Strooper. A framework for the systematic testing of model-based specifications. *ACM Transactions on Software Engineering and Methodology*, 2004. To Appear.
14. D.L. Parnas. "formal methods" technology transfer will fail. *Journal of Systems and Software*, 40(3):195–198, 1998.
15. M. Saaltink. The Z/EVES system. In *Proceedings 10th International Conference on the Z Formal Method*, pages 72–88. Springer Verlag, 1997.
16. S. Schneider. *The B-Method: An Introduction*. Palgrave, 2001.
17. A. Sobel, S Saiedian, A. Stavely, and P. Henderson. Teaching formal methods early in the software engineering curriculum. In *Proceedings Thirteenth Conference on Software Engineering Education & Training*, page 55. IEEE Computer Society, 2000.
18. P. Stocks and D. Carrington. A framework for specification-based testing. *IEEE Transactions on Software Engineering*, 22(11):777–793, 1996.
19. M. Utting and S. Reeves. Teaching formal methods lite via testing. *Software Testing, Verification and Reliability*, 11(3):181–195, 2001.

A   Sample Graph Solution

Graph

$nodes : \mathbb{P}\ Node$
$edges : \mathbb{P}\ Edge$

$\forall\, e : edges \bullet$
$\quad \exists\, n_1, n_2 : nodes \bullet e = \{n_1, n_2\}$

INIT

$nodes = \varnothing$

---

addNode

$\Delta(nodes)$
$n? : Node$

$nodes' = nodes \cup \{n?\}$

removeNode

$\Delta(nodes)$
$n? : Node$

$\forall\, e : edges \bullet n? \notin e$
$nodes' = nodes \setminus \{n?\}$

---

addEdge

$\Delta(edges)$
$e? : Edge$

$\exists\, n_1, n_2 : nodes \bullet$
$\quad e? = \{n_1, n_2\}$
$edges' = edges \cup \{e?\}$

removeEdge

$\Delta(edges)$
$e? : Edge$

$edges' = edges \setminus \{e?\}$

---

findPath

$n_1?, n_2? : Node$
$p! : \mathrm{seq}\ Node$

$n_1? \neq n_2?$
$\{n_1?, n_2?\} \subseteq nodes$
$\#p! = \#\,\mathrm{ran}\ p!$
$p!(1) = n_1?$
$p!(\#p!) = n_2?$
$\forall\, i : 1 .. (\#p! - 1) \bullet \{p!(i), p!(i+1)\} \in edges$

Distributed Teaching of Formal Methods

Peter Pepper

Technische Universität Berlin
pepper@cs.tu-berlin.de

Abstract. This paper argues that the education in formal methods cannot be located in a few distinguished courses. Rather it has to spread throughout the curriculum such that its spirit is found in many courses. To this end, one needs a way of presenting the underlying concepts of formal methods in an informal style that is amenable even to beginner students.

1   Introduction

A faculty member of a mathematics department was once asked: "In which courses do you teach your students, what a proof is?" The surprising answer was: "Nowhere. They watch us doing proofs for five years. Then they know what a proof is."

After a moment's thought, the answer is actually not so surprising. A mathematical proof is mainly a social endeavor: A line of thought is presented in such a way that fellow mathematicians find the reasoning in each step convincing and are satisfied with the overall strategy. Over the centuries a stock of generally agreed proof patterns has evolved that is part of the professional background of every serious mathematician.

One may object that there is the field of *Formal Logic*. But the topic of this field is *not* the stock of accepted proof patterns and its everday usage. Rather it deals with the limits of provability. In this meta-theoretical approach the proof activities become the topic of study and therefore the employed rules and admissible actions must be extremely simplified in order to make reasoning *about* them easier. Such a highly simplified and condensed sysyem is unsuited for everyday mathematical work.

This situation has many parallels with the concept of *Formal Methods* in Computer Science. Like the idea of "mathematical proof" it is a not clearly defined concept, even though professionals have a good understanding of what it means. And like the mathematicians we may be well advised to view "Formal Methods" as something that has to be learned through continuous practice and good examples.

As an aside we may observe that there is a similar situation with the ubiquitous request for teaching the students "soft skills". This request also cannot be fulfilled by introducing a course entitled "Soft Skills for Engineers". There are elements of teaching that need to be distributed throughout the curriculum.

C.N. Dean and R.T. Boute (Eds.): TFM 2004, LNCS 3294, pp. 140–152, 2004.

1.1   What Are Formal Methods?

The first obstacle in planning a formal-methods education is the lack of a clear definition of what *Formal Methods* are. To some people, the use of formal methods starts, when they use UML; others consider UML as a mere tool for drawing sketches of rough design ideas. (The answer is probably somewhere in the middle.) So it is not surprising that the report [7] makes the observation that many people agree on the need to improve formal-methods education: "However, specific recommendations are rare. Pointed questions about what should be taught to undergraduates, or what constitutes a professional skill in formal methods, or even what preparation someone should have to do research, are usually answered with a shrug or the slogan 'teach more mathematics'."

We will make no attempt here to add the n+1st definition of *Formal Methods*, but rather consider it as a general paradigm for approaching the development and analysis of programs in the same attitude in which mathematicians approach proofs. There are at least five major realms, where such an attitude may apply:

- formal reasoning;
- formal modelling;
- formal developmet;
- formal analysis;
- formal theory.

These aspects occur – in varying degrees – in most areas of Computer Science. By taking the idea of Formal Methods more as an attitude than as a concrete method or technique we obtain a very broad view, which includes among other things

- refinement and deduction;
- systematic design;
- verification;
- systematic testing;
- cost analysis.

The Formal Methods page of the World Wide Web Virtual Library has almost 100 entries in its section on "Individual notations, methods and tools", ranging from *Abstract State Machines* to *Z notation*. (And it does not include UML.) So the situation is the same as with programming languages: One has no chance to teach even the tiniest fraction of existing languages. Therefore one has to teach programming language *concepts*, exemplified by one or two, at most three concrete languages.

The teaching of Formal Methods also means the teaching of a paradigm, exemplified with two, three, or at most four concrete instances. The concretely chosen systems and tools are not so important. What counts is to convey a specific state of mind when developing programs. One can use Hoare logic, temporal logic, Z or algebraic specification: in the end the message will be the same. For getting a feel for formal working, Petri Nets are neither better nor worse than StateCharts.

1.2   Success or Failure?

A big issue in the professional debates is the question, whether formal methods are a success or a failure. Again, this heavily depends on the criteria that one is willing to apply.

Let us take *Algebraic Specification* as a point in case. Evidently, the method is not used to a noticeable extent in industry. So, whenever the degree of industrial use is taken as the criterion, Algebraic Specification was a big failure.

Nevertheless many people consider it a success story. And there are good reasons for this viewpoint. The work on Algebraic Specification provided deep insights into the structure and foundations of software systems. This had great impacts on the design of programming languages, on the design of libraries (as can be seen very well at least in parts of the Java packages), on various software methodolgies and so forth. Even considerable parts of UML show influences of these insights.

1.3   Do Formal Methods Matter?

The lack of direct uses of formal methods in industry also poses a problem in connection with education. Virtually all Computer Science students work as programmers in industry at the latest after their second year. So there is a tendency to identify the experiences of their student jobs with "the field".

Moreover, they make the observation (inside and outside university) that ninety percent of the code they write is not amenable to formalization. It is about input/output with plausibility controls, about graphical user interfaces, about lengthy data layouts and so forth.

Therefore it is important that students accept the spirit of formal methods "subconciously". This means that they should not be confronted with heavy formal notations and tools initially (which they would consider as academic ballast anyhow). Rather they should work with formal methods like mathematicians work with proofs: They come in different degrees of precision, but they are part of the daily routine. This way, the issue of success or failure – which is linked to every concrete method and tool – does not even come up.

Moreover, the daily-routine applications should be chosen such that the students have an actual gain from the formal or semiformal way of proceeding. (We will show examples for this in Sec. 3.) In other words, the students see from their own experience that they can actually solve certain tasks relatively easily by employing formal methods that would be extremely cumbersome otherwise. Maybe there are even a couple of exercises that would be intractable at all without formal reasoning.

Such positive experiences will have a much deeper effect than even strong statements like "It is irresponsible to produce safety-critical embedded systems without formally ensuring their quality."

2   Distributed Teaching

Based on these observations we come to the conclusion that there is no single course, where "formal methods" can be taught. Rather, we have to view *formal methods* as an overall paradigm that has to be integrated into many courses. This leads to an overall curriculum design along the following lines:

- The first-year courses can provide a first look-and-feel of formal design, however, still presented in informal terms.
- The higher level of undergraduate education can already utilize concrete methods and/or tools.
- The first two years of the undergraduate level are accompanied – as it is the case in all engineering desciplines – by a sound mathematical education.
- The graduate education offers courses that are usually heavily influenced by the research focus of the faculty members, thus contributing to the university's profile. This applies to Formal Methods as well.

Since the other issues are quite standard in todays'curricula, we will only focus on the first one of these points in the following.

"Educators are starting to consider teaching formal methods at the undergraduate level." (Clarke and Wing in [3]) This statement from 1996 is by now a reality in some universities, but they are probably still a minority. I beleive that there are at least two reasons, why educators are hesitant:

- Learning how to program is a hard intellectual endeavor, since it requires a high degree of abstraction. Formal methods add a second level of abstraction, which makes the task much harder, if not unbearably hard, for beginners.
- Many people have the perception that formal methods need a plethora of specialized mathematical notations.

These prejudices lead to statements like: "Formal methods are hard. I feel that most mortals like me just need more help in it than in other subjects." (an anonymous educator quoted in [7]).

In order to overcome this attitude one may proceed along the following lines (which is essentially the curriculum at the TU Berlin). In the first semester the students start with functional programming, using the language Opal [5]. Functional languages are inherently closer to formal reasoning and development than imperative or (even worse) object-oriented languages, which struggle much more deeply with technical issues. In the second semester this is followed by Java. And in the third semester this leads into preliminary concepts of Software Engineering and advanced algorithms.

This setting opens the possibility to derive algorithms in a clean functional way and then "transform" them (not formally but intuitively) into Java programs. This may lead to surprising insights by the students. ("It was the first time ever that one of my programs ran bug-free right away." was the astonished comment of an "experienced high-school hacker".)

Besides this derivation-oriented way of proceeding, one may also program directly in, say, Java or Modula. This programming can also be amalgamated with formal reasoning. (This is exemplified in greater detail in Section 3.)

3   Formal Methods in Undergraduate Courses

In the remainder of the paper we focus on the possibilities for leading first-year students towards a style of program development that anticipates the use of formal methods. As stated before, we do not believe in the use of heavy formalisms during this initial stage. Rather we try to inject the ideas in "homeopathic doses".

The programs in this course are all presented in the same style, which may be viewed as a stratified instance of *design patterns*:

- problem specification (informally or mathematically):
  - o task to be solved;
  - o constraints to be observed;
- solution principles (including correctness considerations);
- coding;
- evaluation:
  - o cost analysis ($\mathcal{O}$-notation);
  - o test strategies.

Most of this is self-explanatory. Therefore we only comment on two issues.

By *solution principles* we understand ideas like the coloring metaphor, which has been often used by Dijkstra. Usually this comes in the following setting: *The work space has three colors: The black things are fully processed, the gray things are currently being considered, and the white things have not been touched yet. Every thing passes from white through gray to black.* (Sometimes only black and white are needed.) This can be applied to searching and sorting as well as to graph algorithms.

This way of proceeding is an example of a "formal think pattern" that can be nicely presented in colloquial terms but in actual fact constitutes a formal way of reasoning (just like a mathematical proof). We consider this as a natural first step on a path through methods, which employ more and more rigorous formalisms. The book by Gries [4] contains many beautiful examples of this way of proceeding. Even though the book presents these examples mostly in the strict formalism of Hoare Logic, they can be taught equally fruitfully in semiformal ways.

The *test strategies* entail two aspects. One is the choice of relevant scenarios. (It is well known by now that this is almost identical to the design of verification strategies.) This is standard.

The other aspect is more interesting in our context. It actually goes back to the good old days of electronic tube computers. Since the machines were very unreliable at those times, programmers checked the calculations. For example, when you program a routine for the square root, it is a good test to square the result and compare it to the input value.

More generally, whenever one has $y = f(x)$ for a programmed function f and one knows properties $p_i(x, f(x))$ that must hold, then one should integrate them as plausibility controls into the code (provided that they are easily programmable). The above property $g(f(x)) = x$ is only a special case of this paradigm. (As a by-product the students get in touch with the paradigm of programming by inversion.)

To make this principle of *teaching formal methods informally* more concrete we present its application to a few examples (as they are taught in our first-year course [6]).

3.1   Example: Playing with Fibonnacci's Function

Fibonnacci's function is used in almost every course on programming (to an extent that students may feel annoyed as soon as it is mentioned). But it may be worthwhile to play around with it such that a few less known aspects are presented.

First of all, most people do not know that the original formulation does not use one but two functions, which represent the populations of mature and young rabbits in the population. The development of the population over (discrete) time is described by the following equations.

$$
\begin{aligned}
mat(0) &= 0 \\
yng(0) &= 1 \\
mat(t+1) &= mat(t) + yng(t) \\
yng(t+1) &= mat(t)
\end{aligned}
\tag{1}
$$

(The interested reader may reformulate them in colloquial terms in order to see the rules of rabbit reproduction according to Fibonnacci.) A first exercise for the students may be to derive the standard one-function version based on the definition $fib(t) = mat(t) + yng(t)$:

$$
\begin{aligned}
fib(0) &= 1 \\
fib(1) &= 1 \\
fib(t) &= fib(t-1) + fib(t-2) \qquad \text{for } t \geq 2
\end{aligned}
\tag{2}
$$

It may be interesting to contrast two ways of proceeing: The first one is an actual *derivation* of the recursive equations (2) from the definition by using the the equations (1). The second one is an *induction proof* showing the validity of (2) based on (1) and the definition.

In a next step, one may give yet another variant, viz. the tail-recursive function

$$
\begin{aligned}
fb(0, a, b) &= a \\
fb(t, a, b) &= fb(t-1, a+b, a) \qquad \text{for } t \geq 1
\end{aligned}
\tag{3}
$$

Then one can ask the students to show by induction that the following lemma holds:

$$
fb(t, a, b) = a \cdot fib(t) + b \cdot fib(t-1)
\tag{4}
$$

From this the alternative definition of fib is immediately obvious:

$$
fib(t) = fb(t, 1, 0)
\tag{5}
$$

At this stage one can present the "obvious" Java implementation of *fib* based on *fb*. (One may or may not tell the students that this is an instance of a formal transformation known as tail recursion elimination.)

```
public int fib ( int t ) {
    //ASSERT t >= 0
    int a = 1;                      // initialize a, b according to
    int b = 0;                      //           fib(t) = fb(t, 1 ,0)
    for (int i = t; i > 0; i--) {   // realizes recursion of fb
        int aOld = a;
        a = a + b;
        b = aOld;
    }//for
    return a;                       // realizes termination case of fb
}//fib
```

This way, the students have covered the whole range from an initial informal modelling (Fibonnacci's original rules of the game) via a sequence of mathematical equations that bridge the gap between the original model and a computer-oriented model to the final Java or C code.

As a nice by-product one can demonstrate the difference between an exponential and a linear algorithm – independent of the programming language. These demonstrations work particularly nicely, if the students can transliterate the equations directly into a functional language.

3.2   Example: Gauss Elimination

An area, where formal programming methods are surprisingly ill established, is Numerical Analysis. In particular when the subject is taught by mathematicians, there is a formal discussion of all kinds of numerical properties, followed by a piece of code that abounds in index calculations, which are claimed to implement the mathematical algorithm.

We will demonstrate that this need not be so. On the contrary, the area of numerical programs allows elegant formal derivations that can be easily presented to first-year students.

The well-known *Gaussian elimination* is a point in case. We consider its main part, viz. the LU-factorization. It can be illustrated as in Figure 1.

Since the students know the basics of matrix calculation, in particular matrix multiplication, the scenario of Figure 2 can be used.

From this scenario the following set of equations can be deduced by simple matrix multiplication. (One has to view the elements 1, u und a als one-element matrices.)

$$
\begin{array}{lcl}
1 \cdot u + \vec{0} \cdot 0\!\downarrow = a & \Rightarrow & u = a \\
1 \cdot \vec{u} + \vec{0} \cdot U' = \vec{a} & \Rightarrow & \vec{u} = \vec{a} \\
l\!\downarrow \cdot u + L' \cdot 0\!\downarrow = a\!\downarrow & \Rightarrow & l\!\downarrow = a\!\downarrow \cdot \frac{1}{u} \\
l\!\downarrow \cdot \vec{u} + L' \cdot U' = A' & \Rightarrow & L' \cdot U' = A' - l\!\downarrow \cdot \vec{u} \stackrel{def}{=} A''
\end{array}
$$

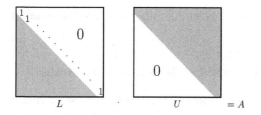

Fig. 1. LU-Partitioning

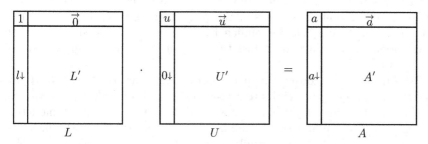

Fig. 2. LU-Partitioning (recursive step)

These equations immediately yield a recursive algorithm for the *LU* factorization.

```
private void factor ( int k ) {
   //ASSERT 0 <= k < N
   L[k][k] = 1;                             // diagonal element of L
   U[k][k] = A[k][k];                       // diagonal element of U
   System.arraycopy(A[k],k+1,U[k],k+1, N-k-1);   // copy row u
   double v = 1/U[k][k];                    // factor for column l
   for (int i = k+1; i < N; i++) {          // compute column l
      L[i][k] = A[i][k]*v;
   }//for
   for (int i = k+1; i < N; i++) {          // compute A''
      for (int j = k+1; j < N; j++) {
         A[i][j] = A[i][j] - L[i][k]*U[k][j];
      }//for
   }//for
   if (k < N-1) { factor(k+1); }            // recursively for A''
}//factor
```

As can be seen, this program is nothing but the one-to-one translation of the above mathematical equations into Java notation. As a simple additional exercise one may have the students convert the tail recursion into an encompassing loop.

This example makes a strong point for the value of formal derivations. Even beginners realize that it would be extremely hard to come up with the proper indexing in the program *factor* without the mathematical equations. These equations, in turn, are relatively simple, since they are the result of a straightforward matrix multiplication.

3.3 Example: Use of Models as a Formal Method

One of the most important formal methods is the *use of models*. They are usually taught (in Software Engineering) in the following setting: There is a real-world scenario into which the given programming task is embedded. This real-world scenario has to be captured by a model (ideally a formal one). Then the model has to be implemented in terms of the constructs provided by the given programming language. (And the implicit hypothesis in Java-based courses is that object-oriented languages have just the constructs needed by most real-world scenarios.)

We would like to convey this paradigm to first-year students. But applying Software Engineering principles to real-world scenarios is way beyond the manageable problem size at this stage. Nevertheless the value of using models can be conveyed by nice and small examples. As a matter of fact, the message is even stronger: It may be worthwhile to introduce a model, even if the problem is already formulated in programming-language terms.

A beautiful point in case is **heapsort**. If we were to describe heapsort on the basis of arrays, we would have to draw pictures like the following:

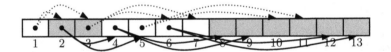

This is obviously useless. And the situation does not improve, if we augment the programming by Hoare-style assertions about the array indices.

There is only one decent approach: *a change of model*. Let us briefly consider the technique from a theoretical point of view (which is *not* the explanation given to first-year students). As can be seen in Figure 3, we state the problem within the realm of trees. Then we have two independent aspects:

1. We can solve the problem within the realm of trees. Formally, this establishes a morphism from the specification *tree view* to the specification *tree program*.

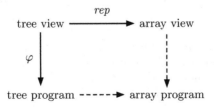

Fig. 3. Change of model

2. We give a representation of trees – actually only of the subclass of heaps – by arrays. Formally, this is again a morphism from *tree view* to *array view*.

By combining these two aspects, we obtain our desired array-based solution *array program*. In formal terms, this amounts to the building of the pushout of the diagram.

It is evident that this category-theoretical phrasing cannot be used in a course for first-year students. But this is not necessary. It suffices to present the method as such. This is easily understood, even little complications don't spoil the effect. On the contrary, they make the concept even more convincing.

(1) Let us begin with the representation morphism *rep*. The drawing of a simple tree like the one on the right convinces every student that trees of this kind are in a one-to-one correspondence to arrays. This motivates the heap conditions, in particular the famous formulas $left(i) = 2 * i$, $right(i) = 2 * i + 1$ and $parent(i) = i/2$.

But there is a complication. The underlying programming language is Java. And in Java array indices start from 0! It is immediately seen that the formulas are no longer so nice, if we start numbering the tree nodes from 0. This motivates the introduction of an additional function $index(i) = i - 1$ (the use of which will be seen in a moment).

(2) Now it remains to solve the problem within the realm of trees. This paper is not the place to repeat the derivation of the well-known heapsort algorithm in full detail, therefore we only sketch one fragment here in order to demonstrate the embedding of formal ideas into a mostly informal setting.

We use the first phase of the algorithm, that is, the conversion of a totally unordered tree into a heap. We assume that students are by now familiar with the principle of using induction/recursion for solving problems. The following statements are easily seen:

- *Base case*: Every leaf is – by definition – a heap.
- *Recursion step*: For any tree, where both the left and right subtree are already heaps, the operation *sink* illustrated below effects the conversion into a heap.

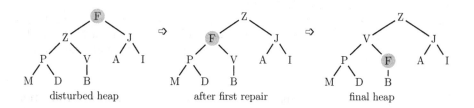

These two cases together with the illustration make the following case distinctions evident. The first case is the base case for leaves, in the other two cases the current node has to be compared with the maximal child. Let a be the array/heap and i be the current node.

$$let \ m = maxChild(a, i):$$
$$i > N/2: \qquad\qquad\qquad\qquad sink(a, i) = a$$
$$i < N/2 \land node(a, i) \geq node(a, m): sink(a, i) = a$$
$$i < N/2 \land node(a, i) < node(a, m): sink(a, i) = sink(swap(a, i, m), m)$$

These equations are formulated within the realm of trees. Therefore it remains to reformulate them in terms of arrays, using the auxiliary functions derived in part (1) of the process. In category speak this amounts to the building of the pushout.

```
private void sink ( char[] a, int i ) {
    //ASSERT left subtree and right subtree of i are already heaps
    //ASSERT there is at most one disturbance in tree i
    //ASSERT the disturbance (if any) is at node i
    int k = i;
    while (k <= (a.length)/2) {
        //ASSERT left subtree and right subtree of k(!) are already heaps
        //ASSERT there is at most one disturbance in tree i(!)
        //ASSERT the disturbance (if any) is at node k
        int m = maxChild(a,k);
        if (a[index(k)] >= a[index(m)]) { break; }
        swap(a, index(k), index(m));
        k = m;
    }//while
}//sink
```

As can be seen, the invariants are stated as semi-formal comments. (The third one follows directly from the first two ones.) Moreover, they are only mentioned at selected decisive points. This illustrates the way, in which even first-year students can be accustomed to the principles of Hoare-style reasoning without overtaxing them by a huge amount of formal noise.

It should also be noted, how the auxiliary functions are used without exceptions in order to hide away the low-level indexing aspects of Java. This can be seen even more clearly in the function maxChild.

```
private int maxChild ( char[] a, int i ) {
    if (right(i) > N)                                       { return left(i); }
    else if (a[index(left(i))] >= a[index(right(i))]) { return left(i); }
    else                                                    { return right(i); }
}
```

About termination. The example also provides a nice exercise for termination proofs (again being done by semi-fromal reasoning). In most first-year curricula the loops normally are of the kind that in C/Java is based on i++ or i--. In such examples it is hard to make a strong case for the assessment of termination.

In the heapsort example one can show that in each pass through the while-loop the index k gets strictly closer to the end of the array (such that it will eventually be beyond $a.length/2$). But this argument requires a closer look at the function $maxChild$. Here one has to argue – based on the auxiliary functions $left$ and $right$– that the result is larger than i.

About complexity. Finally, the example is ideally suited for a cost analysis. The students may have seen other tree-based examples before, at least tree-style recursions like in mergesort and quicksort. So their assumption will be an $\mathcal{O}(N \log N)$ behaviour.

However, the above induction argument leads to the following main method for phase 1 (remember that the leaves need not be considered):

```
private void arrayToHeap ( char[] a ) {
    for ( int i = a.length/2; i >= 1; i-- ) {
        //ASSERT left subtree and right subtree of i are already heaps
        sink(a, i);
    }//for
}//arrayToHeap
```

This program entails the following cost analysis that is based on the *height* of nodes (which is defined such that leaves have height 0).

For a node of height h there are at most h swaps. And there are at most $2^{\log N - h}$ nodes of height h (since $\log N$ is the height of the root). This leads to the following calculation, where the last step can be found in a booklet of mathematical formulae.

$$\mathcal{O}(\sum_{h=1}^{\log N} h \cdot 2^{\log N - h}) = \mathcal{O}(2^{\log N} \cdot \sum_{h=1}^{\log N} \frac{h}{2^h}) \leq \mathcal{O}(N \cdot \sum_{h=1}^{\infty} \frac{h}{2^h}) = \mathcal{O}(N \cdot 2)$$

This kind of reasoning is doable for first-year students, in particular, since they have accompanying courses on higher mathematics.

4   Summary

In this paper I have made the point – based on experiences gained at the TU Berlin – that the education in formal methods has to be distributed over the whole curriculum. Moreover, it has to be introduced in light-weight form already in the very first years. This means that one has to convey the spirit, but not the full notation.

Yet, there is one major problem, which has not been addressed so far. This approach necessitates a general agreement in the faculty. When the principles of formal methods shall be employed in many courses, then there must be many teachers, who cooperate in this endeavor. This, however, is rarely the case in today's universities.

Nevertheless, if there is at least a selected group of educators who follow this line (more or less strictly), then formal methods have a good start. And with the increased number of chairs on Embedded Systems (which is one of the major trends these days) the number of colleagues who are sympathetic to formal methods is likely to increase.

Acknowledgement. I am grateful to Bernd Mahr not only for making concrete suggestions for improving the paper, but even more for the many valuable discussions about the topic of teaching Computer Science in general and Formal Methods and Theroy in particular.

References

1. Jonathan P. Bowen and Michael G. Hinchey. Ten commandments of formal methods. *IEEE Computer*, 28(4):56–63, 1995.
2. Michael G. Hinchey Jonathan P. Bowen. Seven more myths of formal methods: Dispelling industrial prejudices. In M. Bertran, M. Naftalin, and T. Denvir, editors, *FME'94: Industrial Benefit of Formal Methods*, volume 873 of *Lecture Notes in Computer Science*, pages 105–117. Springer-Verlag, 1994.
3. E. M. Clarke and J. Wing. Formal methods: State of the art and future directions. *ACM Comp Surveys*, 28(4):626–643, 1996.
4. D. Gries. *The Science of Programming*. Springer-Verlag, 1981.
5. P. Pepper. *Funktionale Programmierung in Opal, Ml, Haskell und Gofer*. Springer-Verlag, 1999.
6. P. Pepper. *Programmieren mit Java*. Springer-Verlag, 2004.
7. S.D.Johnson, W.P.Alexander, S.-K. Chin, and G. Gopalakrishnan. 21st century engineering consortium workshop (XXIEC): a forum on formal methods education. Technical report, http://www.cs.indiana.edu/formal-methods-education/xxiec/report.html, March 1998.

An Undergraduate Course on Protocol Engineering – How to Teach Formal Methods Without Scaring Students

Manuel J. Fernández-Iglesias and Martín Llamas-Nistal

Grupo de Ingeniería de Sistemas Telemáticos
Departamento de Ingeniería Telemática
Universidade de Vigo, Spain
manolo@det.uvigo.es,
http://www-gist.det.uvigo.es/

Abstract. At a first sight, teaching formal methods to future telecom engineers seems to be a simple task. Last-year engineering undergraduates have already taken demanding courses on Mathematics, Computer Science and Computer Networking, among other engineering-related subjects. Consequently, they should be prepared both for the theoretical foundations of formal methods and to apply them to practical problems. The benefits of formal methods would be evident, and students would rush to register in this course. However, when we designed a course shaped as the rest of the courses in our engineering school, it was a complete failure. This paper discusses this experience, and how it was re-engineered into a successful one to conclude that protocol engineering serves to teach formal methods without scaring students.

Keywords: Protocol engineering, undergraduate courses, Promela, Spin, case-based learning.

1 Introduction

This paper discusses our experience teaching formal methods to last-year undergraduate students at the Technical School of Telecommunication Engineers, University of Vigo, Spain. Telecommunication Engineering at Vigo is a five-year program. The first three years are common to all students, and are devoted to fundamentals on Mathematics, Physics, Electronics, Signal Processing, Computer Science and Communications. The last two years are oriented towards specialisation: students can choose among Electronics, Signal Processing/Communications, and Computer Networking.

Our course — Communication Protocol Engineering — corresponds to the fifth year of the Computer Networking specialisation. It has a workload of 4.5 credits/45 lecture hours and is devoted to the design and validation of computer protocols. The course is organised into 15 2-hour theoretical lectures and 15 hours of laboratory work. Example course topics from previous years were:

C.N. Dean and R.T. Boute (Eds.): TFM 2004, LNCS 3294, pp. 153–165, 2004.
© Springer-Verlag Berlin Heidelberg 2004

- Academic year 1999/00 and 2000/01. Wireless ad-hoc networks. Mobile auction protocols.
- Academic year 2002/03. Wireless ad-hoc networks. Location-aware services.

The course is optional. Instead of taking this course, students may take courses on local, metropolitan and satellite networks, or on advanced microprocessor architectures. The recurring question when taking a decision on which course to select can be summarised as follows:

> I am already a skilled programmer. I have also constructed and tested some protocol code using *traditional* software techniques and tools. Incidentally, these techniques work pretty well for me. Why should I spend additional time learning how to design and validate this kind of software?

This paper is the story on how we tried to answer this question along the years, to convince students that protocol engineering supported by formal techniques is something worth to learn, or at least something worth to be familiar with. First, we offer some details on the profile of the students taking this course. This will help to understand the expectations and motivations of our students. Then, we describe how the first edition of the course was organised, and the results obtained. The lessons learnt from this initial approach motivated the authors to introduce dramatic changes in course organisation and contents, changes that had as a result the new course model described in Sect. 4. Finally, we summarise the results of this process and propose some conclusions.

2   Student Profile

As discussed above, Communication Protocol Engineering is an optional course corresponding to the fifth and last year of the Computer Networking specialisation at the Telecommunication Engineering School, Universidade de Vigo. The course is organised into 15 2-hour theoretical lectures — 66% of the workload — and 15 hours of laboratory work — 33% of the workload.

On average, students are 23 years old, and they have already taken courses on programming, software engineering, operating systems, computer networking, database management systems, computer architectures, real time systems and distributed computing. They are familiar with the most relevant programming paradigms: structured programming, object-oriented programming and Internet programming, and most of them have some basic knowledge of functional programming.

Although they have built along the four previous years a robust theoretical foundation in all aspects related to networking — information theory, coding, communication protocols, etc. — their previous knowledge is only introductory in some relevant cases. For example, they know the syntax and behaviour of the constructors of common programming languages, and the most used life-cycle models in software system design, but they have not studied the semantics of programming languages in general, either operational, denotational or axiomatic.

As another example, they know how to design an object-oriented application, but they are not aware of the theoretical foundations of object-oriented programming.

To sum up, our average students can be characterised as follows:

- They are interested in the subject of formal methods. They have chosen to take this course among other options.
- They have a solid foundation on networking, distributed computing and protocol analysis. They understand and can identify the basic — desired — properties of protocols and distributed systems.
- They are used to the classical waterfall and stepwise refinement software life-cycle models [12], where all the planning and design is done at the beginning of the project, and all testing and verification is done at the end of the project. They have also been introduced to better models like the iterative development or the spiral model, but they have been introduced as just several instances of the waterfall model.
- They have taken courses on algebra and discrete mathematics.
- They have not taken previous courses on formal methods or Formal Description Techniques.

This course was first offered during academic year 1998/99. For the first edition, the syllabus of the course was designed according to the discussion in Sect. 3. After this initial experience, the course was redesigned as presented in Sect. 4.

3 Initial Approach

Taking into account the student profile discussed above, we had to develop a course on formal methods focused on protocol engineering. The basic objective of the course would be to introduce the basic formal methods concepts and tools needed to design and validate computer protocols. This have to be done in 30 hours of classroom lectures and 15 hours of laboratory practice.

Our initial approach was to devote the time available to:

- Introduce the subject. What are formal methods?
- Provide a basic introduction on the foundations of formal methods.
- Introduce some of the most relevant formal description techniques around.
- Show examples of how formal methods work.

With this approach, we thought that students would gain some insight in an approach to design previously unknown to them. They would be aware of the existence of formal methods and their benefits and, after taking the course, they would study further the subject on their owns because they would feel the benefits are worth the effort.

The syllabus of the course included:

1. An introduction to formal methods. The objectives of formal methods in protocol design: a common framework for requirements capture, system specification, design and deployment; early detection of errors; support for verification and validation; etc.
2. Semantic foundations: introduction to process algebras, labelled transition systems, state machines, automata, etc.
3. Examples of formal methods: SDL [9], Estelle [8], LOTOS [7] and Promela [4]. Basic constructors. Specification of simple protocols.

Practical lectures at the laboratory consisted on the specification of well-known protocols used traditionally in educational settings or to illustrate contributions to the field: alternate bit protocol, sliding window protocol, leader election protocol, dining philosophers, etc.

After the first academic year, we asked the students about their experiences. Most comments from students can be summarised as follows:

- I will have to learn a lot of advanced mathematics to be able to use formal methods at their full capabilities. Formal languages are really powerful. You can specify practically any situation that may appear when designing a protocol. However, to understand many operators I will have to understand the underlying semantics, which is not straightforward.
- The field of formal methods is a mess. There are lots of approaches, languages and techniques to solve the same problems, and few seem to fit seamlessly to real world situations. Besides, in many cases tools available are arcane and difficult to use, they seem to be designed for experts in the field.
- Protocol engineering is not fun. The learning slope seems to be insurmountable. I am lost among so many techniques and tools.

From these reactions, we inferred that teaching formal methods on their own, as a field of study, was not the correct approach for last-year telecom engineering students. We had to find a way of transmitting the principles and benefits of formal methods in a way that these benefits become apparent after applying them to a field of study our students are familiar with. We will teach how to design and verify communication protocols, and we will rely on formal methods as the supporting tool to do so.

4   Case-Based, Tool-Oriented Approach

Thus, the rationale for the new version of the course was as follows: in the same way as you do not need to be an expert on the theoretical foundations of programming languages to be a skilled programmer — although it would be an asset if designing a new compiler or new programming language — you do not need to learn the details of process algebras or Buchi automata to be a skilled protocol engineer. In both scenarios, you use a *tool* to solve a problem —

construct a software system or validate a protocol design. Obviously, you still need some — basic — background to understand why things work that way.

Now, each year the course is organised around a specific topic. The topic is selected from previous or ongoing experiences from our research group. Course activities are as follows:

- Classroom lectures to introduce basic formal methods concepts from a practical, hands-on point of view. Classroom lectures are basically the same every year. The most relevant concepts introduced are [4]:
  - Introduction to Protocol Engineering. Brief history. Protocol models. Protocols as languages: vocabulary, syntax, grammar, semantics. Aspects to consider when designing a communication protocol.
  - Methods to specify, model and validate protocols. Formal description techniques. Brief summary of most common formal languages and tools.
  - Protocol elements: service, environment, vocabulary, encoding, protocol rules.
  - Desired protocol properties: modularity, simplicity, robustness, completeness, soundness, fairness, liveness.
  - Representation of protocols machines: state space, protocol behaviour, state sequences, reachable states, execution trace.
  - Validating protocols with Promela and Spin. Specification language. Linear time logic. Labelling states. Temporal claims. Using Spin as an oracle.
- The discussion of a real protocol engineering project, preferably from our research group. This project defines the topic for the corresponding year. Students have information about the contractor, what are its requirements, which product is pursued, which problem is intended to solve, etc.
- The successful completion of a work assignment. It is given over to students at the beginning of the course, and is based on a simplified, educational-biased version of the project selected for this year. As a general rule, students have to develop a prototype of the protocol or protocols selected, and verify a set of properties the prototype must satisfy. Properties are selected to cover all major aspects of verification (security, liveness, fairness, race conditions, etc.).

As can be inferred from the course organisation discussed above, Promela [4] and the accompanying tool Spin [6] were selected to support the validation process. Spin targets efficient software verification, and uses the high level language Promela (PROcess MEta LAnguage) to specify system descriptions. Spin has been used to trace logical design errors in distributed systems, such as data communication protocols. Basically, this tool checks the logical consistency of a specification, and reports on deadlocks, unspecified receptions, flags incompleteness, race conditions, and unwarranted assumptions about the relative speeds of processes.

Students follow the typical mode of working with Spin (c.f. Fig. 1). First, they develop a Promela specification of a model of the system described in the work assignment (step 1 in Fig. 1). Then, they perform interactive simulation

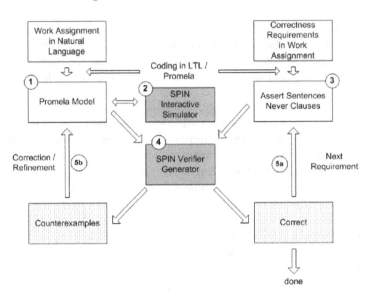

Fig. 1. Working with Promela/Spin

using the provided Spin simulator until basic confidence is gained that the design behave as intended (step 2). After this, students use Spin to generate an optimised on-the-fly verification program from the high level initial specification, which includes the corresponding correctness requirements. This verifier is compiled and executed for the correctness requirements rephrased as Promela assert sentences and never clauses (steps 3, 4, 5a). If counterexamples to the correctness claims are detected, they would feed them back into the interactive simulator and inspected in detail to establish and remove their cause, that is, to propose an alternate version of the protocol having the desired properties, as described in the work assignment (steps 3, 4, 5b).

Students work in pairs, and they are free to organise their work as best suits them. They have to identify tasks, define a calendar of activities and propose a validation programme.

Spin was selected because it is comparatively easy to learn, and Spin or variations thereof are among the most widely used tools in the field of protocol design and verification.

Next, we briefly describe two course topics to give some insight on the actual case studies selected.

4.1   Year 1999/00 and 2000/01. Mobile Auction Protocols

Students had to model the protocols for the base station and mobile terminals in a mobile auction setting designed by our research group [1] [11]. The original research work was assisted by the formal description technique LOTOS [7], mainly in the testing phase.

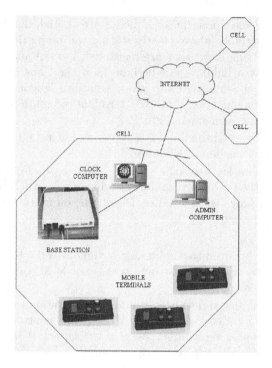

Fig. 2. Wireless Auction System

Each user owns a mobile terminal with a unique serial number. When the user enters a new auction room, the terminal initiates an automatic dialog with the base station placed there, and obtains a local working code. Once users are registered they can participate in all forthcoming auctions, provided they have enough credit.

Entities participating in the auction are (c.f. Fig. 2):

- *Cell.* A cell is an auction room. All active terminals entering a cell are assigned to it.
- *Base station.* The core of the bid system. It is responsible of assigning transmission slots to user terminals, resolving conflicts, recognising present terminals, transmitting messages to them, and deciding who wins an auction.
- *Terminal.* A terminal is a mobile hand held computer that sends bids to the base station and receives messages from it.
- *Clock computer.* During auctions, it displays a price count-down. A terminal bid stops the clock computer when a user is interested in the current price. Also, the clock computer sets terminal recognition mode or auction mode in the base station, transmits a list of valid users and their balance to the base station, receives the list of present users, and generates messages to be transmitted to terminals.

Students were given a description of the service desired, that is, an elaborated version of the paragraphs above clearly stating the properties of the intended wireless auction setting: how users are registered, how an auction evolves, how bids are made, how a bidding user becomes a winner, how users are credited and debited, etc. Students were also given a natural language specification of the supporting communication protocols: terminal recognition, bidding, winner identification, product assignment, etc.

Students were required to model this system in Promela, to simulate it using Spin, and to verify it as described above.

To guarantee — at least to some extent — that results from different groups were comparable, the protocol vocabulary and syntax — i.e. frame formats and types — were also provided in advance. Depending on frame type, two different data loads had to be considered:

1. A user frame — transmitted from user terminals to the base station — had a two-byte data load. The first byte is the user local code. The second one is a checksum, for robustness.
2. A base station frame transmitted from the base station to user terminals — had a 17-byte data load. Additional *MODE* bits controlled auction working mode: *Terminal recognition, Auction activation, Winner identification, Winner acknowledgement,* or *Purchase mode.*

The auction protocols included the possibility of sending ASCII messages to the terminals, to be shown on their displays. Typical messages are current account balance and the total amount of items purchased. Any base station frame could be used to send a 12-byte message to any terminal, by setting the adequate control bits.

Bidirectional handshake ensured that all bids arrived to their destination, which guaranteed a finite bid time for a given number of present users, which incidentally is a basic characteristic of real-time systems.

As introduced above, students were required to model this system in Promela, to simulate it using Spin, and to verify a set of 12 properties including invariants, safety and liveness properties, temporal claims, and key features of the system. They were also asked to identify the class each property belongs to. Some of the properties students were asked to verify were:

- Terminals do not generate traffic before the base station initiates *Terminal recognition.*
- After *Terminal recognition* is initiated, each terminal registers only once.
- When the working mode is *Auction activation,* only registered terminals may issue bids.
- All terminals receive all broadcast messages submitted by the base station.
- If a terminal issues a bid, the base station changes from *Auction activation* to either *Winner identification* or *Purchase mode.*

4.2   Year 2002/03. Location-Aware Services

Students have to model the configuration protocol of a Bluetooth Location Network (BLN) that was also designed by our research group [2]. As in the previous case, formal methods were applied to support the design process. BLN is targeted to location-aware or context-driven mobile services, such as m-commerce, e-museums, or electronic guidance where exhibition visitors receive specific information associated to their current location. In any of these scenarios, there exist service servers that need to know user location in real time to send context-specific information to users' handhelds.

Users carry a Bluetooth terminal, or any mobile data terminal and an independent Bluetooth location badge. Users must access the Web/WAP servers from their handhelds and enter their badge address. Then, the Bluetooth address of the badge becomes valid from the BLN point of view. The server binds users' IP addresses or WAP session identifiers to badge numbers for all subsequent transactions. The badge interacts with the BLN, which in turn provides service servers with user location estimated in real time. The service servers may use this information to push Web/WAP contents into user terminals. Thus, no action from the users is required to generate context-driven updates.

Two protocols implement BLN functionality. The first — configuration — protocol is used to construct the *ad-hoc* location network, discovering active network nodes in the designated area and creating the corresponding routing tables. The second — location — protocol supports the identification and location of users within the are covered by the network constructed using the configuration protocol:

- The *BLN configuration protocol*, which is used to create the spontaneous location network discovering the network topology (i.e. active stations and their communication links) in a process initiated by the master node. This process propagates through the network until stable routing tables for all nodes are created. This protocol also provides network survivability and fault tolerance. The BLN configuration protocol handles network recovery when a node fails. In this case, routing tables should be automatically updated to reflect the new network status.
- The *BLN location protocol*, which handles badge detection and generation of location information to be transmitted to the master node. The paths needed to transmit location information are created during network configuration. Basically, a node detects active badges in its area of influence (Bluetooth cell) and transmits both cell identification and badge numbers to the master node. Note that, once the BLN has been configured, transmission of location information is straightforward: location packets generated in nodes detecting an active badge are sent through an adjacent node as defined by the corresponding routing table, and packets received by a node are forwarded to the master node, either directly when the closest neighbour is the master node, or through a subsequent node, also as defined by routing tables.

As stated above, we selected the first — configuration — BLN protocol as the case study for academic year 2002/03. Incidentally, along the research work towards this Bluetooth Location Network, we detected some errors affecting network survivability in the initial solution proposed by the research team.

The proposed BLN configuration protocol fails during automatic reconfiguration if several adjacent nodes failed according to a specific failure pattern. Altough in most cases the new routing tables were correctly created for the surviving nodes, in some specific cases some surviving nodes in the vicinity of the failing nodes will construct new routing tables that will include loops, preventing location messages to reach the master node.

Incidentally, this error was not detected by the research team in a first — published — survability analysis based solely on simulation [3]. There, it was assumed that node failures were independent, and were generated according to a uniform distribution. In that case, it was possible to disconnect a large number of nodes without finding inconsistencies.

We provided the students with the initial – erroneous – specification of the BLN configuration protocol, without informing them that the specification was indeed erroneous. We expected the students to find errors by themselves and propose a protocol update — although all groups detected the erroneous behaviour, some groups failed in proposing a correct protocol update. Note that this was *not* a straightforward task.

As in the previous case discussed in Sect. 4.1, we asked the students to verify a set of properties covering the most relevant aspects in protocol verification. Examples of these properties were:

- Eventually, are minimum distance routes generated for all nodes?
- Eventually, an entry is created for all nodes in the network?
- Are loops possible? That is, a route can be generated from node n where the corresponding path includes n?
- In case of one node failure, are new (correct) routes eventually created for all nodes?
- What happens if two adjacent nodes in the same layer fail? And if there are three failing adjacent nodes? Use a 3-layer network where failing nodes are placed in the second layer.

5   Benefits of This Approach

The most satisfying conclusion that can be extracted from this course is that students feel that formal methods work. There are tools that you can use and apply to real problems. You can write a validation model, check it for errors, run it, and obtain useful information about the properties of the code you wrote. For the purist, this might not be a *real* course on formal methods, but we think that the initial objectives were fulfilled. Our students see formal methods as a tool that contributes to improve the quality of software, and more specifically communication protocols.

Another conclusion extracted from this experience is the usefulness of rapid prototyping. In most cases, communication protocols are pretty simple. This is most evident when you have to develop your own custom protocol for specific situations where available, standardised protocols are over-featured (e.g. embedded solutions, microcontroller-based systems, ad-hoc networks, etc.). In theses cases, it is very convenient to construct a working model of the protocol from initial sketches, to play with it and gain confidence in your design. This initial prototype is also useful to complete the requirements capture phase. Contractors and designers can study the prototype together to analyse the basic behaviour of the pursued product, to detect as earlier as possible any misunderstandings or misinterpretations of the system specification.

Incidentally, the benefits of rapid prototyping were among the first positive aspects discovered by our students. They had previous experiences from other practical courses where the initial assignments had to be modified by the lecturers to correct errors that prevented the correct completion of the work. In many cases, these errors were detected by the students themselves when testing their software, perhaps several weeks or even months after the course started. As a consequence, deadlines would be delayed, which interfered with other courses and caused many inconveniences to the students. In our case, errors in the assignment — i.e. errors in the initial specification — were detected earlier, and their impact on the course was dramatically reduced.

With respect to the subject of the course — protocol engineering — the use of formal methods permitted a better understanding and detection of protocol issues that are not evident from specifications, and difficult to find in normal operation: race conditions, livelocks, under-specification and over-specification, etc. This helped our students to better understand how protocols work, and which are the basic design principles that should always be taken into account when designing a communication protocol.

6   Conclusion and Future Plans

Once the course was publiziced according to the new approach, we managed to keep around 15% of the students interested in taking this course (c.f Fig 3), with a slightly positive tendency.

Protocol Engineering serves to teach Formal Methods without scaring undergraduates. Although this subject is not as popular as the other two approaches discussed above — advanced architectures and networking technologies — it can be considered a promising result when compared to the results of the first year, where only 7% of the students chose Communication Protocol Engineering.

In the case of professional studies — e.g. Escuelas Técnicas in Spain, Institutos Politecnicos in Portugal, Teknikums in Austria, Fachhochschule in Germany or Politechnics in Finland and other countries — we think that there is a niche for formal methods as a field of study. However, due to the nature of these studies and the profile of students, we think that formal methods should be approached

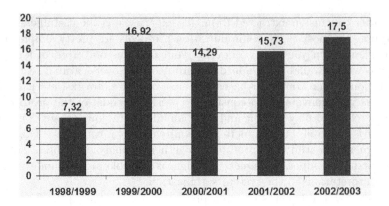

Fig. 3. Registration Statistics. Percentage of students taking this course w.r.t. the total number of students registered in all three optional curses

as a tool that can improve the professional skills in the corresponding professional fields, and this is more evident in the case of software-related technologies.

In our case, the next step will be to use formal methods as a tool to be applied to other problems besides communication protocols, interpreting formal methods in the sense of Vienneau [13]:

> [...] as methods that provide a formal language for describing any software artifact — e.g. specifications, designs, source code — such that formal proofs are possible, in principle, about properties of the artifact so expressed.

More specifically, we are planning to apply formal methods to new paradigms as Internet Programming or Web Services. Some positive results have already been obtained [10], and we feel that it should not be difficult to find case scenarios suitable for the approach discussed in this paper.

Acknowledgements. The authors wish to thank the students of course 305-010-795 *Ingeniería de Protocolos de Comunicaciones* at Universidade de Vigo for their feedback and suggestions when developing this course and preparing this paper. The authors also wish to thank the anonymous referees for their comments and suggestions, which definitely contributed to improve the final version of this paper.

References

1. Burguillo-Rial, J.C., Fernández-Iglesias, M. J., González-Castaño, F. J., Llamas-Nistal, M: Heuristic-Driven Test Case Selection from Formal Specifications. A Case Study. Procs. of FME 2002. Lecture Notes in Computer Science **2391**, 436-448, 2002.

2. Fernández-Iglesias, M. J., Burguillo-Rial, J.C., González-Castaño, F. J., Pousada-Carballo, J. M., Llamas-Nistal, M., and Romero-Feijoo, A.: Wireless Protocol testing and validation supported by formal methods. A hands-on report. The Journal of Systems and Software, 2004. To appear.
3. González-Castaño, F.J. and García-Reinoso, J.: Survibable Bluetooth Location Networks, Procs. of IEEE Int. Conf. on Communications, 2003.
4. Holzmann, G.: Design and Validation of Computer Protocols, Prentice Hall, 1991.
5. Holzmann, G.: The Model Checker Spin, IEEE Transactions on Software Engineering **23(5)**, 279-295, 1997.
6. Holzmann, G.: The SPIN Model Checker : Primer and Reference Manual. Pearson Education, Englewood Cliffs, New Jersey, 2003.
7. Information Processing Systems - Open Systems Interconnection. LOTOS: A Formal Description Technique Based on the Temporal Ordering of Observational Behaviour. IS 8807, ISO, 1989.
8. Information Processing Systems - Open Systems Interconnection. ESTELLE: A Formal Description Technique Based on an Extended State Transition Model. IS 9074, ISO, 1989.
9. ITU-T. SDL: Specification and Description Language. Z.100, CCITT, 1993.
10. Narayanan, S., and McIlraith, S.: Simulation, Verification and Automated Composition of Web Services. Proceedings of WWW 2002, 77-88. ACM Press, 2002.
11. Rodríguez-Hernández, P. S., González-Castaño, F. J., Pousada-Carballo, J. M., Fernández-Iglesias, M. J., García-Reinoso, J.: Cellular Network for Real-Time Mobile Auction. Wireless Personal Communications **22(1)**, 23-40, 2002.
12. Scacchi, W.: Process Models in Software Engineering, in J. Marciniak (ed.), Encyclopedia of Software Engineering, 2nd. Edition, Wiley, 2001.
13. Vienneau, R.: A review of Formal Methods, Kaman Sciences Corporation, 1993.

Linking Paradigms, Semi-formal and Formal Notations

Henri Habrias and Sébastien Faucou

I.U.T. of Nantes, University of Nantes,
3 rue Ml Joffre 44041 Nantes Cedex 01, France.
{habrias, faucou}@iut-nantes.univ-nantes.fr

Abstract. In this paper, we expose some of the techniques that we use in Nantes to link paradigms and formal notations in formal specification lectures for 1st year students. The notion of model is the core of our teaching.

Symbol: From the Greek sumballein, to compare: sun (together) + ballein (to throw), the Greeks used "throw together" (/sumballein/) very frequently to signify the making of a contract or convention."[1].

1 Introduction

Students meet with different programming languages with their own idiosyncrasies. Most of the time, they have difficulty in separating the fundamental from the idiosyncrasy. And some professors want to present another layer of languages! These professors say that they teach specifications. But the students are used to write programs without having written any specification. And specifications are not taught by the other professors whose subjects are "well" known: mathematics, programming languages, logic, databases. All these professors write some mathematics or something looking like mathematics [2]. But nobody would try to input such mathematical texts in a computer for syntax checking, type checking etc. Each professor has his own syntax which is not always exposed to the students. Hence "$\forall x \bullet P(x)$" (as written in Z), can also be written "$\forall x P(x)$", "$(\forall x)P(x)$", "$\forall x, P(x)$" or $\forall x P x$" without any further justification.

Many professors also use pictures, sometimes called "graphical notations". Some professors are even specialized in "semi-formal notations"[3]. No legend is generally provided and the same graphical sign can have a lot of meanings depending on the professors.

Thus, the danger in teaching formal methods is to extend the patchwork of notations (formal, graphical), vocabularies, courses, etc. The number of patchwork items was limited in France until now. We were not used to considering a university as a supermarket or as a self-service cafeteria. The organization was more that of a classical French restaurant with menus. But our institute (two years of studies after the end of high school diploma) was in advance, following

C.N. Dean and R.T. Boute (Eds.): TFM 2004, LNCS 3294, pp. 166–184, 2004.

the way of universities of "northern european countries". Hence, for 5 years, the "specification" course has been split into different "modules". In the first year, we have two "modules": spec1 and spec2. In spec1, we teach graphical logic and set notations (Euler *vs* Venn, Peirce, etc.) [4] [5], the semiotics triangle [6], "complexité" vs "complication" [1], the four meanings of the verb "to be" according to Frege [7], a short history of logic (logic of terms *vs*. logic of propositions, the consequences of the structure of the phrase of Aristotle[8] until the inventions of the relations, with illustrations), B, n-ary relational model. In spec2, we teach automata (without output, with outputs, structured), regular expressions, Petri nets and GRAFCET [2][9], communication between processes, CCS [10] [11], Event B [3][12] [13] [14], and lastly JSD[15] [16] [17] as an application of both modules. The books we recommend are [18] [19] [20] [9] [21] [22] [23] [10] [24] [16] [25] [26] [15] [27] [11] [28]. Some of them can be considered as "popular science books" in English words: [19] [21] [22] [23].

From [22] we emphasize on "abstraction *vs* generalization", "abstraction as idealization" and "abstraction as extraction". Our philosophy is to give not only paradigms, concepts and techniques but also their *precondition* of use because in the "real-world", the problems are not exercises of Z, CCS, etc. or *ad-hoc* example for a thesis. Following such a goal, we are subject to criticism: "you say too many things, you're going to mislead the students". To answer this criticism:

— we formalise each notation using basic set theory and first order logic, and we use the syntax of the B notation (we chose B after having used Z because: it covers the whole development process, it is supported by tools, it is taught, and it is applied in the industry). The B notation is taught during the first courses through simple examples. These examples are also used to illustrate basic concept like predicates *vs.* expressions, predicates *vs.* substitutions;

— we try to present the students with the limits and the implicit assumptions of notations, techniques and paradigms (see section 2). Indeed, if we don't warn the students, they will eventually face difficulties and will believe that it comes from their lack of "expertise". This problem partly explains the low use of formal methods by graduate students.

— we link notations, techniques and paradigms by using the same examples as much as possible (see section 3).

---

[1] Intricacy in English (?). "complexité" is intrisic with the domain problem. "complication" depends on notation (ex: roman numeration *vs.* decimal numeration), data abstraction, etc. We use the example of M. Jackson about the "American film star" who gets married, divorces, signs and cancel a contract and who is monogamous and has no more than one contract at the same time (automata *vs* regular expression).

[2] The "Sequential Function Chart", defined in the I.E.C. 848 Standard ("Preparation of function charts for control systems", International Electrotechnical Commission, Publication 848) inherits from the French item GRAFCET.

[3] Named also "B System"

2   Some Limits and Implicit Assumptions

2.1   Examples of Implicit Assumptions

Closed world, unicity of names, closure of the domain. When we were not teaching formal methods, we paid attention a lot to the implicit assumptions made when we were specifying a database schema: (1) closed world assumption (2) unicity of names (3) closure of the domain. These assumptions are often forgotten when an invariant of state is written.

Consider the following exercise: specification of a relational database schema to register a Petri net (fig 1(a)). Configurations of fig. 1(b) are not allowed. A solution is given in fig. 1(c).

Fig. 1. (a) A correct configuration (b) Two non-correct configurations (c) The relational schema (Codd notation)

If he considers the "closed world assumption", the reader knows that in the database there are no other transitions than the transitions respecting the invariant (the "relational schema" is an invariant). Idem for the places. Therefore the constraint expressing that places not connected to a transition and transitions not connected to a place are forbidden is taken into account. If the closed world assumption is not supposed, then we need the following schema (Codd notation):

PlacesAbove(transitionWithPA, place)
PlacesBelow(transitionWithPB, place)
Transitions(transition)
Marks(place, NAT)

and the constraint:

ProjOn_transitionWithPA(PlacesAbove) ∪
ProjOn_transitionWithPB(PlacesBelow) =
Transitions

Completeness of the operation repertoire of a B machine. If we look at the Little_Example of the B-Book [29] p. 508-509), we see that to refine the machine, we have to take into account the repertoire of the machine operations (fig. 2).

We can lose information relatively to the abstract machine. But as the lost information was not accessible (no operation to observe it), no problem! J.R.

MACHINE
   $Little\_Example\_1$
VARIABLES
   y
INVARIANT
   $y \subseteq NAT1$
/* the implementable integers
without zero */
INITIALISATION
   $y := \emptyset$
OPERATIONS
   enter (n) $\widehat{=}$
      PRE $n \in NAT1$ THEN $y := y \cup \{n\}$
   END;
   $m \leftarrow maximum \ \widehat{=}$
      PRE $y \neq \emptyset$ THEN $m := max(y)$
   END
END

REFINEMENT
   $Little\_Example\_2$
REFINES
   $Little\_Example\_1$
VARIABLES
   z
INVARIANT
   $z = max(y \cup \{0\})$
INITIALISATION
   $y := 0$
OPERATIONS
   $enter(n) \ \widehat{=}$
      PRE $n \in NAT1$
      THEN $z := max(z, n)$
   END;
   $m \leftarrow maximum \ \widehat{=}$
      PRE $z \neq 0$ THEN $m := z$
   END
END

Fig. 2. B machines of the little example

Abrial writes *"the state of the first machine is too rich with regard to the op-erations the machine offers. In other words, that richness (...) is only needed for a convenient, and easy to understand, specification of the machine. (...) The first is made for human readers to understand what the problem is. The sec-ond describes the model of a possible computation as prescribed by the first"*[29]. We consider that it is very important, when we present a specification, to an-nounce if the set of given operations is complete. Sometimes, the specifier does not include an operation in the repertoire of a machine to express the fact that this operation cannot be called (a way to express some constraints that are not easily expressed in the invariant). That must be explicitly written. The client has to be aware that he has to look at the repertoire because he can be sur-prised to discover that a piece of information he thought was present in the database is not in the database and is definitively lost. In fact, in B, a clause $CONCRETE\ VARIABLES$ exists. It allows to declare a variable that will be retained during the refinement process even if no operation produces the value of this variable as a value of its output parameter. This variable is not refined and can be used "inside" operations. We will indicate the variables that the client wants to retain, to read it when he wants. It allows the specifier to forget, first, to specify an observation operation (an operation with an output parameter) on the value of this variable.

2.2   When the Constraint Does Not Fit a Specification Paradigm

Consider the text: *"A person only teaches a subject if this person is qualified to teach this subject."* It is easily modeled as a subset constraint. Now, consider this other text: *"Students make their choice for one or more industrial training(s) - say training. Several students can choose the same training. We assign to a student one of the training he has chosen. The same training is not assigned to more than one student. A student cannot include an already assigned training in his choices."*. Of course, the rule must be specified in the invariant properties, in order to be used for proof obligations of operations (*Precondition* $\wedge$ *Invariant* $\implies$ *[Substitution]Invariant*). If the rule is expressed only in the precondition, the proof approach of B is bypassed! If we write *assignement* $\subseteq$ *choice* $\wedge$ *assignment* $\cap$ *choice* $= \emptyset$, we obtain a vacuous specification. A specification taking into account the requirements is given fig. 3. This exercise is a real life application and it is not easily specified in B. Some readers of the requirements will ignore a part of the text (even experimented B-practitioners[30])! It's perhaps a verification of the Sapir-Whorf hypothesis[31].

2.3   "Click and Prove"[4]   Without Awareness Is Nothing but the Ruin of Formal Specifications

Nowadays, the students are used to "working on the machine" and it is easy to put the Atelier B in their hands, as it is (more and more) the case in other courses. If we ask them to prove, they prove![5] We know that nowadays, some students in France are very far from the meaning of what they read or write ("the crisis of meaning"). In B, they are forced to prove for every operation that *Precondition* $\wedge$ *Invariant* $\implies$ *[substitution]Invariant*. We insist on the "*Ex Falso Quodlibet*". But in practice, many students modify their specification until the proof is discharged, forgetting the semantics of the problem domain. They have the behavior of an "automaths" in Stella Baruk's words [19]. We give them 4 proved operations to comment on:

– one with a precondition inconsistent with the invariant,
– one with a false precondition,
– one with such a precondition as the operation does not modify the state,
– one where the right part of the implication that the prover cannot prove has been put in the precondition.

And we must confess that, at the end of the laboratory sessions, we find many machines where these techniques have been put into practice.

---

[4] "Click'n'Prove" (or "La Balbulette" for the French name) is the new proactive interface of the interactive prover of Atelier B and its free version B4free. This interface has been developed by Jean-Raymond Abrial and Dominique Cansell see http://www.loria.fr/~cansell/cnp.html. See also http://www.cs.unh.edu/~charpov/PhD/dada.html.

[5] Every researcher knows the joke: "If you ask me to do research then I will do research. If you ask me to find then I will find."

```
MACHINE
   Trainings
SETS
   STUDENTS; TRAINING
VARIABLES
   tr, st, choice, assignment, dateC, dateA, clock
INVARIANT
   clock ∈ NAT ∧ st ⊂ STUDENTS ∧ tr ⊂ TRAINING∧
   choice ∈ st ↔ tr ∧ assignment ∈ st ⇸ tr∧
   /*to express bijection with Atelier B*/
   assignment ∈ st ⤀ tr ∧ ran(assignment) = tr ∧ assignment ⊆ choice∧
   dateC ∈ choice → NAT ∧ dateA ∈ assignment → NAT∧
   /* For every student (having done one/several choices and one
   assignment), there are no choices more recent than the assignment:*/
   ∀(ss) • (ss ∈ (dom(choice) ∩ dom(assignment)) ⇒
   max(ran(({ss} ◁ choice) ◁ dateC)) < dateA(ss ↦ assignment(ss)))∧
   /* And for every chosen and assigned training there are no choices
   more recent than the assignment:*/
   ∀(tt) • (tt ∈ (ran(choice) ∩ ran(assignment)) ⇒
   max(ran((choice ▷ {tt}) ◁ dateC)) < dateA(assignment⁻¹(tt) ↦ ss))
INITIALISATION
   clock, st, tr, choice, assignment, dateA, dateC := ∅, ∅, ∅, ∅, ∅, ∅, ∅
OPERATIONS
   choose(ss, tt) ≙
      PRE
         ss ∈ st ∧ tt ∈ tr ∧ ss ∉ dom(assignment)∧
         tt ∉ ran(assignment) ∧ clock + 1 ∈ NAT
      THEN
         choice := choice ∪ ss ↦ tt||dateC := dateC ∪ {(ss ↦ tt) ↦ clock + 1}||
         clock := clock + 1
   END;
   assign(ss, tt) ≙
      PRE
         ss ∈ st ∧ tt ∈ tr ∧ ss ↦ tt ∈ choice∧
         ss ∉ dom(assignment) ∧ tt ∉ ran(assignment) ∧ clock + 1 ∈ NAT
      THEN
         assignment := assignment ∪ {ss ↦ tt}||
         dateA := dateA ∪ {(ss ↦ tt) ↦ clock + 1}||clock := clock + 1
   END
END
```

Fig. 3. The B machine for the "training assignment" problem

3 Linking Notations, Techniques, and Paradigms

3.1 Linking Proof and Model Checking

The following example is used to link techniques: proof and model checking;
notations: formal and non formal graphical notations. It is also used to illus-

trate the refinement and the differences between a guard (for an event) and a precondition (for an operation).

We want to model a buffer. To expose its behaviour, we give to the students some examples of accepted execution sequences ([in, in, out, in, out, in, out, out, in, in]) and refused execution sequences ([in, in, out, out, out], [in, out, out], [in, in, in]). We ask them to formally model the system following a top-bottom approach and to formally prove the correctness of their process (i.e. refinement proof).

We present a solution with B[6] using proof and an other with MEC [18], using model checking.

Solution with B. In B, events can be modelled as non-called guarded operations without parameters. In our teaching, we focus on the differences between preconditioned operations and guarded operations (in the B Book, we do not find a single example of an operation beginning with a guard!). In course, we also give a solution of this problem using Event B with the associated proof obligations: invariant preservation, no deadlock, no livelock and refinement.

Before writing in B, the behaviours are described using formal graphical notation: labelled transition system (LTS) and Jackson tree. When refining, we use a non formal graphical notation to describe the structure.

Fig 4 gives the behaviour of the M1 system with graphical notations and fig. 5 is the corresponding B machine. The structure of M2 (the system that refines M1) is given fig. 6. Its behaviour is described with graphical notations fig. 7 and B fig. 8.

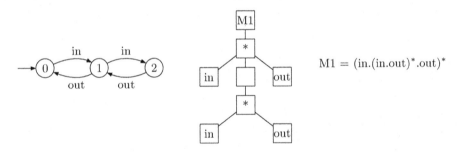

Fig. 4. Description of the behaviour of M1 using LTS (left), Jackson tree (middle) and regular expression (right)

Solution with model checking. After the B solution, we present the students with a solution using model-checking. We use the MEC model-checker which allows to verify properties of LTS. We use the same names than the B specification. Moreover, we just give here our comments, the LTS being given above.

---

[6] Thanks to Steve Dunne.

```
MACHINE
    M1
VARIABLES
    state
INVARIANT
    state ∈ 0..2 /*number of data in the buffer */
INITIALISATION
    state := 0
OPERATIONS
    in ≙
        SELECT state = 0 THEN state := 1
        WHEN state = 1 THEN state := 2
    END;
    out ≙
        SELECT state = 1 THEN state := 0
        WHEN state = 2 THEN state := 1
    END;
    move ≙ skip
END
```

Fig. 5. Machine M1

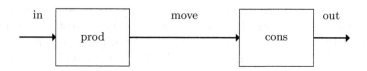

Fig. 6. Opening the box: informal graphical description of the structure of the system

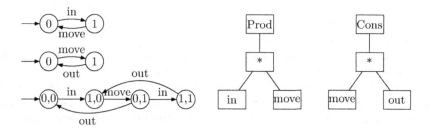

Fig. 7. Description of the behaviour of M2. On the left (from top to bottom): LTS for Prod, Cons and M2; on the right: jackson trees for Prod and Cons.

MACHINE	MACHINE	MACHINE $M2$
$PROD$	$CONS$	INCLUDES
VARIABLES	VARIABLES	$PROD, CONS$
$pstate$	$cstate$	PROMOTES
INVARIANT	INVARIANT	in, out
$pstate \in 0..1$	$pstate \in 0..1$	OPERATIONS
INITIALISATION	INITIALISATION	$move \,\widehat{=}\, pmove \| cmove$
$pstate := 0$	$pstate := 0$	END
OPERATIONS	OPERATIONS	
$in \,\widehat{=}\,$	$out \,\widehat{=}\,$	IMPLEMENTATION $M1\_I$
SELECT $pstate = 0$	SELECT $cstate = 1$	REFINES
THEN $pstate := 1$	THEN $cstate := 0$	$M1$
END;	END;	IMPORTS
$pmove \,\widehat{=}\,$	$cmove \,\widehat{=}\,$	$M2$
SELECT $pstate = 1$	SELECT $cstate = 0$	PROMOTES
THEN $pstate := 0$	THEN $cstate := 1$	$in, out, move$
END	END	END

Fig. 8. M2 and related B machines. MI_1 is used to prove that M2 simulates M1 using the techniques of K. Robinson.

Modelling system M1: no problem.

Modelling system M2: M2 has two components (prod and cons), and a new event (move). The new event occurs when the two components communicate: prod sends its value to cons and, at the same time, cons receive the value from prod. It was hidden in M1 because it is an "internal" event of M2. In a first time, the LTS for prod and cons are given (no problem). The next step is to compose prod and cons, so as to obtain M2. As a composition operator, we use the synchronized product[18]. It leads us to explicitly write the set of overall actions of the system. Some actions involve both components (move) and some action involve only one component (in, out). With the synchronous interpretation, we have to explicitly write when a component "idles" during a global actions. Thus, we have to modify the LTS of prod and cons to introduce "idle" transitions (labeled e) that loop on each state. The set of overall actions is: $\{\langle in, e\rangle, \langle move, move\rangle, \langle e, move\rangle\}$.

Proving that M2 refines M1: the last step is to prove that M2 refines M1. In a first time, we express the refinement relation as a safety property: *"M2 must never have an observable behavior that is not a behaviour of M1"*. The next step is to write a LTS that captures this property[27]: we give a system M1' that is based on M1, plus: (a) a state Error that denotes *"a wrong behaviour has occurred"*, (b) a new action e, that denotes unobservable (internal) events, (c) new elements in the transition relation: $\{(s0, e) \rightarrow s0, (s0, out) \rightarrow Error, (s1, e) \rightarrow s1, (s2, e) \rightarrow s2, (s2, in) \rightarrow Error\}$.

We now have to check that M2 does not violate the property. We compute the synchronized product of M2 and M1' so that observable events of M2 are synchronized with the corresponding event in M1' and unobservable events of M2 are synchronized with e. The set of global action is (the order is [prod, cons, M1']): $\{\langle in, e, in\rangle, \langle move, move, e\rangle, \langle e, out, out\rangle\}$. The resulting LTS is isomorphic to M1, so M2 refines M1.

4   Linking Algebraic and State-Based Specifications

As a very good and pleasant introduction to axioms and models, we use chapter 16 of [32] written by E. Semienov about the concept of point and line.

Here (fig. 9), we use the PROPERTIES clause of B to specify the signature and the axioms of the algebraic specification of a stack. A complete developement is presented by K. Robinson[7] in [34].

MACHINE
   Stack
SETS
   $STACK, ELT$
CONSTANTS
   $pop, push, pEmpty$
PROPERTIES
   $pEmpty \in STACK \wedge pop \in (STACK - \{pEmty\}) \rightarrow ELT \wedge$
   $push \in STACK \times ELT \nrightarrow STACK \wedge$
   $\forall(ss, el) \bullet (ss \in STACK \wedge el \in ELT \Rightarrow pop(push(ss, el)) = el$
VARIABLES
   st
INVARIANT
   $st \in STACK$
INITIALISATION
   $st := pEmpty$
OPERATIONS
   $res \leftarrow op\_pop \,\widehat{=}$
      PRE $st \neq pEmpty$ THEN $res := pop(st) || st := pop(st)$ END;
   $op\_push(el) \,\widehat{=}$
      PRE $el \in ELT$ THEN $st := push(st, el)$ END;
  . . .
END

Fig. 9. "Algebraic" specification of a stack in B

---

[7] S. Schneider [33] and K. Robinson [34] write equality between a SET and a relation (example: STACK = ELT). As $SETS$ are sets of atomic values, Atelier B considers such equalities as badly typed.

5   Linking Codd Relational n-ary Model, B, and Phasing

A large majority of our students have industrial trainings ("stages" in French) whose the subject is to develop an application with MS Acces and VB or with mySql and PHP. If we do not take into account this fact and the fact that B or Z use the same paradigm as the "relational model" of Codd, we have very few chances that our students use one day what we teach in formal methods.

But we have to take into account a certain number of problems! The n-ary relational notation is often (if we specify few constraints) easier to use than the B notation: very often the functions are total, so it is shorter to specify with n-ary relations. Moreover, the projection operator of the n-ary relational model is easier to use that the proj of B. And we have to decide which SETS to use.

In the following example, we can decide to use a set STUDENT only. But why not to use also a set NAME , a set GROUP and even GROUP_ALLOCATION? In the following example, we do not take into account the identification of the students, of the groups. This aspect is very important. Identifiers have to be useful to the users, and we must be sure that we did not register the same student with different identifiers (When the student enters a relational schema without specifying a "key", Access offers to produce a "key". That is very dangerous!) First, we can decide to only specify with "concepts", then, second, to introduce the identifications. Fig. 10 gives an example:

SETS
$\quad STUDENT$
VARIABLES
$\quad Students$
INVARIANT
$\quad Students \subseteq STUDENT$

. . .
SETS
$\quad STUDENT, NAME$
VARIABLES
$\quad Students, StudentSurname, StudentFornames$
INVARIANT
$\quad StudentSurname \in Students \rightarrow NAME \land$
$\quad$ /* No student has two similar fornames! */
$\quad StudentFornames \in students \twoheadrightarrow iseq(NAME) \land$
$\quad$ /* A student can have one or two fornames. */
$\quad \forall(ss) \bullet (ss \in students \Rightarrow size(StudentFornames(ss)) \in 1..2) \land$
$\quad StudentSurname \otimes StudentFornames \in Students \rightarrowtail$
$\quad NAME \otimes iseq(NAME)$

Fig. 10.

And we have to take into account the facts that the constraints are not the same during all the life of a process. This is very rarely considered in n-ary relational schemas and, in general, in the database community. The invariant is a weak invariant or an invariant for a single phase only. In the following example, we consider a part of the life of a school.

During phase 1, the number of students to recruit is set. This number gives the number of groups of students. We only so pass to phase 2 when this information is recorded. During phase 2, we register the students. It is also possible to cancel a registration. We only so pass to phase 3 when we have a number of students in the database equal to the number we decided to recruit. During phase 3, we assign students to groups. Students can change group. We only so pass to phase 4 when we have all the students in the database registered to groups. Every group has 20 students. We give the relational schema without a null value corresponding to the B specification for each phase. It appears that if we just give the schemas of relations without other constraints, it is not sufficient as a specification. At first, we specify (fig.11 the "common" part (common to each phase) using B.

SETS
    $STUDENT$
VARIABLES
    $Phase, Students, Nb\_Students\_decided, Group\_allocation$
CONSTANTS
    $CardGroup = 20$
INTERPHASE INVARIANT
    $Phase \in NAT \land Students \subset STUDENT \land Nb\_Students\_decided \in NAT \land$
    $Nb\_Students\_decided \bmod 20 = 0 \land card(Students) \le Nb\_Students\_decided \land$
    $Group\_allocation \in Students \nrightarrow 1..Nb\_groups\_decided \land$
    $\forall gg \bullet gg \in 1..Nb\_groups\_decided \Rightarrow$
    $card(Group\_allocation^{-1}[\{gg\}]) \le CardGroup$
DEFINITIONS
    $Groups \mathrel{\widehat{=}} ran(Group\_allocation);$
    $Nb\_groups\_decided \mathrel{\widehat{=}} Nb\_Students\_decided \cup CardGroup$
INITIALISATION
    $Phase := 0 \| Students := \emptyset \| Nb\_Students\_decided :\in NAT \|$
    $Group\_allocation := \emptyset$

Fig. 11. Interphase specification (B and Codd)

We give the details of each phase: list of the operations that can be called in this phase (the phase is part of the precondition of the operation), the phase invariant and the Codd relational schema without null values (we use a Identification field for every SET and fields prefixed by Nb for field taking their value in NAT). See table 1.

Table 1. Details of each phase

Phase 1	Operations	$Op\_Set\_Nb_Students\_decided$
	Invariant	$Phase\ =\ 1 \wedge InterPhaseInvariant \wedge Students\ =\ \{\} \wedge$ $Group\_allocation = \{\}$
	Codd schema	RS_students(Id_Students) RS_ Nb_Students_decided(Nb_Students_decided) RS_ Group_allocation(Id_Students_Alloc, Nb_group)
	Remarks	Plus other constraints. It is not explicit that the relations *students* and $Group_allocation$ are empty and that a relation respecting the $RS_students$ schema has one 1-uple only and that $Nb_group \in 1..Nb\_Students_decided$. Operations are preconditioned by the phases where they can be called.
Phase 2	Operations	$Op\_Student\_registration, Op\_Registration\_cancellation$
	Invariant	$Phase = 2 \wedge InterPhaseInvariant \wedge Nb\_groups\_decided \neq$ $0 \wedge Group\_allocation = \{\}$
	Codd schema	Idem phase 1.
	Remarks	It is not explicit that $Nb\_groups\_decided > 0$
Phase 3	Operations	$Op\_Group\_allocation, Op\_Group\_change$
	Invariant	$Phase\qquad =\qquad 3\quad \wedge\quad InterPhaseInvariant\quad \wedge$ $card(dom(Group\_allocation)) \leq Nb\_Students\_decided$
	Codd schema	RS_students(Id_Students) RS_ Nb_Students_decided(Nb_Students_decided) RS_ Group_allocation(Id_Students_Alloc, Nb_group)
	Remarks	It is not explicit that $Nb\_Students\_decided > 0$.
Phase 4	Operations	$Op\_\ldots$
	Invariant	$Phase\qquad =\qquad 4\quad \wedge\quad InterPhaseInvariant\quad \wedge$ $Group\_allocation \in Students \rightarrow 1..Nb\_groups\_decided \wedge$ $ran(Group\_allocation) = 1..Nb\_groups\_decided$
	Codd schema	RS_ Nb_Students_decided(Nb_Students_decided) RS_ Students(Id_Students_Alloc, Nb_group)
	Remarks	Now, the projection of *Students* on *Id_Students* is equal to the set of the *Id_Students* of all the registered students. So we do not need RS_students(Id_Students) and the cardinal of the projection of *Students* on *Nb_group* is equal to $Nb\_Students\_decided20$.

Last, we specify the interphase operation (the operation that changes from one phase to another, see fig. 12).

5.1   Linking Semi-formal and Formal Notations. The Example of the "Qualified Association" of UML

The definitions of the "qualified association" written in natural language are very confuse[8]. As an exercise, we give these definitions to our students, then we

---

[8] http://archive.eiffel.com/doc/manuals/technology/bmarticles/uml/page.html

$Op\_change\_phase \;\widehat{=}$
PRE
$\quad Phase = 0 \vee$
$\quad Phase = 1 \wedge Nb\_groups\_decided \neq 0 \wedge$
$\quad Group\_allocation = \emptyset \vee$
$\quad Phase = 2 \wedge Nb\_groups\_decided \neq 0 \wedge$
$\quad Group\_allocation \in Students \nrightarrow Nb\_groups\_decided \vee$
$\quad Phase = 3 \wedge Group\_allocation \in Students \rightarrow 1..Nb\_groups\_decided \wedge$
$\quad ran(Group\_allocation) = Students$
THEN
$\quad Phase := Phase + 1$ END;

Fig. 12. Interphase operation

give one example in UML, then with the Niam notation[35][36][16] which allows
to express set constraints (fig. 13), then a translation into B and in Codd notation. Students must get used to interpreting a semi-formal specification through
a formal notation (see the conlusion of this paper for more details on interpretation)[9]. By so doing, we are "pioneers" in UML. Indeed, here are some words
extracted from the last version of the MOF (April 2002, v1.4, 4.9.2, p. 4-15): *"in
a rigourous, mapping independent fashion (...) the sets of all possible instances
(...) the Cartesian product (...) a Link, which is a member of All_Links, can be a
tuple of the form '⟨c1, c2⟩' where 'c1' and 'c2' are members of Classe1_Instances
and Class2_Instances respectively. (...) a subset (...)"*. Elementary mathematic
on set and relations is now in the luggage of the specifiers of the XXIst century!

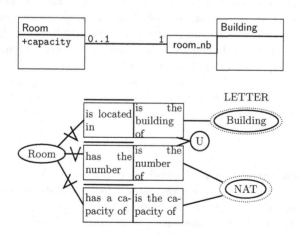

Fig. 13. The example in UML and NIAM

---

[9] As another application of this principle, our presentation of Harel's statechart semantics is given in classic B [37] and Event B.

Here is a translation into B, using the direct product ($\otimes$)

...

INVARIANT

$\quad IsLocatedIn \in Room \rightarrow Building \wedge$

$\quad HasTheNumber \in Room \rightarrow NAT \wedge$

$\quad Id\_Building \in Building \rightarrowtail LETTER \wedge$

$\quad Capacity \in Room \rightarrow NAT \wedge$

$\quad IsLocatedIn \otimes HasTheNumber \in Room \rightarrowtail Building \times NAT$

...

And now, a translation into the Codd notation for the "n-ary relational model":

$\quad$ Room(Building_letter, Room_number, capacity)

$\quad$ Building(Building_letter)

5.2 Linking B to Law and Management: Interpretation of Juridical Texts

Forewords: beside computer science, our students have mandatory courses in economics and law. They are teached the basic concepts of law before learning law applied to software. The formal methods are used in these courses as an analysis grid.

Specification of a roman law precept. We follow the Socratic method to make the student discover the structure of the Code Civil using mathematics on sets and relations and the B notation. Here is an example where we specify (fig. 14) a precept of the Roman law [38]: *Infans conceptus pro jam nato habetur quoties de commodis ejus agitur.* (child conceived is to be treated as born every time it is his interest, Code civil, art. 725, 906, 961). This principle infringes on the general principle implying that the personality is by the birth and at moment of the birth. Article. 725-1° of the CC decides that to inherit, a person must be conceived at the time the legacy is open. It results that a child will dispose of the legacy of his father, as if he was born at the time of the opening of the succession.

Measures of administrative procedure complexity. We use also B to study the complexity of administrative procedures used in different countries in the world to follow the "automotive vehicles" (what concept under the registration number?). The complexity is measured in terms of the number of the necessary operation (and the number of their parameters), of the number of elementary substitutions of the minimal operations respecting the invariant. A minimal operation is the operation with the less substitutions as possible. In the following example, $Op1$ is a minimal operation. $Op2$ is not because rr is not total.

SETS
  $PERSON; TYPE\_P = \{artificial, natural\}; SEX = \{male, female\}$
DEFINITIONS
  $natural\_person \triangleq Type\_Person^{-1}[\{natural\}],$
  $Men \triangleq sexOf^{-1}[\{male\}], Women \triangleq sexOf^{-1}[\{female\}]$
VARIABLES
  $type\_Person, persons, sexOf, date\_of\_conception,$
  $date\_of\_opening\_inheritence, inherits, father, mother, affected\_by\_inher\_on$
INVARIANT
  $persons \subset PERSON \wedge type\_Person \in persons \rightarrow TYPE\_P \wedge$
  $sexOf \in natural\_person \rightarrow SEX \wedge$
  $date\_of\_conception \in natural\_person \nrightarrow DATE \wedge$
  $date\_of\_inheritance\_opening \in natural\_person \nrightarrow DATE \wedge$
  $inherits \in natural\_person \leftrightarrow natural\_person \wedge$
  $father \in natural\_person \nrightarrow Men \wedge$
  $mother \in natural\_person \nrightarrow Women \wedge$
  $affected\_by\_inher\_on \in natural\_person \nrightarrow DATE \wedge$
  $affected\_by\_inher\_on = (mother; date\_of\_conception) \cup$
  $(father; date\_of\_opening\_inheritence) \wedge$
  $\forall(d1 \mapsto d2) \bullet (d1 \mapsto d2) \in (date\_of\_conception^{-1}; affected\_by\_inher\_on)$
  $\Rightarrow d1 < d2$

Fig. 14. "Infans conceptus pro nato habetur quoties de commodis agitur" in B

SETS
  $AA; BB$
VARIABLES
  aa, rr
INVARIANT
  $aa \subset AA \wedge rr \in aa \nrightarrow BB \wedge$
...

OPERATIONS
  $Op1 \triangleq$
  ...
    THEN $aa := aa \cup \{eb\}$
  END;
  $Op2 \triangleq$
  ...
    THEN $aa := aa \cup \{eb\} \| rr := rr \cup \{aa \mapsto eb\}$
  END;

Fig. 15. Example of minimal (Op1) and non minimal (Op2) operations.

6   Conclusion

Teaching specification is not teaching mathematics. Teaching specifications is to be situated between Russell: *"Mathematics is the only science where one never knows what one is talking about nor whether what is said is true"* and Emile

Borel: *"Mathematics is the only science in which one knows exactly what one is talking about and one is certain that what on is saying is true"*[39]. The core of our problematic is the concept of model. We think that it is necessary to pay attention that our attitude (our methods) do not contradict our principles. If we claim to sever the links to metaphysics (Dijkstra writes that: *"[...] To further sever the links to intuition, we rename the values {true, false} of the boolean domain as {black, white}"*[40]) we must not continue to apply the structure of the phrase of Aristotle (see model "entity - relationship - property") with all its metaphysics consequences. What is our philosophy of mathematics? What is the philosophy of this student and of this other student?

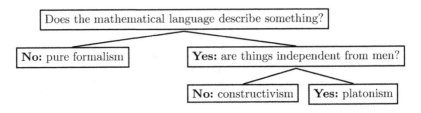

Fig. 16. Mathematics and reality[41]

We can distinguish two meanings for the term model: (1) A model is an interpretation: assigning a meaning to formal sentences in such a way that this sentences be verified. Geometry becomes a model of a formal language, rather than the formalization of idealized properties from the observation of the sensible space. We then study the relations between sets of sentences and sets of models of these sentences. A model (of a sentence) written in a formal language is an interpretation (assigning meaning to symbols of the language) in which this sentence is true. (2) A model is the assignment of a formal sentence to an "empirical reality" ("To an observer B, an object A* is a model of an object A to the extent that B can use A* to answer questions that interest him about A" [42] "the two meanings of the concept of model are nothing else than the two complementary faces of the same activity: to interpret. To interpret[10] is inevitable: to interpret formalism, or, conversely to interpret mathematically a set of data. One the one hand, a language without model has no interest, on the other hand and reciprocally, the expression is not the mirror of the experience." [44].

In the debate on *"the cruelty of teaching computing science"* [40], we must consider not only the proposal of E. W. Dijkstra *"The programmer's task is...to give a formal proof that the program he proposes meets the equally formal functional specification."* but also the answer of T. Winograd [45] *"This is a noble goal, but it presupposes that someone else has done all the hard work by managing to create a formal functional specification that is appropriate to the task*

---

[10] We use the example of Frege: "The proposition 'Cato killed cato' , can be interpreted in 4 different ways: 1) killed (Cato, Cato) 2) killed himself (Cato) 3) killed Cato (Cato) 4) Cato killed (Cato)" Frege quoted by J.L. Gardies [43].

at hand." We cannot reject the hard work in a "new discipline" or an "interdisciplinary haven" , (Dijkstra) or in a new "level". We consider that it is the software developer's role to ask the good questions to the customer (as it is the doctor's role to ask the right questions to his or her patient). We consider that it is the specifier's responsibility –ultimately, isn't it what we want?– to write the specification.

Several centuries were needed to invent what is called "clinical" medicine [46]. Clinicians are doctors in medicine. They don't consider that they don't need medical science. On the contrary, they know that with their science, they can make observations, find questions, make and verify hypotheses, make deductions, etc. We hope that in using and liking different concepts, paradigms and technics we help our student to be responsible specifiers.

References

1. Paper, P.E.P., ed.: The Essential Peirce Selected Philosophical Writings. Volume 2 (1893-1913). Indiana University Pres (1998) ISBN: 0-253-21190-5.
2. Lee, E., Varaiya, P.: Introducing signals and systems: The berkeley approach. In: First Signal Processing Education Workshop, October 15-18, 2000, Hunt, Texas (2000)
3. OMG: Mof web pages (2002)
4. Blanché, R., Dubucs, J.: La logique et son histoire. Armand Colin (1996)
5. Davenport, C.: The role of graphical methods in the history of logic in Methodos, Milano (1952)
6. Eco, U.: Le signe. Le livre de poche, Paris (1992) ISBN: 2-253-06094-1.
7. Frege, G.: Collected papers on mathematics, logic, and philosophy. Blackwell, B. (1984) ISBN: 0631127283.
8. Schmitz, F.: Wittgenstein. Les Belles Lettres, Paris (1999) ISBN: 2-251-76020-2.
9. David, R.and Alla, H.: Petri nets and Grafcet, Tools for Modeling Discrete Event Systems. Prentice Hall, New York (1992) ISBN: 0-13-327537-X.
10. Fencott, C.: Formal Methods for Concurrency. Thompson (1996) ISBN: 1-85032-173-6.
11. Milner, R.: Communication and Concurrency. Prentice Hall (1989) ISBN: 0-13-115007-3.
12. Abrial, J.R.: Extending B without changing it (for developing distributed systems). In Habrias, H., ed.: 1st Conference on the B method, I.U.T. de Nantes, France (1996) 169–190 ISBN: 2-906082-25-2.
13. Abrial, J., Mussat, J.: Introducing Dynamic Constraints in B. In: B'98, Second Int. B Conference Montpellier. (1998) 82–128
14. Abrial, J.R.: Etude Système: méthode et exemple. (1998)
15. Jackson, M.: System Development. Prentice Hall (1983) ISBN: 0-12-379050-6.
16. Habrias, H.: Introduction à la spécification. Masson (1993) ISBN: 2-225-82768-0.
17. Jackson, M.: Software Requirements & Specifications, a lexicon of practice, principles and prejudices. Addison-Wesley (1995) ISBN: 0-201-87712-0.
18. Arnold, A., Begay, D., Crubillé, P.: Construction and Analysis of Transition Systems with MEC. World Scientific (1994) ISBN: 981-02-1922-9.
19. Baruk, S.: Echec et Maths. Editions du Seuil, Paris (1979) ISBN: 2-02-004720-9.
20. Bérard, B., et al.: Systems and Software Verification. Springer (2001) ISBN : 3-540-41523-8.

21. Davis, P., Hersh, D., Marchisotto, E.: The Companion Guide to "the Mathematical Experience". Birkhauser Verlag AG (1995) ISBN: 0-817638490.

22. Davis, P.J.and Hersh, D.: The Mathematical Experience. Haughton Mifflin Co (1999) ISBN: 0-395-929687.

23. Fearn, N.: Zeno and the tortoise - How to think like a philosopher. Atlantic Grove (2001) ISBN: 1-903809-13-4.

24. Frappier, M., Habrias, H.: Software Specification Methods, An Overview Using a Case Study. FACIT. Springer (2000) ISBN : 1-85233-353-7.

25. Habrias, H.: Dictionaire encyclopédique du génie logiciel. Masson (1997) ISBN: 2-225-85328-2.

26. Habrias, H.: Spécification formelle avec B". Lavoisier-Hermes (2001) ISBN: 2-7462-0302-2.

27. Magee, J., Kramer, J.: Concurrency: State Models & Java Program. Wiley (1999) ISBN: 0-471-98710-7.

28. Monin, J.: Understanding Formal Methods. Springer (2003) ISBN: 1-852-33247-6.

29. Abrial, J.R.: The B-Book, Assigning Programs to Meanings. Cambridge University Press (1996) ISBN: 0-521-49619-5.

30. Habrias, H., André, P.: Writing constraints that do not fit to a specification paradigm. Technical report, LINA, Nantes (2004)

31. Mandelbaum, D.G., ed.: Selected Writings of Edward Sapir in Language, Culture and Personality. University of California Press (1986) ISBN: 0-520055942.

32. Quant: Diabolo math. Belin (1983) ISBN: 2-701-10452-1.

33. Schneider, S.: The B-Method: An Introduction. Palgrave (2001) ISBN: 0-33379284-X.

34. Robinson, K.: Reconciling Axiomatic and Model-Based Specifications Using the B Method. In: ZB 2000. (2000) 95–106

35. Nijssen, G., Halpin, T.: Conceptual Schema and Relational Database Design. Prentice Hal (1989) ISBN: 0-7248-0151-0.

36. Habrias, H.: Le modèle relationnel binaire, Méthode NIAM. Eyrolles, Paris (1988)

37. Sekerinski, E.: Graphical design of reactive systems. In: B'98 Second Int. B Conference Montpellier. (1998) 182–197

38. Roland, H., Boyer, L.: Adages du droit français. Litec, Paris (1999) ISBN: 2-7111-3003-7.

39. Le Lionnais, F.: Les grands courants de la pensée mathématique. Hermann (1997) ISBN: 2-7056-6332-0-27.

40. Dijkstra, E.W.: On the Cruelty of Teaching Computer Science. CACM **32** (1989) 1398–1414

41. Dosen, K.: Le programme de Hilbert. In: Le concept de preuve à la lumière de l'intelligence artificielle,. (1999) ISBN: 2-20001472-4.

42. Minsky, M.L.: Matter, mind and models. In: Semantic Information Processing. MIT Pres (1968) ISBN: 0-262130440.

43. Gardies, J.: Esquisse d'une grammaire pure. Vrin, Paris (1975) ISBN: 2-7116-4057-4.

44. Sinaceur, H.: Modèle. In Lecourt, D., ed.: Dictionnaire d'histoire et de philosophie des sciences. PUF (1999) ISBN: 2-13-049992-9.

45. Winograd, T.: Debate: On the Cruelty of Teaching Computer Science (a response to Dijkstra). CACM **32** (1989) 1412–1413

46. Foucault, M.: The Birth of the Clinic. Pantheon (1973) ISBN:0-394710975, translated from the french by A. S. Smith.

Teaching Formal Methods in Context

Jim Davies, Andrew Simpson, and Andrew Martin

Software Engineering Programme
University of Oxford
Wolfson Building
Parks Road
Oxford OX1 3QD

Abstract. The Software Engineering Programme at Oxford teaches formal methods as an integral part of its programme of professional education in software engineering. This paper explains how the methods are taught—in the context of emerging trends in software development, and in the context of existing practice—and how their use is promoted through course design and motivating examples.

1 Introduction

The Software Engineering Programme at Oxford began in the early 1980s as a set of 'industrial courses': employees of organisations such as IBM would come to Oxford for an introduction to formal methods such as Z [27] or CSP [16]. An 'integrated programme' of six one-week modules was established in 1993; this has evolved into a comprehensive programme of education in software engineering, with modules in 26 different subjects, and students from more than 100 different organisations.

Formal methods are at the heart of the expanded programme. There are two modules that teach Z, two that teach CSP, one that teaches B [1], and another that shows how Z, CSP, and UML can be used together in the design, development, and testing of object-oriented software. Other modules adopt a similar, principled approach: rigorous modelling with UML; techniques for the analysis of security protocols; grammars for design patterns; relational and schema calculus for database design; precise process descriptions for service-based architectures; notions of abstraction and refinement for model-based testing.

These methods are taught in the context of emerging trends in software development, as characterised by terms such as *programming in the large* (a term first popularised in the 1970s: see, for example, [10]), *model-driven architecture* [19], and *model-based testing* [7]. They are taught also in the context of current practice: students are shown how formal methods can be used to complement informal and semi-formal techniques, and to faciliate communication between stakeholders and developers. This teaching is informed by the questions and contributions of the students themselves, all of whom are practising designers, programmers, managers, or developers.

C.N. Dean and R.T. Boute (Eds.): TFM 2004, LNCS 3294, pp. 185–202, 2004.
© Springer-Verlag Berlin Heidelberg 2004

In this paper, we explain the two contextual approaches taken to the teaching of formal methods: in Section 2, as part of an emerging discipline of model-driven software engineering; and in Section 3, as part of a programme of advanced education for current practioners. In Section 5, we report upon the experience of delivering such a programme of education, and discuss the issues raised.

2   Formal Methods and Software Engineering

When our industrial courses were first introduced, the promotion of formal methods for software development was a challenging task: for every acknowledged success, there were many more failures; neither the methods nor the industry were ready for technology transfer on the scale required. Twenty years later, the situation has changed: there is now a widely-recognised need for precise, abstract descriptions with enough formality to support design-level validation, test generation, and formal verification.

However, the challenges still remain. We are no longer asked 'why should we use these methods?', but instead: 'how should we use them?', 'where is the tool support?', and 'how does this particular technique relate to (for example) JUnit, UML 2.0, XDE, eXtreme Programming, .net, web services, or the latest model for threading in Java?' To answer such questions, we have to understand more about the methods that we teach: their qualities, their limitations, and how they might be positioned in a software engineering curriculum.

2.1   Software Engineering

To consider formal methods in the context of software engineering, we must first arrive at a suitable characterisation of that discipline. In 1969, Bauer [22] defined *software engineering* as

> "the establishment and use of sound engineering principles in order to obtain, economically, software that is reliable and works efficiently on real machines"

While this is a good definition, it says very little about the principles involved. It is the nature of these principles, and the processes in which they are applied, that has been the focus of so much engineering and scientific endeavour.

A more satisfactory definition may be obtained by re-using the definition of *systems engineering* presented by Blanchard [5]:

> "The application of scientific and engineering efforts to (1) transform an operational need into a description of system performance parameters and a system of configuration through the use of an iterative process of definition, synthesis, analysis, design, test and evaluation, and validation; (2) integrate related technical parameters and ensure the compatibility of all physical, functional, and program interfaces in a manner

that optimises the total definition and design; and (3) integrate reliability, maintainability, usability (human), safety, producibility, supportability (serviceability), disposability, and other such factors into the total engineering effort to meet cost, schedule, and technical performance objectives."

This casts more light upon both principles and process. The context in which formal methods are used includes:

- the comprehension and transformation of requirements;
- an iterative process of design, development, and testing;
- questions of consistency and compatibility of interfaces and components; and
- the need to address issues that arise in use: non-functional requirements such as dependability and usability.

Of equal importance is the fact that all formal methods have been *developed* in this context. Their purpose, their features, their semantics—all of these arise out of trying to solve particular problems in software engineering. To teach formal methods without (communicating) an understanding of this context is to separate them from their meaning.

2.2   Changes in Context

The discipline of software engineering is evolving, with significant developments in the following areas:

Programming languages. The adoption of languages such as Java, with improved support for abstraction, encapsulation, reflection, and concurrency, has reduced the amount of effort required to relate abstract models to executable code.

Modelling languages. The widespread use of the Unified Modeling Language (UML) has meant that most software developers are familiar with the use of abstract or 'conceptual' descriptions, even if these descriptions are lacking in appropriate, behavioural semantics.

Model interchange languages. The development of standard formats (such as XMI—XML Metadata Interchange) for the storage and transformation of models is a prerequisite for the application of formal methods on an industrial scale.

Metamodelling approaches. The definition of UML profiles and object models for formal languages supports the use of different methods—whether formal or informal—in combination; the definition of UML 2.0 allows the use of formal notations as extensions to an elegant, well-understood core.

Open components and services. Aspects of a design that might have been programmed from scratch, or would have required adaptations towards closed, proprietary technology, can now be addressed using standard components with open, well-defined standards and interfaces; this both invites and rewards the use of precise, abstract representations.

Outsourcing and offshoring. Where software development is undertaken outside an organisation, or across different sites within the same organisation, precise descriptions of functionality become increasingly important.

Tools and frameworks for validation and verification. The combination of Ant and JUnit/JML, for example, allows the user to automate regression testing based upon precise, abstract characterisations of correctness.

Collaborative working. Open source development strategies and inter-enterprise computing encourage the formulation and exchange of information at the conceptual level, and an emphasis upon compliance and verification.

Project administration systems. Applications such as Maven [24] that support the automated configuration and integration of development support applications such as Ant, JUnit, Bugzilla, PMD, and CVS provide an ideal platform for the deployment of tools employing formal techniques.

This list is not intended to be exhaustive, and in each of the areas there are also factors that discourage or delay the adoption of formal methods, but there is a clear, emerging trend towards a context in which precise models, and hence formal techniques, are seen as an essential part of software development.

The visibility of projects such as Microsoft's SLAM/SDV [3] both acknowledges and contributes to this trend. It is indicative that Bill Gates, speaking at the Windows Hardware Engineering Conference, could state: "...even software verification, this has been the Holy Grail of computer science for many decades but now in some very key areas, for example, driver verification, we're building tools that can do actual proof about the software and how it works in order to guarantee the reliability."

2.3   Model-Driven Software Engineering

The routine, integrated application of formal methods in software engineering will realise (and greatly extend) the promise of the *model-driven architecture (MDA)* [19]. In MDA, a platform-independent model of the system is automatically transformed, using fixed implementation libraries or strategies, into a platform-specific executable version of the system, ready for deployment.

This form of automatic refinement, in which the current level of programming concepts is replaced by components, patterns, and constraints, is simply the next step in increasing levels of abstraction: from machine code, to Cobol, to C, and then to environments such as the Java 2 Enterprise Edition. Each of these levels of programming abstraction could be regarded as formal: the difference now is that we are reaching a level of abstraction where the programs, or the models, can more readily support the use of formal, mathematical methods.

There is no clear distinction to be made between levels: the applicability of techniques, and the nature of the abstraction, depends upon the way in which the languages are used, and the supporting framework. The developments in the software engineering discipline mentioned above mean that the support (and the demand) for abstract modelling is increasing. To understand the support required, consider the five categories of models shown in Figure 1:

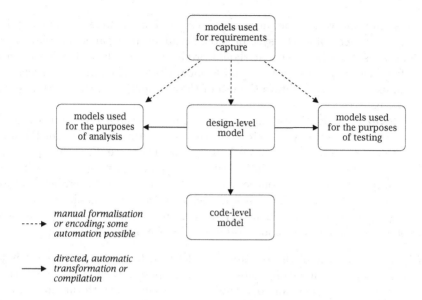

Fig. 1. Model-driven/model-based software engineering

Models used in requirements capture. These are typically unfaithful, or impressionistic, rather than informal. They are created with precise syntax, in a language—usually graphical—that has at least one precise semantics, but they are intended to convey impressions of requirements, rather than final characterisations. For example, in terms of UML: state diagrams might include transitions which, after further consideration, would be redirected or removed; sequence charts might omit interactions later found to be crucial; class diagrams, often inappropriate in any case, might present only an approximate distribution of data and functionality.

Design-level models. These record design decisions, and are intended as faithful representations of the final implementation; they are precise, but lack some of the detail necessary to generate a complete, working system; they may be expressed formally, in a precise subset of UML, but they will typically contain too much information to support the direct application of formal methods. Instead, we may take advantage of developments in modelling languages, model interchange languages, and metamodelling approaches to first extract only that information that is required for our purpose.

Models used for the purposes of analysis. Using appropriate model transformation technology—possibly mapping from the syntax and semantics of the design-level models to that of another language, but certainly abstracting some of the information contained in those models—we may produce models that are more amenable to the application of formal methods. We may then use these methods to reason about properties of the design.

Models used for the purposes of testing. Again using transformation technology, we may create projections of design models, containing strictly less information, for the purposes of testing. For example, the model might explain exactly how the system should respond to a particular sequence of messages: the output that it should produce, or the state that it should be left in. Developments in tools and frameworks for automatic test generation and execution [7] facilitate the use of these models, and thus better reward their construction.

Code-level models. These are no more than structured presentations of the executable code; they contain all of the information necessary for the automatic generation of the final working system. These are the models presented in programming tools, or interactive development environments (which often describe the return journey between structured representation and executable as 'round-trip software engineering'). Developments in programming languages, components, and services continue to narrow the gap between code-level models and models produced for the purposes of design.

An important aspect of the necessary model transformation technology is the means of expressing modelling intentions or purposes. Each of the solid arrows in the diagram represents an opportunity for automatic transformation, or compilation. Such transformations need to be directed if the resulting model is to be fit for purpose: we must supply analysis directives, compilation directives, and testing directions for each of the three kinds of transformation shown.

Analysis directives may be obtained automatically from precise components of requirements-level models; others must be constructed from scratch, although this construction may be in a language better suited to their expression than the language used for the design models. We might expect to find some degree of complementarity between compilation and test directives: aspects of the design model that are automatically may not need to be tested; models for testing might focus instead upon hand-written code and integration issues.

2.4   Current Practice

At present, the use of precise, abstract models—that is, at a level of abstraction above the level of executable code—is extremely limited. The underlying reason is the immaturity of the tools, languages, frameworks, and model transformation technologies. The changes mentioned above are underway, but their impact has only recently started to have an effect on perceptions and practices.

Developers and designers have neither the time nor the inclination for manual translation between models. Where circumstances demand, they are happy to spend time directing transformations, selecting aspects of a design to explore, but manual transcription—any suggestion that they might need to re-enter information that is already present, albeit in a slightly different form, in an existing model—is regarded as completely unacceptable: an indication that the tools and methods are not ready for industrial application.

However, there is still considerable value in teaching the concepts and principles of formal methods, along with the formal notation, to industrial practitioners. Not only does this prepare them for (and hasten the introduction of) the more widespread use of precise, abstract models, but also these concepts, principles, and notation can be applied with a lighter touch, to illuminate particular aspects of a problem or design.

This illumination is particularly effective when (ideas from) formal methods are used in combination with less formal approaches to modelling. As Fowler [14], suggests, these approaches are regarded as useful:

> "Most graphical modeling languages have very little rigor; their notation appeals to intuition rather than to formal definition. On the whole, this does not seem to have done much harm. These methods may be informal, but many people still find them useful—and it is usefulness that counts."

Using formal notation, or the insight gained through experience in the application of appropriate formal methods, the value of these informal models is greatly increased: the 'intuition' is enhanced.

The use of formal methods 'with a light touch' requires a deep understanding of both methods and context. The importance of teaching formal methods in context, explaining their application within software engineering, will decrease only when the methods themselves are more widely used, and their use becomes more automatic.

3   A Programme of Professional Education

The Software Engineering Programme is a part-time, *post-experience* programme of education: it teaches software engineering to people already in full-time employment. All students are expected to have at least two years' experience of 'large-scale' software development, designing or programming as part of a development team. The formal methods taught in the Programme are thus taught, unavoidably, in the context of existing practice.

3.1   The Design of the Programme

Most industrial software engineering activity is project-based, driven by the demands of customers and/or corporate strategy. As a result, there are often times during the year when students are simply unable to attend courses, or complete assignments: their working commitments leave them no time to do so. Furthermore, adult students may have other responsibilities that can, from time to time, interrupt their studies.

To make the programme accessible to working professionals, the taught component is delivered as a collection of residential, one-week modules, repeated once or twice a year, with a minimum of prerequisites or dependencies. During a teaching week, students are insulated, as far as possible, from the demands of the workplace: the intention is that they should do little else but concentrate upon the subject matter of the course.

We have employed the same mode of teaching for students on the full-time MSc in Computer Science, and found it to be surprisingly effective. The only concern raised—by faculty, not by students—was that there would be insufficient time to reflect upon the material from one lesson before the next began. In our experience, this seems to be outweighed by the benefits of concentrated teaching, as opposed to a few hours a week across a semester: a significant momentum is achieved, carrying the students further into the subject.

Where students from the same cohort have had the choice between the two modes of delivery—in courses in object-oriented design, Z, and CSP—those attending the one-week modular version appeared to attain a deeper understanding of the subject. Of course, there are other factors in play: the structure of classes is different, and a teaching week requires greater preparation, and greater (intensity of) commitment from the lecturing staff. Nonetheless, we are reassured that one-week modules can be at least as effective as conventional lecture courses.

Each module is preceded by a period of preparatory study. This may entail reading chapters from a set text, examining relevant research articles, attempting preliminary exercises, gathering data, or preparing a brief presentation. It is then followed by a written assignment, to be completed during the six weeks following the teaching week, that allows students to develop and demonstrate their understanding of the material.

A candidate for the MSc has five years in which to complete their programme of study, consisting of ten modules, a project, and a dissertation. This duration might seem surprising, in comparison with the single year allowed for our full-time MSc in Computer Science, but it reflects the pressures upon working professionals—most are unable to attend more than three or four modules in a year—as well as the likelihood of a significant 'life event' occuring during the period of study; most of our students will experience a change in professional or private circumstances between admission and graduation.

3.2   Teaching Formal Methods

The Programme is divided into five themes, each of which contains five modules addressing different aspects of the software engineering discipline:

- *formal techniques*: modules in Z, CSP, process and data refinement, and B.
- *object orientation*: modules in programming (Java, J2EE, Corba) and design (UML notations and design patterns);
- *software development*: modules in requirements, management, risk, quality, and testing;
- *enterprise computing*: modules in web services, databases, XML, functional programming, and performance modelling;
- *computer security*: modules in security principles, human and social factors, risk analysis and management, and secure implementation.

Students are free to select any combination of modules. Where it is unlikely that a student would be able to follow one module without first attending another—for example, the *design patterns* module assumes complete understanding of *object-oriented programming*—the two modules are placed in the same theme.

In addition to the constraints of current practice mentioned in Section 2.4, the teaching of the *formal techniques* theme is influenced by the fact that the greater part of software engineering activity in industry involves the maintenance, extension, and integration of existing systems—complete, formal descriptions of such systems are not available; neither is there time to develop them. Accordingly, we emphasise the use of formal methods, in combination with other techniques, to capture and communicate separate aspects of a system or design.

This contrasts with the approach implied by the characterisation of formal methods found in Sommerville [26]:

"Formal methods may be used at two levels in the development of critical systems:

1. A formal specification of the system may be developed and mathematically analysed for inconsistency. This technique is effective in discovering specification errors and omissions...
2. A formal verification that the code of a software system is consistent with the specification may be developed. This requires a formal specification and is effective in discovering programming and some design errors."

Our emphasis upon the use of formal methods for communication is supported by the characterisation of formal methods given by Wing [31]:

"formal methods can be used to

– identify many, though not all, deficiencies in a set of informally stated requirements, to discover discrepancies between a specification and an implementation, and find errors in existing programs and systems;
– specify medium-sized and non-trivial problems, especially the functional behaviour of sequential programs, abstract data types, and hardware; and
– provide a deeper understanding of the behavior of large, complex systems."

Our emphasis upon the use of formal methods in combination with other techniques is supported by the similarity between this characterisation of formal methods and the following account of UML, given by Bennett et al. [4]:

"The diagrams in a modelling language such as UML also conform to agreed standards. Diagrammatical models are used extensively by systems analysts and designers in order to:

– communicate ideas,
– generate new ideas and possibilities,
– test ideas and make predictions,
– understand structures and relationships."

The widespread adoption of UML, and the displacement of more formal notations such as SDL, owes much to its presentation as a means of abstraction and communication, rather than analysis.

In our formal techniques stream, we teach formal proof: we show how a natural deduction system can be used within predicate calculus; how equational reasoning can be used to establish properties of sets and relations; how structural induction can be used to reason about recursively-defined objects; how to calculate preconditions; and how to show data refinement by simulation.

However, we do not expect our students to construct their own proofs beyond the scope of the module assignment. Our purpose in teaching proof techniques, and the theories of refinement, is simply to convey a proper understanding of the semantics of statements *and models* constructed using formal notations. Without this, students would lack the intuition required to support the successful use of formal methods.

A proper, working understanding of model semantics is required for the anticipated transition to model-driven or model-based software engineering, enabled by the changes in context described in Section 2.2. It is needed for the construction of analysis, testing, and compilation directives for model transformation, and also for the comprehension of feedback—counterexamples, warnings, or errors—from the analysis and testing tools.

Outside the *formal techniques* theme, we use the notations and concepts of formal methods—set theory, logic, schema calculus, process notation, preconditions, and refinement—but we do not present formal proofs. There may be formal methods in use—for example, the *Casper* tool is used during one of the security models—but any formal reasoning is fully automated. Nevertheless, the use of these notations and concepts helps to convey an understanding of their semantics.

These links between modules promote a progression of learning in both directions. Applications of formal techniques such as

- the use of CSP to reason about transactions within a module on distributed objects,
- the use of the Z schema notation used to explain the semantics of relational algebra in databases, and
- the use of Haskell to provide a precise, concise explanation of XSLTs

outside the formal theme prompt students to register for later modules in Z, CSP, and Functional Programming. When they attend these modules, the fact that they have already seen an application provides both confidence and context to support their learning.

In the other direction, the material in the modules of the formal theme is motivated through applications that link to other modules: for example, the module on mathematics makes connections between typed set theory and the relational model of data, shows how logic can be used in statements of requirements, and demonstrates the use of predicates to constrain object models. If the students attend later modules in the corresponding subjects, then these links help reinforce the lessons learnt.

In either case, when links are made between two modules in different themes, care is taken to ensure that the modules can still be studied separately, or in either order. However, we would argue that an integrated programme, in which theory is linked to practice, and methods are linked to their application, offers the potential for deeper, more effective education.

It is not clear that this argument would attract universal support: [2] examines the role of formal methods within Computing Curricula 1991 [30], Computing Curricula 2001 [29], and the SoftWare Engineering Body of Knowledge [17], and observes that "the computing education community has adopted a curriculum strategy of dividing curricula elements into areas of 'theory' and 'practice'."

Our own perspective is informed in part by the familiar quotation from Christopher Strachey, almost a 'mission statement' for the Programme:

> It has long been my personal view that the separation of practical and theoretical work is artificial and injurious. Much of the practical work done in computing, both in software and in hardware design, is unsound and clumsy because the people who do it have not any clear understanding of the fundamental design principles of their work. Most of the abstract mathematical and theoretical work is sterile because it has no point of contact with real computing.

Although Strachey was talking about computing, we would argue that this sentiment is equally applicable to software engineering. The shift towards higher levels of abstraction, and increasing importance of model semantics, only makes it more imperative that such a separation is not allowed to occur.

3.3   Examples

To show how the notations and concepts of formal methods are used in modules outside the *formal techniques* theme, we will present two simple examples.

Overlapping intervals. Students work in groups of three or four to complete the development of a distributed diary: a system for arranging meetings between groups of users. The system is specified using UML; the students are asked to implement the system using Java, and test their implementation using JUnit.

The design of the system includes a class called Meeting, which has—amongst others—two attributes called start and finish. After an extremely brief introduction to, or reminder of, predicate logic and set theory, the students are asked to produce a precise description of the method overlaps(), called to determine whether or not one interval of time overlaps with another. The reader could be forgiven for thinking that the same answer—perhaps

$$\_overlaps\_ : (Date \times Date) \leftrightarrow (Date \times Date)$$

$$\forall start_1, finish_1, start_2, finish_2 : Date \bullet$$
$$(start_1, finish_1) \; overlaps \; (start_2, finish_2) \Leftrightarrow$$
$$start_1 < start_2 < finish_1 \lor start_2 \leq start_1 \leq finish_2$$

—might be presented by each of the groups, but this is not the case; instead, the groups consider:

- whether intervals of zero length should be allowed;
- whether intervals of non-zero length that meet at a single point should be described as 'overlapping';
- how overlaps() should respond to pairs of dates that are not ordered as expected: that is, what happens if $start_1 > finish_1$?
- whether a simpler definition is possible

This debate serves to underline the need for precise descriptions and abstract design: students are likely to appreciate immediately the advantage of identifying and resolving this issue at the design stage, using concise, formal notation, rather than waiting until later in the development process.

They are likely also to appreciate that some issues can be resolved only through a better understanding of purpose and context. For example, should the system work like a video recorder, and allow the user to book timeslots end-to-end? Is a reminder event, set for 10.00, to be regarded as a meeting?

The example offers the opportunity to demonstrate the value of proofs in propositional calculus. Starting from a characterisation of the problem that all present can agree with—that the two intervals *do not* overlap if the first starts strictly after the second finishes, or *vice versa*—an application of De Morgan's laws will produce a more economical answer.

It offers also the opportunity to demonstrate the concept of preconditions, as we note that the economical answer relies on the assumption that the intervals are represented in a canonical fashion, with the start time listed as the first element of the pair. The relationship between preconditions in Z, the behaviour of the implementation, and testing using JML, can also be explored.

Schemas and the relational model. The module on database design uses Z schema notation to help explain the semantics of relational schemas, building on the observations of, amongst others, [8], [12] and [21]. The relational schemas

$$CountryDetails\ (\ name : Country, capital : City,$$
$$population : \mathbb{N}, currency : Currency)$$
$$CityDetails\ (\ name : City, country : Country,$$
$$population : \mathbb{N}, area : \mathbb{N})$$

are presented alongside a series of Z definitions

$$[Name, Currency]$$

$$City, Country : \mathbb{P}\ Name$$

$$
\begin{array}{l}
\_\_CountryDetails_____ \\
name : Country \\
capital : City \\
population : \mathbb{N} \\
currency : Currency \\
\hline
\end{array}
$$

$$
\begin{array}{l}
\_\_CityDetails_____ \\
name : City \\
country : Country \\
population, area : \mathbb{N} \\
\hline
\end{array}
$$

and the following tuples, members of the *Country* schema:

(Austria, Vienna, 8 004 000, Euro)(Colombia, Bogotá, 34 984 000, Peso)

are presented also as bindings:

$$\langle name == \text{Austria}, capital == \text{Vienna},$$
$$population == 8\,004\,000, currency == \text{Euro} \rangle$$
$$\langle name == \text{Colombia}, capital == \text{Bogotá},$$
$$population == 34\,984\,000, currency == \text{Peso} \rangle$$

Although this presentation is more verbose, it records more accurately the model being used, since the operations of the relational calculus and algebra typically operate on *named* attributes, rather than referring to them by position.

This correspondence between relational schemas and Z schemas is then exploited to support early reasoning about constraints, something is not possible in many of the popular, commercial tools for entity-relationship modelling. It supports also the introduction of the relational calculus, with an accompanying explanation in terms of Z-style set comprehensions. Feedback from students on the database module suggests that the additional insight is extremely helpful.

4   Experiences and Results

The value and feasibility of this approach to teaching formal methods in context, as part of an integrated approach to software engineering, can be measured in terms of the success of the Programme: its ability to attract good students; the feedback from the students; and the attitudes of the teaching staff.

4.1   Recruitment

Although the cost of participation is significant, the programme is aimed squarely at individuals, not their employers. From 1993 to 1998, the student body consisted mainly of employees of large organisations in the computing and telecommunications industries. This mode of recruitment was not satisfactory:

- The working environment is becoming more pressured, and more uncertain. It is difficult to obtain management support for any programme that would mean a fixed schedule of absences from the workplace.
- During restructuring in the computing and telecommunications industries: human resources and training budgets are cut; research and development activity is curtailed, making employee education appear less of a priority.
- Partnerships with companies can sometimes suffer from a 'project mentality': successful or not, after three years, it may be time to do something else.

In 1999, a new strategy was adopted: instead of working through management initiatives and human resources departments, the promotional activity would be focussed almost exclusively upon the individuals who might attend. Since then, interest in the Programme has increased steadily, and the fact that participation is driven by individuals, and not by organisational or management initiative, has led to a tangible increase in student motivation.

There has also been an increase in the proportion of students who elect to pay the full cost of the course themselves. The current distribution of current students according to funding source is: 30% funded by self; 47% funded exclusively by employer; 23% funded partly by employer, partly by self. This has led to greater diversity in the student body: fewer assumptions can be made about the nature of previous experience, or the culture of the student's workplace. At the same time, a wider variety of experiences can be drawn upon in the classroom. The overall effect has been one of improvement: in the quality of course material; and in the learning experience of the students.

At present, 36% of the student body are employed by large, multinational enterprises—companies such as IBM, Nokia, Motorola, Chase, Barclays, and Microsoft—and another 14% are employed by the public sector in the UK. Because of the perceived importance of smaller organisations as a source of innovation within the industry, we took steps to promote the programme to employees of small-to-medium enterprises (SMEs). Our expectation was that smaller organisations would be more reluctant to release employees for advanced education: their training needs are more immediate, and the opportunity cost of a single employee's absence from the workplace is that much greater.

In practice, we found that this was not the case: SMEs were at least as willing to release their employees. It appears that direct financial cost is a more significant factor: we conducted a confidential survey of SMEs, asking them to allocate a score to identified factors in selecting and purchasing courses. On a scale between 1 and 5, with 5 being 'very important', the responses with the four highest means were: *direct financial cost*, 4.7; *local availability* 4.0; *cost in staff time* 4.0; *staff interest* 3.9.

Below these came: *quality of tuition, value to the business, relevance to current and future software development environments*, and *relevance to company objectives*. This suggests that smaller companies might not place any great importance upon advanced education. However, it seems that their employees *do*, perhaps more so than the employees of larger organisations: a subsequent bursary scheme for employees of SMEs was quickly oversubscribed.

Levels of recruitment have increased considerably since the first 22 students were admitted in 1993. The number of new admissions in each of the last five years are (1999) 30; (2000) 60; (2001) 56; (2002) 54; (2003) 69. The complement of academic staff (faculty) on the Programme has increased: from 1 to 7. The number of modules delivered each year has also increased: from 6 to 48.

4.2   Student Feedback

In a survey of which skills are most important to software engineers [20], 'formal specification methods' was ranked 37th, and predicate logic was ranked 39th. Although, on a positive note, these topics weren't completely dismissed, it was clear that—at the time the survey was conducted—'formal methods' lacked industrial credibility.

Our own experience, in working with industrial software engineers, suggests that the results of this survey may be somewhat out of date; the developments listed in Section 2.2 have started to affect attitudes in industry. Nevertheless, there are many practitioners who fail to appreciate the increasingly important role of formal methods in software engineering, just as many undergraduates who fail to appreciate the role of mathematics in computing [18]).

The operation of the Programme, including staff salaries, is funded entirely from the fees charged to students; student feedback is taken quite seriously. For the purposes of this paper, one of the most interesting statements on the module feedback form is *I think the techniques taught during the course will be valuable to me in the future.*

Students are asked to indicate their agreement or disagreement with this statement, a score of 5 indicating strong agreement, and a score of 1 indicating strong disagreement. Interestingly, there is little difference between the mean response for modules in the formal techniques theme and the mean response for other modules. For 2003, the mean scores included

- discrete mathematics (first Z course): 3.9
- schemas (second Z course): 4.2
- concurrency (first CSP course): 4.0
- functional programming (Haskell): 4.4
- object-oriented design (UML): 4.2
- object-oriented programming (Java): 4.3
- extensible markup language (XML): 4.3

Comments from the students suggest that the perceived relevance of the first Z course increases as other modules are studied. The following student comments received for the functional programming course, although not itself part of the formal techniques theme, provide a good illustration of the attitude that we hope to engender:

- "I might not use the ideas immediately but it gave me a different way of thinking about programming."
- "The theory can only help me understand my work better in the future."

With a relatively small student population, and several complicating factors, these results and comments cannot form the basis of a detailed scientific study. However, as in the case of our experiments with modes of delivery, the fact that there is no significant difference is reassuring.

4.3   Staffing

A typical application of formal methods will involve the introduction of formality above the level of the code, modelling some aspect of design or intended behaviour. There are then two separate issues to be addressed:

- reasoning about the model, using mathematical methods, perhaps with the support of model-checking or theorem-proving technology;
- understanding and maintaining the relationship between the model and the system under development.

The first of these is easier to address in an academic programme: the lecturer will usually have an academic background, probably in computer science or mathematics, a good knowledge of the modelling language, and a sound grasp of the reasoning techniques. The second is much harder: the lecturer may have relatively little experience of using the language in context, either in combination with other tools and techniques, or as part of a large software development project; and there is still a great deal of research to be done in this area.

Fortunately, there is also more to be gained from teaching formal methods in context. Not only does the context demand more in terms of explanation, adding to the understanding and experience of the lecturer, but also the meeting of theory and practice will often suggest new extensions and new applications, pushing their research in new directions.

Teaching formal methods in context requires links across the software engineering curriculum of the kind described in Section 3.2. This is facilitated by close collaboration between members of the academic staff in matters of course design, over and above the 'buy-in' from colleagues that the teaching of formal methods already requires [32,23].

In the case of the Software Engineering Programme, all of this has been achieved through the establishment of a separate group of academics, comprising six lecturers and four teaching assistants. *All* of the teaching and administrative activity for these individuals falls within the Programme, and their research is closely related to the modules that they teach (and made easier by the fact that this teaching occurs in one-week bursts). Each academic teaches six one-week courses a year, with up to 16 participants on each course; in most cases, the academic is joined by an assistant for the duration of the teaching week.

This is a slightly unusual situation, and may prove difficult to recreate at another institution. However, collaborative groups of an equivalent nature may be established, within or across instiions, to promote the teaching of formal methods as an integral part of the software engineering discipline.

5   Conclusions

The challenges of teaching formal methods are well documented: in the proceedings of workshops [11]; in books [9]; in the results of surveys [15]; on web sites [13]; and in the reports of working groups [2]. In this paper, we have addressed ourselves to one of the most significant challenges: that of student motivation.

Several different approaches have been suggested: lightweight [6]; informal [28]; weaving [32]; and subterfuge [25]; the approach that we advocate owes much to these suggestions. It has been informed by our experience of teaching formal methods as part of a programme of professional education in software engineering; although the students on this programme have experience of industrial practice, the challenge of motivation remains.

We have argued that formal methods should be taught in the context of software engineering practice. We have attempted to characterise emerging practice in terms of developments that will effect a change in the discipline: a move towards model-driven or model-based software engineering. We have argued also that they should be taught in the context of an integrated software engineering curriculum, the design of which should reflect emerging practice. In support of this argument, we have presented a brief account of our own curriculum, together with some evidence regarding its viability.

The applicability of this approach to full-time education—in particular, full-time undergraduate education in computer science—might seem at issue. Teaching formal methods to practitioners affords a greater opportunity to connect with current practice, and to observe the effects of doing so. However, such a connection is not made automatically: it must be made by the lecturer, either in the class, or in the preparation of teaching material. The same kind of connection can be made for full-time students, and we would hope to see the same benefit: that they should stop asking 'why?', and start asking 'how?'.

References

1. J.-R. Abrial. The B-Book: Assigning Programs to Meanings, 1996.
2. V. L. Almstrum, C. N. Dean, D. Goelman, T. B. Hiburn, and J. Smith. Support for teaching formal methods. *ACM SIGCSE Bulletin*, 33(2):71–88, June 2001.
3. T. Ball, B. Cook, V. Levin, and S. K. Rajamani. SLAM and Static Driver Verifier: Technology Transfer of Formal Methods inside Microsoft. In *Integrated Formal Methods 2004*, volume 2999 of *LNCS*. Springer, 2004.
4. S. Bennett, S. McRobb, and R. Farmer. *Object-Oriented Systems Analysis and Design*. McGraw-Hill, 1999.
5. B.S. Blanchard. *System Engineering Management*. Wiley, 1998.
6. R. Boute. Can lightweight formal methods carry the weight? In *Proceedings of Teaching Formal Methods 2003*, pages 47–55, 2003.
7. A. Cavarra, C. Crichton, and J. Davies. A method for the automatic generation of test suites from object models. *Information and Software Technology*, 46, 2004.
8. R. S. M. de Barros. *On the Formal Specification and Derivation of Relational Database Applications*. PhD thesis, Department of Computing Science, The University of Glasgow, 1994.
9. C. N. Dean and M. G. Hinchey, editors. *Teaching and learning formal methods*. Academic Press International Series in Formal Methods, 1996.
10. F. DeRemer and H. Kron. Programming-in-the-Large versus Programming-in-the-Small. In *International Conference on Reliable Software*, volume 10 of *SIGPLAN Notices*, 1975.
11. D. A. Duce. *Proceedings of Teaching Formal Methods 2003*. BCS, 2003.
12. D. Edmond. Refining database systems. In J. P. Bowen and M. G. Hinchey, editors, *Proceedings of ZUM'95: The Z Formal Specification Notation, 9th International Conference of Z Users, Limerick, Ireland*, pages 25–44. Springer-Verlag Lecture Notes in Computer Science, volume 967, September 1995.

13. Formal Methods Educational Site.
    www.cs.indiana/edu/formal-methods-education/.
14. M. Fowler. *UML Distilled: A Brief Guide to the Standard Object Modeling Language*. Addison-Wesley, 3rd edition, September 19, 2003.
15. H. Habrias. Investigation into the teaching of B worldwide. www.iut-nantes.univ-nantes.fr/ habrias/coursb/questionnaireEnglish.html, 2003.
16. C. A. R. Hoare. *Communicating Sequential Processes*. Prentice-Hall International, 1985.
17. IEEE Computer Society. The SoftWare Engineering Body of Knowledge, 2004. www.swebok.org.
18. C. Kelemen, A. Tucker, P. Henderson, K. Bruce, and O. Astrachan. Has our curriculum become math-phobic? (an American perspective). In *Proceedings of the 5th Annual SIGSCE/SIGCUE Conference on Innovation and Technology in Computer Science Education*, pages 132–135, July 2000.
19. A. Kleppe, J. Warmer, and W. Bast. *MDA Explained: The Model Driven Architecture(TM): Practice and Promise*. Addison-Wesley, 1st edition, 2003.
20. T. C. Lethbridge. What knowledge is important to a software professional? *IEEE Computer*, 33(5):44–50, 2000.
21. A. P. Martin and A. C. Simpson. Generalizing the Z Schema Calculus: Database Schemas and Beyond. In *Proceedings of APSEC (Asia-Pacific Software Engineering Conference) 2003*, pages 28–37, 2003.
22. P. Naur and B. Randall. Software Engineering: A Report on a Conference Sponsored by the NATO Science Committee, 1969.
23. R. L. Page. Software is discrete mathematics. In *Proceedings of the 8th ACM SIGPLAN International Conference on Functional Programming*, pages 79–86, 2003.
24. The Apache Maven Project. Maven, 2004.
25. A. C. Simpson and A. P. Martin. Supplementing the understanding of Z: a formal approach to database design. In *Proceedings of Teaching Formal Methods 2003*, pages 65–70, 2003.
26. I. Sommerville. *Software Engineering*. Addison-Wesley, sixth edition, 2001.
27. J. M. Spivey. *The Z Notation: A Reference Manual*. Prentice-Hall International, second edition, 1992.
28. D. Stiles. Informal formal methods in a computer engineering curriculum. In *Proceedings of Teaching Formal Methods 2003*, pages 40–46, 2003.
29. The Joint Task Force on Computing Curricula, IEEE Computer Society, Association for Computing Machinery. Computing Curricula 2001. http://computer.org/education/cc2001/, 2001.
30. A. B. Tucker, editor. *Computing Curricula 1991: Report of the ACM/IEEE-CS Joint Curriculum Task Force*. IEEE Computer Society Press, 1991.
31. J. M. Wing. A specifier's introduction to formal methods. *IEEE Computer*, 23(9):8–24, September 1990.
32. J. M. Wing. Weaving formal methods into the undergraduate computer science curriculum. In *Proceedings of the 8th International Conference on Algebraic Methodology and Software Technology (AMAST)*, 2000.

Embedding Formal Development in Software Engineering

Ken Robinson[1,2]

[1] School of Computer Science & Engineering
University of New South Wales,
NSW 2052 Australia,
`kenr@cse.unsw.edu.au`
[2] National ICT Australia

Abstract. Formal methods have had considerable success in developing the theoretical fundamentals of many areas of computing, but have had considerably less success at penetrating the areas where those formal techniques could be applied. This can be regarded as a failure of formal methods. This paper is concerned, in particular, with the lack of impact of formal techniques on software development, and especially on software development curricula. The paper presents some diagnoses of the cause of the problem and discusses attempts at integration of formal development into a Software Engineering program.

1 Background

As a general observation the use of formal methods in system development appears to have had very little penetration into practice. One reason we submit is because *Formal Methods* has developed as though it is a separate discipline sitting in glorious isolation from the rest of Computer Science, Software Engineering and Computer Engineering. While members of the Formal Methods community have a common concern, namely to use rigorous and formal techniques in computing, they are motivated by a variety of problems and there are no foci. For fundamental research in formal methods this is not a disadvantage, but it is a serious obstacle to the transfer of formal techniques to application areas.

1.1 Curricula

The effect of the isolation and separation of formal methods from "the rest" is frequently mirrored in curricula and tends to lead to curricula that are ineffective in the integration of formal techniques into computing applications. A curriculum may contain one or more —frequently only one— course called Formal Methods, but with no connections to other courses. Consequently and conversely, it is frequently the case that the *other* courses make no reference to, or use of, the formal techniques studied in the Formal Methods course. Most damaging is the

C.N. Dean and R.T. Boute (Eds.): TFM 2004, LNCS 3294, pp. 203–213, 2004.

result that students, having seen no application of the formal methods, tend to dismiss them as irrelevant.

The most recent draft of the Software Engineering Curriculum from IEEE Computer Society and ACM [6] has a core course called *Formal Methods in Software Engineering*. This course is at least heading in the right direction as far as its name is concerned, but its content is a mixture of many formal methods and it is clear that no significant application of formal techniques will be able to take place in the time available.

1.2   From Computer Science to Software Engineering

Much of what passes as formal methods would be classified by this author as *computer science*, where the intended connotation is that "computer science" is a science concerned with the study of computing phenomena. To apply those methods and techniques in *software engineering*, attention must be given to the form of the development process and the need for system decomposition and composition. These requirements are non-trivial and formal techniques will only succeed if they can work within and support those requirements.

In a software engineering program it is imperative that formal methods be integrated at some level in the software development process. The techniques must be exposed and tested at some reasonable level to the requirements mentioned above. Only by demonstrating some capability in dealing with those requirements can there be any expectation of acceptance of the methods.

At the author's university we have attempted to address some aspects of those requirements and to use a formal method in non-trivial practical situations. The rest of this paper reports on the aims, content and experience of that exercise.

2   Experience at UNSW

At The University of New South Wales (UNSW), we first introduced a formal method into a project based course in 1991. At that time we used Z and we devised a process for approximating Z specifications from Data Flow Diagrams (DFD) [13]. In 1997 we introduced a Software Engineering program [20], in which we run a series of workshops over the first three years. In each workshop we cover some phase of the software development process and the students work in teams on a project. The workshops are practice-based not lecture-based.

In the second year of the program we run a course on *Software System Specification* [4], in which we initially taught Z and now teach the B Method (B). In parallel with that course we run a workshop, *Software Engineering Workshop 2A* [16], in which B (initially Z) is used to model the requirements for some system. In the next semester we run another workshop, *Software Engineering Workshop 2B* [17], in which the specification is taken though design to a prototype implementation.

2.1 Experience with Z

Z provides elegant structuring of the mathematics of a formal specification, but it provides no intrinsic structuring for specifying the components of a system. This is a significant problem for students and worse it is a significant obstacle to the validation of specifications presented by students. In the initial stages we used the ZTC [7] type checker and that at least ensured that the mathematics was well formed; it did little to provide any confidence that the specification was sensible, let alone "correct". Later, towards the end of our use of Z we used the Z/EVES [3] proof assistant. This allowed us to do a small amount of proof, but did little to raise confidence in the specifications presented by students.

2.2 Changing to B

In 2000, after a number of years teaching B to senior students, we decided to switch to B in the courses described above. The following is a list of the properties of B that helped inform that decision.

- B is a method and not simply a notation; B covers the complete software development process from specification to implementation, and even beyond to evolution.
- B distinguishes between the different phases of the development sequence: *specification*, *refinement* and *implementation* as follows:

  Specification: Non-determinism and only concurrent composition makes imperative specification impossible and enforces concentration on the modelling of single state changes. While it is possible to make a valid case for the possibility of using sequential composition in specifications, it's absence is extremely valuable for teaching students, who are inexperienced in abstract modelling but well acquainted with imperative programming.

  Refinement: Introduces the refinement relation and sequential composition. Sequential composition provides the opportunity for the inspection of results returned from B's operations; something that is not possible in specifications.

  Implementation: No state, imported machines and total hiding of the state of imported machines, no non-determinism, only sequential composition, unambiguously sets the scene for imperative implementation using only the operations of the imported machines. Implementation is identified as a terminal step in refinement.

  The distinctive phases of a B development make the progress from abstract to concrete tangible. In some other refinement scenarios, specifications, refinements and implementations are not distinguished.
- B has modular composition rules that recognise, not only the needs for textual composition and de-composition, but also development modularity including proof.

In contrast, Z is purely a specification notation, and while Z can be refined [11,8], it is not a method and does not offer any substantial assistance for the design and implementation phases.

From the student viewpoint:

Z leads them to a point from which there appears to be no further path. This considerably diminishes the credibility of Z as software development tool.

while

B addresses formal software engineering requirements as well as being based on formal computer science.

There is no clearer example of the difference between *computer science* formal methods and *software engineering* formal methods than Z and B.

2.3   The B Method and Software Engineering

B [1] is a formal method that comes with a framework that fits the software development lifecycle. There are separate constructs for specifications, refinements and implementations all sharing a mathematical toolkit of set theory, logic, generalised substitutions and refinement. B is supported by two toolkits: the B-Toolkit [10] and Atelier B [19]. The toolkits provide a form of configuration management and carry out, or assist with the tasks of analysis, specification validation by animation, proof obligation generation, proof, documentation, translation to executable code and management of a development.

2.4   Embedding B Developments

In the first second year workshop (2A) the teams develop a specification of some system in B. Examples of systems developed in the last few years are:

> an airline reservation system
>
> a voting system
>
> a warehouse management and distribution system

Then in the following second year workshop (2B) the teams develop an OO design of a prototype from their B specification. Their prototype is then implemented by embedding a B implementation of a lower layer in their informally developed upper layers. The upper layers are typically implemented in Java or C++.

As well as providing some form of "closure", demonstrating that there is life after specification, this exercise demonstrates a pragmatic fusion of formal and informal development techniques.

2.5   Embedding B Designs in OO Designs

One of the ideas that we have been pursuing at UNSW is the embedding of formal designs in OO designs. We have been developing and using this strategy over the last four years. Formal embedding commenced as an experiment and has remained optional for the students. Given the size of the projects being undertaken by students, this is not a simple exercise and not all teams choose to participate. As experience has enabled greater support, a larger percentage of student groups have been able to complete their projects with an embedded B component. In 2003, 60% of teams managed to achieve the embedding.

Formal embedding provides a strategy for carrying out a formal development on some critical part of a system and embedding the product of that development into a larger context. It is arguably a practical way of pursuing formal development, as it is going to be unlikely in practice for a complete system to be formally developed.

B machines provide an encapsulation of state and operations. Thus they can be regarded as modelling an object. However it is simple, and very common, to model a class. The basic schema for modelling the class is illustrated in fig 1.

Class
+attri: ATTR
+Methodi(args:ARG): RESULT

MACHINE *Class*
SETS *CLASS* ; *ATTR* ; *ARG* ; *RESULT*
VARIABLES *objects* , *attri*
INVARIANT
  $objects \subseteq CLASS \land$
  $attri \in objects \nrightarrow ATTR$
INITIALISATION *objects* , *attri* := {} , {}

OPERATIONS
  $object \longleftarrow$ **MakeObject** (*INITattr*) $\widehat{=}$
    PRE $CLASS - objects \neq \{\} \land INITattr \in ATTR$ **THEN**
      ANY *obj* **WHERE** $obj \in CLASS - objects$ **THEN**
        $object := obj \parallel objects := objects \cup \{ obj \} \parallel attri (obj) := INITattr$
      END
    END ;
  $result \longleftarrow$ **Methodi** (*self* , *args*) $\widehat{=}$
    PRE $self \in objects \land args \in ARG$ **THEN**
      $result :\in RESULT \parallel attri :\in objects \nrightarrow ATTR$
    END
END

Fig. 1. B Model of Class

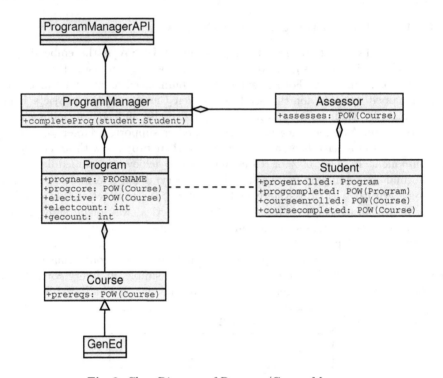

Fig. 2. Class Diagram of Program/Course Manager

Fig 2 shows a class diagram of a program/course management system, modelled initially in B. The "classes" are representations of a system fully specified and implemented in B. Notice that although we are using UML the attribute types are more abstract than normally found in a class diagram. We are utilising UML's lack of semantics. A presentation of the full development can be found on the LectureNotes page of the SENG2020 website [17] and also on the B resource site [2].

2.6   The Development Process

The development process proceeds as follows:

1. a B specification is developed from the requirements;
2. the B specification is translated to a class diagram;
3. an architecture for the complete system is determined, which for simplicity here we will take to be a simple 3-layer architecture consisting of a UAI, a middle layer and a lower layer consisting of "B classes";
4. the classes for the UAI and middle layer are developed;
5. the attributes of the B classes are used to create a *base* specification for the Base Generator of the B-Toolkit;
6. the B-Toolkit is used to automatically develop a base machine;

7. the B machines corresponding to the B layer are implemented by importing the base machine created in step 6;

8. the implementation in step 7 is automatically translated to C code by the B-Toolkit;

9. the UAI and middle layer classes are implemented in Java or C++ and the code from step 8 is embedded using the appropriate interface, as described in sec 2.7.

2.7   Interfacing a B Implementation

The B-Toolkit is used currently in the workshops. This toolkit translates B implementations to C code. The toolkit also provides interfaces in C. To facilitate interfacing the C code to a Java layer, Thai Son Hoang modified the B-Toolkit in 2001 to provide a Java Native Interface (JNI). This JNI enables a layer implemented in Java to call the operations of the embedded B implementation as native methods.

In the summer of 2003–2004, Wei Ming Chen (a second year Software Engineering student, who had recently completed the Software Engineering Workshop 2B) further modified the B-Toolkit to provide an interface to C++ using Qt. The interface can be extended using Qt Designer.

The UNSW modified B-Toolkit is fully downward compatible with the toolkit released by B-Core and is downloadable from the B Resource site [2].

3   Experience

3.1   Teaching Experience

The B coursework and the software engineering workshops have attempted to present formal development techniques in a reasonably realistic context. The following aspects are worthy of comment:

Invariant, preconditions and guards. The students have not seen invariants or precondition before commencing these second year courses. They have, of course seen *guards* but not under that name. These three concepts present the most serious obstacles, that many students take two or more months to understand. To reduce confusion between the roles of preconditions and guards we adopt a strong development discipline: the lowest level models are presented with fragile operations and non-trivial preconditions. Subsequently, an interface machine with robust operations is built "on top of" the fragile machine using machine inclusion. The guards for the robust machine are, of course, derived from the precondition and it is an expectation that there will be zero or very few proof obligations. Further, any proof obligations are expected to be easily discharged by the automatic theorem prover. Non-determinism (using the select construct) is encouraged for mapping the precondition onto guards.

Animation. Quite apart from the primary use of animation to achieve some validation of the specification, animation is very useful for illustrating the role and interaction of invariant and precondition.

Parallel composition. The absence of sequential composition at the machine (specification) level in B is a very powerful device for encouraging students to describe behaviour rather than implementation. Students take some time to adapt to the lack of the ability to think sequentially. With sequential composition, the lack of loops should also be mentioned: loops are a elementary tool in the sequential programmer's toolkit.

Non-determinism. Students are not used to non-determinism and take some time to adapt to this new way of expressing constraints. Of course, non-determinism pairs nicely with the absence of sequential composition.

Proof obligations. Students are strongly encouraged to generate the proof obligations and run the automatic prover, whenever they analyse a construct. This is explained as an extension of the concept of "compiling" to which they are accustomed from programming.

Proof. The course time is inadequate to deal with manual proof beyond a very elementary level. However, students are shown how to use the provers and they are encouraged to at least look at all undischarged proof obligations and to reason whether they are provable or not. Only by doing this will they gain the real benefits of using formally based techniques.

Refinement. Very little time is spent on refinement in the current course. This is a serious deficiency for two reasons: 1) for the fundamental reason of not understanding how formal design and implementation are done in B or any similar methodology; 2) because they will fail to understand that requirements may be distributed across specification and refinement, rather than being concentrated in the specification.

Our objective is to develop the students' ability to think rigorously and quantitatively about system development. We do not expect, indeed we cannot expect, that the majority of students will continue to use B in the later years of their undergraduate program, or after they graduate. Most of them know that as well and this is a serious disincentive for them to learn a method like B. However, we are getting a trickle of students who are interested to learn more; quite a few of whom are interested in developing the interface between formal and informal development.

As was remarked above, students are allowed to opt out of the embedding of the formal development in the informal development. Students who do that have to undertake the complete development in some programming language and this is not a trivial task. Most recognise that having the formal specification and using that as a guide considerably assists their programming task.

Our approach to embedding B developments in OO developments can be compared with the U2B tool developed by Colin Snook [18]. That tool is used to convert B camouflaged as UML to B machines.

It would be nice to be able to give quantitative statistics on the effect of the these courses on students. We do not have such statistics, but we do not expect that students will immediately commence using the methods they have been taught. Subsequent courses do not provide the opportunity and in some cases are positively hostile to formal approaches. We do not take this as failure; we expected this situation before we started. We do know that students are certainly conscious of B and will not forget it in a hurry. This means that students will graduate with an awareness of B and formal software development.

3.2 Tools

We regard it as essential to have a toolkit when using a method such as B. We have access to both the B-Toolkit and Atelier B. We use the B-Toolkit for the courses described in this paper, but will also use Atelier B in more advanced courses. The B-Toolkit provides a very useful range of services: analysis, proof obligation generation, automatic and interactive provers, animation, markup, translation of implementations to executable code, interface generation, a base generator and sundry other services. Atelier B offers similar services with the exception of animation and base generation. The provers in Atelier B are much faster and more convenient to use. The B-Toolkit prover comes with a proof theory library that has many gaps. It is regrettable that both toolkits require the purchase of licences, as this probably deters a number of institutions from using B.

4   Objectives for the Future

4.1   Our Future Plans

We intend to pursue the integration of formal and informal, especially to achieve some closer integration between B and OO development. Semi formal techniques like refactoring and patterns may be of considerable benefit in helping to improve formal developments. It is very clear that formality on its own does not imply clarity, and that the process of system decomposition is largely informal.

We have recently revised the course in which we introduce B, COMP2110, extending it to a full length course [5]. This will allow us to cover refinement and implementation, more on proof as well as exploring relationships with OO development.

All of these changes are aimed at making the practical use of formal methods by the students more effective and hopefully more satisfying.

4.2   Some Research and Teaching Objectives

- we must work on the language used in talking about formal methods, especially as they give strength to a number of myths, for example, infallibility and automatic total correctness;
- we must research and teach the important role of structuring software development (including formal software development);

- we must develop facility in the logic of computing and information structures—logical abstraction and logical computation;
- we must develop formal design patterns, and formal proof patterns;
- we must develop the mathematics of proof to the same level as expected, and accepted, of mathematics in other engineering disciplines. Proof is important here: formal methods without proof is either deceit or delusion.
- we must produce graduates who are comfortable with the discrete mathematics required for proof and mathematical modelling.

Until we achieve some success in the above we cannot expect significant transfer, and we will also have inadequately trained graduates and research students.

Formal Methods is No Silver Bullet! Fred Brook's famous warning, *No Silver Bullet*, also applies to formal methods.

Formal methods offer the promise of higher quality, but that doesn't come without a lot of hard work. Realistic pursuit of formal software engineering will drive that lesson home.

5   Conclusion

This paper has described our motivations for pursuing an integrated approach to the teaching of formal software development methods. We have outlined our approach rather than giving real examples drawn from the workshops. This is because real examples of what students do in the workshops are very large and exceed the space available for a single paper. All the teaching material used in the courses mentioned in this paper are available from the course and resource websites referenced in this paper.

We need to acknowledge that teaching a method like B presents many challenges to both the teacher and the student. In particular, we must recognise that students are likely to be ill-equipped both in mathematical ability and in mindset. Some would use this as an argument for teaching this material at a later stage, perhaps even at the graduate level. We are teaching it early in an attempt to sow seeds early.

Acknowledgments. Most especially, the author would like to thank Thai Son Hoang for his assistance and expertise in modifying the B-Toolkit.

Thanks to both Thai Son Hoang and Wei Ming Chen for the work they have done in extending the B-Toolkit's interfaces.

Thanks to the students in the Software Engineering program for their tolerance and enthusiasm.

The reviewers' useful comments are acknowledged.

Finally thanks to the School of Computer Science & Engineering for the opportunity to develop and teach this material.

References

1. J.-R. Abrial. *The B-Book: Assigning Programs to Meanings.* Cambridge University Press, 1996.
2. UNSW B Resource Site. http://www.cse.unsw.edu.au/b@unsw.
3. ORA Canada. Z/EVES Z proof assistant. http://www.ora.on.ca/z-eves/welcome.html.
4. COMP2110. Software System Specification. http://www.cse.unsw.edu.au/~cs2110.
5. COMP2111. System Modelling and Development. http://www.cse.unsw.edu.au/~cs2111.
6. The Joint Task force on Computing Curricula IEEE Computer Society and ACM. Computing curriculum — software engineering. Technical report, IEEE Computer Society & ACM, 2004. http://sites.computer.org/ccse/volume/Draft3.1-2-6-04.pdf.
7. Xaioping Jia. Ztc: Z type checker. http://se.cs.depaul.edu/fm/ztc.html.
8. S. King. Z and the refinement calculus. In D. Bjørner, C. A. R. Hoare, and H. Langmaack, editors, *VDM and Z – Formal Methods in Software Development*, volume 428 of *Lecture Notes in Computer Science*, pages 164–188. VDM-Europe, Springer-Verlag, 1990.
9. Michael Leuschel. ProB. http://www.ecs.soton.ac.uk/~mal/systems/prob.html.
10. B-Core(UK) Ltd. B Toolkit. http://www.b-core.com.
11. K.A. Robinson. Refining Z specifications to programs. In *Australian Software Engineering Conference*, pages 87–97. I.E.Aust, May 1987.
12. Ken Robinson. Early experiences in teaching the B-Method. pages 291–296, Universite de Nantes, November 1996. Institut de Recherche en Informatique de Nantes.
13. Ken Robinson, Peter Ho, and Martin Schwenke. To Zed and back: Integrating data flow diagrams and Z. pages 127–134. ACM, July 1996.
14. Steve Schneider. *The B-Method: An Introduction.* Cornerstone of Computing. Palgrave, 2001.
15. E. Sekerinski and K. Sere, editors. *Program Development by Refinement.* FACIT. Springer, 1999.
16. SENG2010. Software Engineering Workshop 2A. http://www.cse.unsw.edu.au/~se2010.
17. SENG2020. Software Engineering Workshop 2B. http://www.cse.unsw.edu.au/~se2020.
18. Colin Snook. U2B. http://www.ecs.soton.ac.uk/~cfs/.
19. Steria. Atelier B. http://www.atelierb.societe.com/.
20. UNSW. Software Engineering Program. http://www.cse.unsw.edu.au/seng.
21. John B. Wordsworth. *Software Engineering with the B-Method.* Addison-Wesley, 1996.

Advertising Formal Methods and
Organizing Their Teaching: *Yes, but ...*

Dino Mandrioli

Dipartimento di Elettronica e Informazione, Politecnico di Milano,
P. L. Da Vinci 32, 20133, Milano, Italy
mandrioli@elet.polimi.it
www.elet.polimi.it/~mandriol

Abstract. This position paper aims to address most of the "challenges" suggested by the conference's CFP plus a few others. The style is deliberately informal and colloquial, occasionally even provocative: for every examined point some obvious agreement is given for granted but a few, more controversial, "counterpoints" are raised and hints are suggested for deeper discussion. At the end a constructive synthesis is attempted.

1   Preamble: The Essence of Formal Methods: What Are They?

To optimize the organization of the teaching of formal methods (FMs) and their chances of gaining acceptance, we must first agree on some basic terminology. I very much regret that most terms are often used with fuzzy, often context-dependant, sometimes even contradictory, meanings. For instance, the term "verification" is often used as a synonym of –possibly formal– correctness proof; consequently it is *opposed* to testing. This is particularly unfortunate: first, because, in the common understanding of non-specialized people, the term "verification" is much comprehensive and includes the application of any technique aimed at guaranteeing that an artifact satisfies its requirements and goals; second, opposing different techniques with a common goal fails to show and to exploit their complementarity[1].

The term FMs itself requires some preliminary agreement on its meaning. There is now some wide consensus on claims such as

- "FMs are not mathematics but do exploit it"
- "FMs are not theoretical computer science, or theory of computation, but do exploit it"
- "FMs for Computer and Software Engineering (CSE) are rooted –mainly– in discrete mathematics whereas traditional engineering (civil, industrial, electrical, ... engineering) mainly exploits continuous mathematics"
- "Formal *Methods* should not be confused with formal *models*. Although they *use* formal models, they include much more: mainly guidelines to apply models at best to practical problems; tools supporting them, etc.

---

[1] This habit of using general, widely known terms, with specialized, context-dependant, meaning, occurs unfortunately in many communities: consider, e.g., the use of terms "framework" and "pattern" in the object-oriented culture.

C.N. Dean and R.T. Boute (Eds.): TFM 2004, LNCS 3294, pp. 214–224, 2004.

On the other hand different interpretations of the term FMs range, roughly speaking, between two extreme positions such as:

- "A FM must be fully formal", i.e., it must drive the user through the whole life cycle so that every artifact, from requirements specification to executable code, is documented through a formal syntax and semantics and every step is formally proved correct.

- Any "level of formality" is acceptable: for instance, using a formally defined graphical syntax can be considered as a FM even if a rigorous semantics for the adopted notation is lacking; also, *some* steps of the design process can follow formal guidelines but others can be carried over in a more informal way.

A typical example of such a lack of general agreement between the above positions is provided by UML, which is considered by many practicioners as a FM, whereas many theoreticians do not recognize it at all as such.

Personally, I am in favor of a fairly comprehensive and "liberal" definition of FM, as any method that in some way exploits the use of formalism. In particular, I recommend an *incremental attitude* to the application –and teaching– of FMs: moving from informal documentation to UML is an important initial step in the path that leads to a full exploitation of FMs in industrial activities; as well as, further on, enriching UML with –any kind of– semantic formalization, and augmenting refinement steps by formal correctness proofs. Such a liberal, or incremental, or "modest" attitude is also recommended in the literature as "lightweight formal methods" (see, e.g., [1], [2]).

2   Advertising and Promoting FMs: Yes, but ...

Nowadays, a great amount of effort must be put in the advertising and promotion of any "product"; culture is no exception and the old times of academia compared to an "ivory tower" are perhaps buried forever. Even scientific research requires a lot of "marketing" and publishing deep technical results on major archival journals is by no way warranty of success. Thus, there is now a fairly general consensus on claims such as the following ones:

- At the root of much reluctancy against FMs there is often a "mathfobia", typical of many students.

- Preliminarly to teaching FMs we should strongly *motivate* their use by emphasizing the risks and the costs of poor quality products and the benefits that can derived by the application of FMs. This applies not only to industrial "decision makers" but even to students who are more and more reluctant to accept a course "just because it is proposed by the university".

- "Fun" in the application of FMs should be emphasized through several means (amusing examples, games and competition, user friendly tools, etc.); tedious mathematical details should be avoided and possibly hidden.

- Tools should be used to relieve the user from many, often boring, clerical details, to make the whole process more efficient, reliable and productive.

- As a particular case joining the two above points, so called "push button" tools such as those based on model-checking are strongly recommended since, in principle, they allow the user to be concerned exclusively with the *writing* of properties to be analyzed, leaving all the burden of their verification to automatic tools.

However, most of the above claims hide some subtle traps that could lead to even counterproductive actions. Thus, in their application, one should also keep in mind the following "counterpoints":

- Do not "oversell" FMs; avoid "miracle promises" such as "FMs help producing bug-free software"; "FMs make testing useless"; etc. Such claims can be easily verified as false or at best as overstated and consequently produce the opposite result[2].

- Tools should not be advertised as a "panacea": even outside the FM realm many failures happened due to the fact that managers erroneously hoped that just buying state-of-the-art tools guarantees innovation and improvement in the production process. Also, in some cases, too early distribution of prototype tools could produce a global rejection of the underlying method only because of the poor quality of, say, tool's interface.

- In particular "push-button" itself maybe an example of overselling: in fact, most often such tools are based on brute force algorithms that "do not scale up", i.e., whose complexity becomes soon intractable with the increase of problem size; thus, in order to obtain practical results, users must indeed apply some intellectual skill.

- Not only the contents and the style of the teaching, but even the advertising arguments should be carefully tailored to the particular audience. There are major differences not only between university students and industrial practitioners, between engineers and managers, but even between graduate and undergraduate students, between young and experienced engineers (the former are usually more fresh-minded and open to novelties; the latter only accept minor changes to their current habits); between software engineers and application domain experts (both should be acquainted with FMs but in different ways), etc.

- A particular class of "students" who are often even more reluctant to change their habits than "official students" is the class of ... teachers, both in the high schools (often the deprecated mathfobia is rooted in bad teaching of mathematical bases at junior schools) and even in universities (where far too often professors of Department X ignore and/or disparage the discipline of Department Y. FMs teachers are not absent from this class ...).

- If some "thresholds of commitment and skill" are not guaranteed it is better to downgrade the objective or even to give it up at all. This general claim has several particular instantiations. For instance:

  o If within an industrial environment there is not enough interest and resource commitment in the training of FMs (typically: short term delivery deadlines repeatedly overwhelm time scheduled for training sessions) further insisting may become counterproductive.

  o Students' mathfobia can and should be fought with "fun" and other tools but not up to the point of hiding the fact that some mathematical skill is a necessary prerequisite for successful application of FMs. Even without going to extreme positions such as Dijkstra's [6], FMs teaching should

---

[2] Some classic references about "selling and overselling FMs" are [3], [4], [5].

avoid oversimplified examples that hide the technical difficulties of intricate cases[3].

- (With main reference to the case of teaching to industrial people). In general, "teaching" does not consist exclusively in explaining a topic; a formidable teaching aid is "working together". Building joint teams of application experts and FM experts often produces the best results. This practice should not be applied only during the training activity: in some cases the level of expertise that is needed is such that temporarily "hiring" specialized consultants is more effective than insisting in teaching highly sophisticated technology to not-sufficiently-motivated-or-skilled people. For instance, in several cases of industrial environments, application domain experts could and should be involved in the production of specification documents, but the application of powerful but difficult formal verification techniques such as theorem proving should be left to FMs experts.

3 So What? *Integrating* the Teaching of FMs Within Engineering Curricula

Let me now address the issue of organizing the teaching of FMs. The foundations over which I build my proposal are the following (as usual, some of them are widely shared, others are perhaps more controversial):

- FMs are a very general engineering principle; they have always been a major tool to achieve rigor in analysis and design (one can be rigorous without being formal, but this is usually more difficult). FMs *in general* should be well mastered within any field of science and engineering.
- FMs are, however, "context-dependant": traditional science and engineering (physics, biology, mechanical, industrial, civil engineering, …) have from a long time their own well-established FMs. They are mostly rooted in continuous mathematics. There is no doubt that computer science and engineering have developed their own FMs and that they are –much more, *but not exclusively–* rooted in discrete mathematics and in mathematical logics. It is also a(n unpleasant) fact that FMs are much less exploited within Computer Science and Engineering (CSE) than in other older fields.
- As an obvious consequence, the teaching too of FMs must be somewhat context-dependant: it certainly depends on the specific application field; but it must also depend on the environment within which it occurs: teaching FMs within university curricula may be quite different than teaching them in an industrial environment, perhaps in a few intensive weeks with highly specialized goals and focus.

In this paper my attention is mainly centered on university curricula[4].

---

[3] As a "counter-counter-point" the above argument should not be intended as a generic blame of so-called "toy problems" as opposed to "real-life" problems. In my opinion, *well-designed toy problems* are often even a better teaching aid than real-life projects since they help focusing attention on –few, selected– critical aspects, whereas real projects often bury subtle points under a mass of clerical details.

- However, I consider particularly unfortunate the present state of the art of the organization of university curricula, where, at every level, specialization far overwhelms generality and cross-fertilization among different disciplines. For instance, despite the fact that computer-based applications are mostly part of heterogeneous systems (plant control systems, banks, embedded systems, etc.) not only Computer Engineering (CE) curricula are quite distinct from other engineering curricula, but we have major differences between Computer Science (CS), CE, Software Engineering (SE), etc.
  FMs teaching, unfortunately, is no exception to such an overspecialization: in some cases there have been even proposals of FMs curricula *per se*, forgetting that FMs are a *means* for rigorous and high quality design, *not a goal*; also, many FMs courses focus on single, often fashionable, methods (e.g. model-checking, or theorem proving) failing to show commonalities in their goals and complementarities in their approaches.

In conclusion, I believe that engineering curricula should first emphasize the general usefulness and the common principles of FMs *per se*; a strong interdisciplinary background should also be shared by almost all engineering curricula: CSE majors should know enough of the FMs of traditional engineering (e.g., models for electric circuits) *and conversely* (many non-computer-rooted engineering curricula wrongly consider computer science just as a tool for numerical computations, access to Internet, etc, ignoring its fundamental richness of concepts and principles.)

Only later, the context-dependant part of FMs should be tailored towards the specific needs of the application field.

To state it in another way, the teaching of FMs should be well-integrated in any engineering –and not only software engineering– curriculum and cannot be addressed by itself.

Next, Section 3.1 suggests an example of how the teaching of FMs could be "plugged" into a curriculum for CSE majors, which is the main focus of this paper. To complete the picture, Section 3.2 also provides a few hints on the teaching of (CS) FMs within non-computer engineering curricula.

3.1   A FM Track Within CSE Curricula

Figure 1 provides a synthetic view of the way the teaching of FMs should be integrated within a CSE curriculum. Then, a few explanations and comments are given for some distinguishing elements. Notice that Figure 1 does *not* display the *full structure* of an ideal CSE curriculum: it only deals with the integration of FMs teaching within it; essential –in my opinion– topics such as basics of physics, chemistry, industrial and civil engineering, economics, etc. are omitted.

3.1.1 Mathematical Background

Every scientist and engineer should have a *strong background* both in continuous and non-continuous (this term is more comprehensive than "discrete") mathematics.

---

[4] Some personal experiences and lessons learned in the introduction of FMs-based practices in industrial environments are reported in [7] and [8].

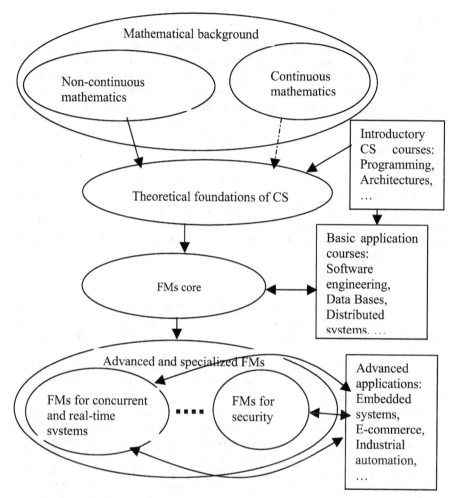

Legend: single-headed arrows denote a precedence relation; double-headed arrows denote mutual dependencies and benefits; dashed arrows denote weak precedence (general culture, beneficial but not mandatory).

Fig. 1. A synthetic view of the relations between FMs and other typical topics of CSE.

Strong background does not mean "many topics" but essential topics well-rooted and well understood. I insist that even CSE students must have such a background on mathematical analysis and calculus: the concept of continuity is fundamental for our community too! Certainly, the impact of non-continuous mathematics is more direct. It should include: elementary algebra and set theory; basics of mathematical logics (propositional and predicate calculus); a little of combinatorics. All in all mathematical background should require *at least* 5 one-semester courses (for CSE majors: 3 courses on non-continuous and 2 on continuous mathematics. A *very minimum* could be 2+2).

Remarks

There is a tendency, mainly imported from the US, to give little and fairly superficial mathematical background at the undergraduate level; later on, graduate and more talented students –it is claimed– will be able to go deeper into mathematical concepts. I am against this approach, as far as it concerns the *mathematical foundations*: foundations must be understood in depth from the beginning to help understand even trivial applications (e.g., the execution of a machine instruction); advanced mathematical topics can and should be taught at the graduate level as well as advanced applications.

Another major hole in the normal way of teaching mathematics is the lack of training in *building deductive proofs*. Often many –maybe complex– proofs are given but the students only have to learn and repeat them –and, sadly, they do so by heart, without even trying to *understand* them; instead, little or nothing is done to increase their skill to develop their own proofs. This unfortunate circumstance is probably the main reason why formal correctness proofs are considered as the most inapplicable formal technique.

3.1.2 Basics of Theoretical Computer Science

Notice that I distinguish between *theoretical foundations* of CS (TFCS) and –basic– FMs: both contribute to the theoretical core of a CSE curriculum, but they are two different things: *TFCS is about models and their properties, FMs are already a first application thereof to practical problems.*

TFCS is often identified with Automata and Formal Language Theory. I disagree, although certainly such topics are important TFCS. My favorite –one-semester– course on TFCS includes:

- **Models for CS:** *Simple* automata and their *basic* properties; simple grammars; (usually I cover much less on these topics than traditional textbooks); use of mathematical formulas (essentially first-order formulas) to formalize simple systems (e.g., formal languages, but also every-day-life objects: railroad crossing systems, elevators, to mention "classical examples"; it is nice and useful to exploit simple examples of hybrid systems, to give the message that often for some system components continuous models are suitable, whereas for others discrete models fit better).

  The fundamental skill of this part is the ability to formalize reality much more than deducing sophisticated mathematical properties from other mathematical properties.

- **Basics of computability.** Despite a few "revolutionary claims" I still believe that the halting problem plays a fundamental role in this topic. It must serve, however, the purpose of going deep into "what can be done and what cannot be done by a computer". In first courses in CS and programming I always get questions whose answer is "there is no algorithm to build algorithms to solve a given problem"; but I also add "I will be able to explain you better this claim in the TFCS course."

- **Basics of complexity theory.** This topic is fairly controversial, at least in Italy: our students usually attend courses on algorithms and data structures (where, typically, they learn tree-managing, sorting, ...) *before* TFCS. Thus, the goal of resuming the complexity issue here is not to teach them to understand whether an algorithm is $O(n^2)$ or $O(n.\log(n))$; rather, it is to teach them to understand when a logarithmic cost criterion is better than a uniform cost criterion and why in some cases the "poor Turing machine" is a better complexity model than the powerful Java Virtual Machine or than counting the statement execution in a C program.

Dave Parnas [9] seems to be in agreement with the above view.

3.1.3 Core FMs Topics

Not surprisingly, "core FMs" coverage should go somewhat in parallel with the basics of design courses such as Software engineering, Hardware design, Operating systems, etc.

Here is a personal proposal for its structure:

- **FMs for System Specification**

  This should exploit the knowledge of basic models such as automata and logic formulas to come up with formalization and analysis of real systems. It should include some examples of requirements elicitation.

  Two important remarks are in order:

  o Accent should be on *methods* rather than on *languages*: e.g. languages such as Z or VDM can certainly be used as vectors to illustrate the methods, but methods should be the real focus just as in programming courses the accent should be –but often is *not*– on programming principles, not on C rather than Pascal or Java.

  o I emphasize the term *system* specification as *opposed to software* specification, the latter being a particular case of the former.

- **FMs for Design**

  Here clearly, the main keyword is *refinement*. Again several linguistic choices are possible (e.g., B) but accent should be on methods.

- **FMs for System Verification**

  Various verification methods should be reviewed and formally treated:

  o "Traditional" formal correctness proofs certainly deserve attention. But FMs for verification are certainly *not only proofs* (this is a common and still hard to fight misunderstanding).

  o Model checking –of course!– should be presented as a major "winner" among FMs.

  o FMs do support also verification techniques traditionally considered as empirical and opposed to FMs: FMs for the derivation, evaluation, ... of testing is a main argument on this respect.

Remarks

- Often "practical courses" such as Software engineering do cover part of the above topics, mainly when the teachers have some "sympathy" with FMs. As an obvious consequence a problem arises of coordination and borderline when plugging a FM track within a CSE (and not only) curriculum. For instance, about system specification, a SE course could introduce to UML and to its use, and a well coordinated course on FMs (see the first horizontal arrow in Figure 1) should mention motivation, problems, and approaches to make a UML specification fully or partially formal.

- As it happens with most "life-cycles" the above structure reflects different phases of system development that in practice should not be necessarily applied in a "waterfall" style. For instance, some amount of verification (V&V) must be applied during requirements elicitation. Of course it is up to the teacher to decide the best organization of the topics.

In my opinion the topics addressed in this section should approximately constitute the part of a FMs track plugged into an undergraduate curriculum.

Of course, –we certainly agree within the FM community– such a track (not my own proposal but *any* track in FMs) should not be an elective track for a minority of theoretically oriented students but should be a core part of the whole CSE curriculum.

The next section outlines, instead, more advanced topics in FMs, that should probably be covered at a graduate level.

3.1.4 Advanced FMs Topics for Specialized Applications

There are, of course, several advanced topics in FMs, usually associated in a natural way with emerging or specialized application fields. In this paper, it is perhaps not necessary to go deep into such an issue.

Typical examples of such topics are:

- Models and methods for concurrent and/or distributed and/or real-time systems
- Models and methods for Artificial Intelligence
- Models and methods for security
- ...

What is most important here –nowadays even more than in the past– is a strong emphasis on critical evaluation, comparison, and *integration* between different methods, which reflect different requirements of more and more integrated applications. A fashionable example of these days is how fault tolerance, real-time, security, all concur to make a system *dependable* as a whole.

In this case too, strong coordination between FMs courses and corresponding applicative courses is demanded. Even more, in such specialized fields one could merge into a single course the treatment of the formal model and its exploitation to the application field; although with this approach there could be the risk of (over)specialization, thus missing important integration and cross-fertilization chances.

3.2   On Possible FMs Tracks Within Non-CSE Curricula

This paper focuses on integrating a FM track within a CSE curriculum. However, I also insist that a suitable track devoted to "CSE FMs", i.e., methods rooted into non-continuous mathematics and devoted to computer-based applications, should be included in other science and engineering fields to complement "their" traditional FMs. The teaching of the various FMs should be somewhat symmetric: on the one side, it is important that CSE majors are exposed to some continuous mathematics and related methods; on the other side the normal CS culture that is provided to physicists, industrial and civil engineers, etc. should not be restricted to describe computers as *tools* for enhancing their job but should include fundamental *concepts* helping to *model and analyze* systems as a whole: after all most systems are hybrid: thus their global understanding requires the managing of both families of models and methods from both communities. Only later on, in the lower and more specialized phases of the design every engineer will go deeper into his own specialized formalism.

As an example, the track described above for CSE majors could be adapted (restricted) to non-majors in the following way:

- One course only for non-continuous mathematics (summarizing the main topics: some predicate calculus and a little of combinatorics and set theory).
- One course presenting a selection of FMs particularly well-suited for the main science or engineering field. Such elements could also be included within a global CS course that integrates informal and formal methods: for instance, a software engineering course for mechanical engineers could include the important issue of specifications and could present some UML possibly integrated with a little formalization: an historical fact that strongly supports such an "open attitude" towards formalisms is that Parnas' SCR has been used to do some specification analysis in cooperation with pilots [10].

4   Conclusions

There is much agreement that teaching is a crucial factor to increase acceptance of FMs in the practice of industrial projects. In this position paper I reviewed, reinforced, and complemented a few suggested clues to improve the state of the art. I also argued in favor of some guidelines that are not often agreed upon, or even adversed, in many university curricula. In essence, I argue for a strongly interdisciplinary approach in the engineering fields as opposed to highly specialized curricula, and for a FMs *track* that is strongly integrated within engineering –and not only engineering– curricula (as opposed to curricula that have FMs as their main topic, and even in the title); that exploits discrete as well as continuous mathematics; that emphasizes the application of formal models as opposed to teaching one or more specific formalism.

References

[1] Easterbrook, S.; Lutz, R.; Covington, R.; Kelly, J.; Ampo, Y.; Hamilton, D.. "Experiences using lightweight formal methods for requirements modeling". *IEEE Transactions on Software Engineering*, Vol. 24, no. 1, pp. 4-14, 1998

[2] Saiedian, H., Bowen, J. P., Butler, R. W., Dill, D. L., Glass, R. L., Gries, D., Hall, A., Hinchey, M. G., Holloway, C. M., Jackson, D., Jones, C. B., Lutz, M. J., Parnas, D. L., Rushby, J., Wing, J. and Zave, P.. "An Invitation to Formal Methods". *IEEE Computer*, Vol. 29, no.4, pp. 16-30, 1996.

[3] Hall A. "Seven Myths of Formal Methods", *IEEE Software*, Vol. 7, no. 5, pp. 11-19, September 1990.

[4] Bowen J., Hinchey M., "Seven More Myths of Formal Methods", *IEEE Software*, Vol. 12, no. 4, July 1995

[5] Bowen J., Hinchey M., "Ten Commandments of Formal Methods", *IEEE Computer*, Vol., 28, no. 4, pp. 56-63, April 1995.

[6] Dijkstra. E.W., "On the cruelty of really teaching computing science". Communications of the ACM, Vol. 32, no.12, pp. 1398-1404, 1989.

[7] Ciapessoni E., Coen-Porisini A., Crivelli E., Mandrioli D., Mirandola P., Morzenti A., "From formal models to formally-based methods: an industrial experience", *ACM Transactions on Software Engineering and Methodologies*, Vol. 8. no 1, pp.79-113, January 1999.

[8] Cigoli S., Leblanc P., Malaponti S., Mandrioli D., Mazzucchelli M., Morzenti A., Spoletini P.: "An Experiment in Applying UML2.0 to the Development of an Industrial Critical Application", Proceedings of the UML'03 workshop on Critical Systems Development with UML, San Francisco, CA, October 21 2003.

[9] Parnas D.L, "Software engineering programmes are not Computer science Programmes", CRL Report 361, McMaster University, Ontario, 1998.

[10] Parnas D.L., Heninger K,. Kallander K., Shore J., "Software Requirements for the A-7E Aircraft", Naval Research Laboratory, Report no. 3876, November 1978.

A   Acronyms

CE: Computer Engineering
CS: Computer Science
CSE: Computer Science and Engineering
FM: Formal Method
SE: Software engineering
TFCS: Theoretical Foundations of Computer Science
V&V: Verification and validation

Retrospect and Prospect of Formal Methods Education in China

Baowen Xu[1,2], Yingzhou Zhang[1], and Yanhui Li[1]

[1] Dep. of Computer Science and Engineering, Southeast University,
Nanjing 210096, China
[2] Jiangsu Institute of Software Quality, Nanjing, 210096, China

Abstract. Formal methods can enhance the security and reliability of software and benefit software developers in comprehending systems. The progress of formal methods, however, will strongly depend on formal methods education that cultivates executive talents. In this paper, we review the present status of formal methods education in China and analyze its features in view of occidental and oriental culture. We present some advice for steady and sustained development of Chinese formal education. We conclude that if carrying out some proper innovation, China will make great contribution in the future to formal methods development in the world.

1 Introduction

Formal methods are software-developing approaches based on the foundations of rigid mathematics. They can clearly, precisely, abstractly and concisely specify and verify the properties of software; and can assist in discovering inconsistencies, ambiguities and incompleteness hidden in the specifications of software. Compared with other methods, formal methods can enhance the security and reliability of software and help the developers of software to understand the systems. After investigating the existing problems and the trend of formal methods, many methodologists point out that formal methods are not all-powerful, and that in current research and practice of formal methods, their potentials are far from being fully exerted [1, 2].

In western developed countries, especially in USA, computer scientists and government departments pay much attention to the development of formal methods. The American Defense Advanced Research Projects Agency (DARPA) sponsored the program of Formal Methods, which focused on the research on the theories and corresponding tools of highly reliable software. The National Aeronautics and Space Administration (NASA) successively issued Formal Methods Specification and Verification Guidebook (I) and (II) in July 1995 and May 1997. The American National Science Foundation (NSF) started the greatest research program heretofore , Information Technology Research, which emphasizes ensuring the correctness and reliability of system performance through verification and formal methods.

C.N. Dean and R.T. Boute (Eds.): TFM 2004, LNCS 3294, pp. 225–234, 2004.

At present, formal methods are introduced into the institutions of higher education, in order that their development and abroad application can be promoted. Some international organizations such as American Association for Computing Machinery (ACM) and Institute of Electrical & Electronic Engineers - Computer Science (IEEE-CS), strongly suggest that formal methods should be introduced to the undergraduate computer science curriculum.

The rest of paper is organized as follows: in Section 2 we review the present status of formal methods education in China, including related curricula, key hindrances in formal methods education and its necessity. In Section 3, we give the features of Chinese formal education from the view of western and eastern culture. We put forwards some advice for the steady and sustained development of formal education in China in Section 4. We conclude this paper in Section 5.

2   The Present Status

Because of the rapid development of software's complexity, especially because of the software's applications in high-technology field, we undertake an important mission to develop secure and reliable software. One effective way to fulfill the mission is using formal methods.

The early application of formal methods in software's verification is the verification for serial programs. Subsequently, applications have been gradually diversified along with the development of researches on and practical applications of software, for instance, using logic and algebraic methods to describe software, and logic inference to verify its properties, or, in another way, applying process algebra to describe concurrent software, and model checking to verify its properties. In recent years much work was done to combine formal methods with graphical software methods and with object-oriented methods, since formal methods, which largely differ from other methods, concentrate on rigorousness. These approaches, i.e. program verification, theorem proofing, model checking, and the combination between graphical methods and formal methods, are not exactly alike, but closely related. Theorem proofing and model checking are reciprocally complementary, with each having its strong point. As for the verification of complex software, it is better to compose multi-methods. All these approaches are important to the research on and application of highly reliable software.

2.1   Formal Methods Curricula

As we know, some traditional colleges in the world have added formal methods in the curriculum of computer studies, including *formal specification* and *formal verification*. In China, some well-known universities such as Peking University, Nanjing University, and Shanghai Jiao Tong University, began to add formal methods into their curricula of graduated computer studies, including *software formal methods*, *formal language and automata*. For example, the following content is about the concrete state of formal methods education in these universities.

Peking University: Its Department of Computer Science and Technology was formally founded in 1978. At present, CS Department has three research institutes, one national key laboratory and one national engineering research center. Among the faculty Prof. Yang Fuqing, member of the Chinese Academy of Science, has done research on program automation since the late 1950s. Her early work was considered as superexcellence one among early researches on program automation. In the CS curriculum, the courses related to formal methods are *formal language and automata, software formal methods, formal semantics* and *Petri net* [4].

Nanjing University: Its CS Department was founded in 1978, however, teaching and research in computer science and technology began as early as in 1958. Several research institutions have been established since then, among which are the Institute of Computer Software, the National Key Laboratory for Novel Software technology, the Institute of Computer Applications, the Institute of Multimedia Computer, and the Software Engineering Center of Jiangsu Province. The courses related to formal methods are *software methodology, formal programming methods, introduction to logic of computer science, software automation,* and *formal semantics* [5].

Beijing University of Aeronautics and Astronautics: As one of the Chinese universities that have pioneered in computer science and technology, BUAA set up its first teaching and research group for solver in 1958 and its first computer software major in 1975. In 1978, Department of Computer Science and Engineering was founded. Within the department reside the National key Lab for Software Development Environment, the key lab of Ministry of Education for Advanced Virtual Technology, the key lab of Beijing Municipality for Advanced Computer Technology. The courses related to formal methods are *formal language and automata, parallel software developing,* and *Petri Net* [6].

Shanghai Jiao Tong University: Its CS Department was founded in 1984. In 2000, the school was authorized to confer doctoral degrees in computer science and technology. In 2001, the school was approved to have the national key discipline on computer software and theory. The courses related to formal methods are *formal language and automata, applied logic* and *formal methods* [7].

Jilin University: Its Department of Computer Science and Technology was founded by academician Wang Xianghao in 1976. In 1981, the school was authorized to confer doctoral degrees in computer software. In 1988 and 2001, the school was approved twice to have the national key discipline on computer software and theory. The courses related to formal methods are *automated reasoning, software automation, formal semantics, symbolic logic* and *programming methodology* [8].

Southeast University: Its CS Department was founded in 1980. In 2002, the school was approved to have the national key discipline on computer application. The courses related to formal methods are *formal language and automata, software formal technology,* and *software developing methods and technology* [9].

Of course, there are many other well-known groups (e.g. Chinese Academy of Science) and researchers (e.g. Prof. Zhang Naixiao, He Jifeng and Zhou Chaochen) in China. For space reason, we don't introduce them in this paper.

The above universities have some advantages, such as solid foundation, strong faculty, good disciplines, long school history and, in all, a high starting level, which make them successful for formal methods education.

In contrast, those unfamous colleges have a large lag in formal methods education. These colleges are often engineering, normal and general schools. The key difficulties these colleges faced can be stated as follows:

(1) Lack of strong faculty
The faculties of these colleges are busy teaching a variety of courses and have no time to investigate the knowledge on formal methods; some even disagree with formal methods education, and to some degree restrict formal methods education in such colleges. Even if some teachers are aware of formal methods, their significance and the benefit from early taking formal methods education, practical actions may be bottle-necked by the positioning of cultivating goals and corresponding teaching programs in these colleges.

(2) Slow development of disciplines
Most of CS majors in these colleges were set up in 1980s following the popular stream, so there are no solid foundation of theory, or good and durable programs for discipline development. Though the leaders of discipline, who are well-known scholars, are employed by some of such colleges with high pay, they still feel difficult to guide faculties and students to fit in with the demand of rapid development of information technology (IT).

(3) Low starting level of cultivating goal
The starting level of cultivating goal in these colleges is low, for they often establish their teaching programs according to the requirement of IT market, in order to relieve their students' employment pressure. Therefore the curriculum of computer science mostly tends to practicality, with little deep theoretics.

(4) Weakness relative to students' research abilities
In contrast to famous colleges, the whole level of the students' aptitude in these colleges is lower. Affected by the objective factors such as faculty strength, discipline development, cultivation goal, and hard facility, students do study or research for practicality, even for faddism. For example, they are zealous for learning many fashionable program languages, for fiddling with various operation systems, all of which are guided by hunting future jobs. Though there are some students who can look ahead, they can only teach themselves with some related materials, and then write some papers using formal methods. So students in these colleges are very difficult to delve into formal methods by themselves.

2.2   The Key Hindrances

Besides the difficulties mentioned in previous subsection, there exists hindrances for all institutions of higher education in China to take formal methods education.

(1) Restrained formal methods environment in China

The hidden troubles in the sustained and healthy development of Chinese software industry are mainly insufficient fund, lack of talent and no kernel technology. The software industry of other countries such as the United States, started early, with sufficient fund and a wealth of talent in software developing. So Chinese software industry is less mature than other countries and Chinese software development often follows other countries. The key to software development is innovation, which is deficient for students taught only in classroom. The innovation depends on not only the ability to learn from other's techniques, but also solid foundation including methodology. Impacted by the whole software environment in China, the Chinese formal methods education has a long way to reach its substantial and steady progress.

(2) Diverse styles of implementation with no criterion

Most of the universities take formal methods education in their own way and in a groping phase. Some schools borrow the teaching style of the famous schools in other countries directly, ignoring the whole environment in China, which causes the effects of formal methods education to appear inconspicuous.

In these institutions of higher education, the courses related to formal methods are mostly elective ones. Because of being taught less or acquainting little, students seldom actively select such courses, except that their advisors require them to do so. Therefore few people come to communicate and discuss such knowledge, diverging from the original intention of teaching formal methods in schools, making it difficult to reach formal education goal, i.e. promoting the application and development of formal technology in software industry.

(3) Others[1]

The Chinese Cultural Revolution destroyed the education system, and then China recovers very slowly from the damage done. In recent years, the Chinese government focused on application- oriented subjects. Thus, there is a lack of funding for foundational research and teaching. There are excellent FM groups in China, but they are rather isolated, both in China and internationally. So they do not form a critical mass to influence the education and research scene in China.

2.3   Necessity for Formal Methods Education

The necessity of formal methods education arises from the significance of formal technology. Being different in the developing principle from other methods, which detect the faults of systems through testing, formal methods are expected to construct the correct systems in so far as possible [10]. The formal methods, which overcome the limitations such as discovering inconsistencies, ambiguities and incompleteness in other methods, can specify system rigidly and exactly; verify the performance of system in different views. At the same time, formal

---

[1] Partly from an anonymous referee.

methods can ensure greatly consistence and completeness in various phases and hierarchy of system development, and guarantee strongly security, reliability and correctness of system performance.

As showed above, formal methods usually include formal specification and formal verification. Formal specification, whose feature is logic precision, removes the ambiguous description showed in other methods inevitably. Its logic precision is beneficial for developers and users to understand requirement consistently and correctly [11], and to improve the developing quality and efficiency as well [12]. Seemingly, the adoption of formal methods makes developers feel inconvenient; increases the designing difficulties because designers need to spend much time and vigor studying and mastering some abstract notations and supporting tools. But in fact, it can reduce the cost of system developing, and improve the developing efficiency as well. The reasons mainly are that the cost of specification is just only a little part in the whole system overhead, but in turn a considerable sum of cost will be saved in testing and maintenance of the late phase. At the same time, the adoption of formal methods can cut down the faults in early phase of system developing so as to improve the developing efficiency.

Formal verification removes ambiguities and subjectivity from requirement analysis, by providing logic-precise verification for system performance described in requirement. Formal specification and formal verification can be applied in all phases of software development, including the earlier period when the analysis approaches are specially required. The cost spent on discovering and locating faults early is lower than doing them later. It can also remedy the existing testing methods, getting a good testing program through offering the precise formal specification.

In addition, formal methods education in institutions of higher education helps students train abstract analytical ability, through letting them concentrate on the essence of things and not be disturbed by complicate details [13].

3   Comparisons in View of Western and Eastern Culture Differences

As an ancient civilization, China possesses the honorable and resplendent culture, which brings us pride together with heavy burden. From the historical view, Chinese culture has two notable features. One is the long feudalism from Zhou Dynasty two thousand years ago to the beginning of Republic of China, since when the social system of hierarchy and grade and Confucianism began to pass off. The other one is the system of imperial examinations which is ingrained in citizens' minds [14].

Feudalistic ideas make Chinese people in long time be affected by the traditional teaching of social order, and make them follow traditions, the system of patriarchal clan and doctrines like sheep. Chinese people often totally accept without any doubt what the saint or ancestors said. This leads later generations to learn the formers' knowledge by rote, and consequently affects affect the students' skepticism and ability of validating their initial ideas in studying formal methods. In addition, Chinese teachers possess dignity, which makes students always follow their advice. The students often think in the way given by teachers or books. Therefore these students who echo what others say fail to consider things independently, or to discover and solve questions by themselves.

In contrast, western people often look up on future, not on tradition. Some of them like to challenge authority, by doubting the preceding theories. They don't unconditionally believe others including their teachers, and only accept the truth instead. These make them be good at discovering and considering questions in their own way during formal methods education. They pursue pragmatism, researching on the actual questions and offering effective approaches to solve questions in order to acquire actual and future benefit. This lets them take advantage of connecting theoretical knowledge with the actual applications of industry during their formal methods learning.

The Chinese education is mainly examination-oriented education. There are two factors leading to this phenomenon. One is the education culture and value concept given by the traditional imperial examinations; the other is the situation of China at present, that is, large population, strong pressure of employment, and bitter competition. Most of what are taught in classroom is theoretical knowledge, so that the theoretical foundation of Chinese students is solider than western students. So this is perhaps a good condition for formal methods education in China if the students have abilities of practice and innovation. But at present, indigent activity of students' thoughts, low enthusiasm and limited fancy all cause the effects of formal methods education inconspicuous.

By comparison, students in western countries are usually at liberty without pressure of examination. They don't care much about their scores, because examination result may not affect their final appraisement. In classrooms, teachers try teaching everything possible to widen students' thought and to flourish students' thinking. The western education attaches importance to sensual cognition and practical skills. They don't require students to remember much information and data; instead they demand students to acquire information and with a view of using it when solving problems. They hate conformism; advocate innovation with attitude; and encourage students to suspect, refute or deny the existing theory. Therefore students can plunge easily into formal methods learning, by considering questions independently and providing their own opinions, which cause the good teaching effects.

4   Suggestions

From the comparisons mentioned above, it is obvious that the implementation of formal methods education in China may be affected by the environment of software industry, the status of institutions of higher education and their disciplines, and faulty strength. There is small gap between the famous universities in China and those in other countries, which makes easy to take formal methods education in such universities. But the quality of implementation in the general colleges can't be ensured. Of course, the effects of formal methods education in China could be notable if the related aspects are reformed. At this point, we give the following pieces of advice for steady and sustained development of formal education in China:

(1) Breaking tradition, taking innovation

Examination-oriented education can be thought as the great barrier of formal methods education. Formal methods education needs innovative thoughts since it started late in China and no local experience could be referred. The traditional examination-oriented education restricts or obliterates to large degree the innovative capabilities of teachers and students. Thus the traditional education system should be first rectified. On the one hand, the chances of obtaining education need to be richened in order to reduce the pressure of examinations. On the other hand, the examination methods should be reformed, by exploding standard answers of questions, judging results flexibly, and encouraging creative thinking. So examinations aim to not just review knowledge on books or memory, but also test on thoughts and aptitude, so that teachers and students pay much attention to train creativity.

In the traditional idea, people attach importance of the grade of examination to the capacity of holding knowledge, which directly cause students to spend much time on learning on rote. However, with the rapid development of modern science and technology, information is continually expanding and updating, with the result that memory loses its predominance. In contrast, more and more attention should be paid on the capabilities of acquiring information, of studying through the whole life, and of coping with actual problems. In the presentday society, only those talents who can study continuously and adapt flexibly to changes, could adjust to the development of future society.

Since the tradition has farreaching effect on us, it needs the whole society (esp. schools and families) to renovate the idea of education in order to cultivate the talents with skills and theory. Teachers should be brave in breaking the bondage of tradition and taking the education of emphasizing innovation during formal methods education. The formal education still needs to strengthen its propaganda for catching more people's attention, so that more students may realize and understand formal methods, and then actively join in its study and discussion.

(2) Improving school environment, establishing long-term planning of teaching

The institutions of higher education can use appropriate funds of state and government to improve their hardware environment, for example, adding network facilities and electronic resources. The institutions should make full use of these resources; adjust the opening time of computer room, library and lab in order to fully satisfy the students' demand for formal methods learning.

As for the development of disciplines and the positioning of cultivating goal, the institutions should show great foresight; survey the world, and at the same time link the current social environment to the plans of discipline development and student cultivation. The courses needn't only aim to reduce the pressure of student employment. Teachers need to steer students correctly, in order to fully exert the advantages of Chinese students' solid theoretical foundation, and then to accelerate the pace of formal methods education in China.

(3) Enhancing teachers' study, arousing students' interest
Teachers need to enhance their study on theory of formal methods; follow the current progress; and change thinking styles and teaching ideas. In addition, teachers should have the consciousness of learning for whole life; exchange with other teachers experiences and the ways of how to steer students better; and build up a new pattern of the student-faculty relation and a good research atmosphere. It is necessary for instructors to understand the target and function of education, and to redesign teaching plans, including the study and mastery of modern education technique.

Since the students' habitual thinking came from the long-term traditional education, the whole schedule of students' formal method learning should develop from easy to hard, in order to make students gradually adapt themselves to the new abstract methods. During this process, teachers should create favorable atmosphere to arouse students' interest, to raise activity of students' thoughts, and to encourage and cultivate students' innovation.

In addition, during formal methods education, it is necessary to eliminate the possible misunderstandings. In literature [1,2], together 14 myths (misunderstandings) are listed and analyzed in detail. We strongly recommend these myths to be explained pertinently in formal methods education.

Though formal methods achieve great progress in the past 20 years, we need to make great efforts and research on many aspects. The progress of all sides in computer science will directly or indirectly promote the development of formal methods. The industry community will accept formal methods with pleasure if their formal supporting tools are apt to use and integrated with others. In the future, formal methods may melt into all fields of information technology, and become the mainstream techniques. It is foreseeable that formal methods will come out as an important role during the developing of applied systems in the future industry.

Hence it is necessary that more people (esp. software engineers) know formal methods well. The formal methods education that takes up the task of cultivating such talents looks especially distinguished. In order to meet the requirement of applied systems in the future industry, formal methods education will be ongoing widely and progressively on the basis of current achievements. With abounding human resource and talents with solid knowledge foundation, China will make great contribution to formal methods development.

Acknowledgements. The authors would like to express their hearty thanks to the anonymous referee for his or her comments.

References

1. Hall, J.A.: Seven Myths of Formal Methods. IEEE Software, (1990) 7(5): 11-19
2. Jonathan, P. B.: Seven More Myths of Formal Methods. IEEE Computer, (1995) 12(4): 34-41
3. NASA JPL: Formal Methods Specification and Verification Guidebook for Software and Computer Systems, Pasadena , CA , USA. (Manual)
   - Vol (I) : Planning and Technology Insertion , (NASA2GB2002295), (1995)
   - Vol (II): A Practitioner's Companion, (NASA2GB2001297), (1997)
4. Website, CS Department of Peking University, Beijing, China,
   http://www.cs.pku.edu.cn/
5. Website, CS Department of Nanjing University, Nanjing, China,
   http://www.cs.nju.edu.cn/
6. Website, CS & Engineering School of Beijing University of Aeronautics and Astronautics, Beijing, China,
   http://scse.buaa.edu.cn/
7. Website, CS Department of Shanghai Jiao Tong University, Shanghai, China,
   http://www.cs.sjtu.edu.cn/
8. Website, CS & Technology School of Jilin University, Jilin, China,
   http://info.jlu.edu.cn/~cs/
9. Website, CS & Engineering Department of Southeast University, Nanjing, China,
   http://cse.seu.edu.cn/
10. Larsen, P.G., Fitzgerald, J., Brookes, T.: Applying Formal Specification in Industry. IEEE Software, (1996) 13 (7): 48-56
11. Hinchey, M.G, Bowen, J.P.: Applications of Formal Methods FAQ. Applications of Formal Methods, Prentice Hall, (1995) 1-15
12. Clarke, E., Wing, J.: Formal Methods: State of the Art and Future Directions. CMU Com-puter Science Technical Report CMU 2CS2962178, (1996) 1-22
13. Chen, H.W., Qi, Z.C., Wang, B.S., Ning, H., Tan, Q.P.: A Framework for Rigorous Software Development (in Chinese). Journal of Software, (1996) 7(3): 187-193
14. Fu Q.: Inquiry Learning under Western and Oriental Cultural Environment (in Chinese). Communications on Education Technology, (2003)

A Survey of Formal Methods Courses in European Higher Education

The FME Subgroup on Education
(Convenor: J.N. Oliveira*)

The Formal Methods Europe Association
education@fmeurope.org
http://www.fmeurope.org/

Abstract. This paper presents a survey of formal methods courses in European higher education carried out by the FME Subgroup on Education over the last two years. The survey data sample is made of 117 courses spreading over 58 higher-education institutions across 13 European countries and involving (at least) 91 academic staff.

A total number of 364 websites have been browsed which are accessible from the electronic (HTML) version of the paper in the form of links to course websites, lecturers and topic entries in encyclopedias or virtual libraries.

Three main projections of our sample are briefly analysed. Although far from being fully representative, these already provide some useful indicators about the impact of formal methods in European curricula on computing.

1   Introduction

In March 2001 the FME association created the *FME Subgroup on Education* (hereafter abbreviated to FME-SoE) targeted at developing and recommending curricular guidelines for *formal method* (FM) *teaching* at undergraduate level. In its aims and motivation, the initiative can be regarded as a "FM replica" of the *Computing Curricula 2001* (hereafter abbreviated to CC2001) proposed by the ACM/IEEE Computer JointTask Force on Computing Curricula [12].

Despite the significant advances in FMs over the last decades, at both foundational or tool support level[1], the only explicit reference to the subject in [12] is elective unit SE10 of the *Software Engineering* area, modestly consisting of the following topics:

- *Formal methods concepts*
- *Formal specification languages*
- *Executable and non-executable specifications*
- *Pre and post assertions*
- *Formal verification*

---

* Correspondig author.

[1] See eg. [2] and world-wide events such as the Toulouse World Congress on Formal Methods (FM99).

C.N. Dean and R.T. Boute (Eds.): TFM 2004, LNCS 3294, pp. 235–248, 2004.

Are formal methods altogether so irrelevant? When CC2001 was released (end of 2001), some may have felt that the curricula were biased towards the pragmatism of US higher education, arguing that different approaches could be found elsewhere, notably in Europe. This viewpoint had in fact been expressed, some years earlier, by J. Cuadrado [3] who — in such a widespread journal as the BYTE MAGAZINE — criticized US curricula for lack of mathematical support for FM-based software design courses. However, the planned structure of the CC2001 report included 3 more volumes: one on Computer Engineering, another on Information Systems and another one on Software Engineering.

The last draft of the latter was released in February 2004, hereafter referred to as the SEEK report [13]. This report offers a broad and more eclectic body of knowledge, in particular exhibiting a far more expressive FM-component:

CMP.fm.1 — *Application of abstract machines (eg. Paisely, SDL)*
CMP.fm.2 — *Application of specification languages and methods (eg. ASM, B, CSP, VDM, Z)*
CMP.fm.3 — *Automatic generation of code from a specification*
CMP.fm.4 — *Program derivation*
CMP.fm.5 — *Analysis of candidate implementations*
CMP.fm.6 — *Mapping a specification to different implementations*
CMP.fm.7 — *Refinement*
CMP.fm.8 — *Proofs of correctness*
FND.mf.11 — *Algebraic structures*
MAA.md.2 — *Pre & post conditions, invariants*
MAA.md.3 — *Introduction to mathematical models and specification languages (Z, VDM)*
MAA.md.4 — *Model checking and development tools*
MAA.md.5 — *Properties of modelling languages*
MAA.md.6 — *Syntax vs semantics (understanding model representations)*
MAA.tm.4 — *Domain modelling*
MAA.rsd.3 — *Spec. languages (eg. structured English, UML, formal lang. such as Z, VDM, SCR, RSML, etc)*
DES.nst.6 — *Formal design analysis*
EVO.ac.7 — *Program transformation*

That this collection of topics is still incomplete can be checked by looking at the (long) list of individual notations, methods and tools of [2]. However, the questions arise: which of these methods are mature enough to reach every school desk? Can newcomers trust them and embark on embodying them in their (FM-specific or other) curricula? Because its main purpose is to support research, the information available from [2] is not structured as an educational body of knowledge and so it does not provide an effective answer to the questions raised above.

This has motivated FME-SoE to perform a survey of existing courses which actually adopt and teach such methods. The main purpose of this paper is to publish a summary of this survey, thus closing what has been regarded as the starting point of FME-SoE's activity. This summary includes some *preliminary* conclusions about the collected data.

When the FME-SoE survey started a list of courses could already be found in the Indiana web-page on *Formal Methods Education Resources* [9]. Anticipating the risk inherent to a world-wide survey, doomed to be incomplete and inconsistent, it was decided to restrict it to European curricula. In this way, we could learn with the exercise before embarking on such a voluminous task, which would demand more resources than those available in the subgroup.

1.1 Structure of the Paper

The remainder of this paper is structured as follows. In the next section we mention some related work in the area of formal method education. Section 3 presents the FME-SoE strategy and the structure of a provisional FM body of knowledge which underlies data classification in the survey. In section 4 we proceed to a brief analysis of our data sample. The paper ends with an evaluation of the work carried out so far, which leads to plans for future work.

2 Related Work

There is currently a world-wide concern with "mathphobia" and the increasing loss of mathematical consistency in higher-education, the ultimate resource base of science. Among many pointers to this topic, and further to [9], we select the following two, which share our concerns with respect to FM-teaching:

- *Working Group on Integrating Mathematical Reasoning into Computer ScienceCurricula* (hosted by the Geneseo's CS Dept. at SUNY, USA)
- Support for Teaching and Learning Formal Methods (University of Texas, USA).

The following workshops have addressed formal methods education:

- *Industrial Training and University Education in Formal Methods* tutorial at FME'97, an earlier FME attempt to address the topic.
- *Teaching Formal Methods: Practice and Experience* — a one day workshop at Oxford Brookes University (12 December 2003) organised by the Applied Formal Methods Group (Oxford Brookes University) in association with BCS-FACS.

3 Survey Description

The WWW has been the main information source for the FME-SoE survey carried out so far. This was completed by individual email contacts with course lecturers and by the information provided by the people who have replied to the FME-SoE call for participation, which was put on-line as soon as the subgroup was created.

At the time of writing, FME-SoE has surveyed 117 courses at 58 higher-education institutions spread across 13 European countries and involving (at least) 91 academic staff.

In addition to objective information (course name, contact person, WWW links etc), courses have been tagged with *subjective* information in the form of keywords intended for contents classification ("subjective" meaning that in many cases it was not obvious what to write, often because the course contents were not readily available).

Three different kinds of keyword were found to be relevant to the survey:

- main topics, or broad areas (38 keywords)
- notations/languages (24 keywords), and
- tools (38 keywords).

A glossary of all keywords can be found in the electronic (HTML) version of this report [14], where pointers to WWW sites describing such acronyms have been recorded wherever available. A total number of 364 websites have been browsed and recorded in the survey at the time of writing.

As soon as the collection of main topics, notations/languages and tools was found to be minimally representative, the prospect of organizing them in an FM *ontology* was considered. However, ontologies are hard to build and it was soon realized that such a task would demand far more effort and team-work than initially planned. So, it was decided to organize the available data in a *provisional*, simple *FM body of knowledge* structured in five broad areas:

- *Foundations*
- *Formal specification paradigms*
- *Correctness, verification and calculation*
- *Formal semantics*
- *Support for executable specification*
- *Other topics*

At a lower level of rank, fourteen sub-areas could be identified:

- *Set-theoretic/topological foundations of Formal Methods*
- *Logical foundations of Formal Methods*
- *Type-theoretic foundations of Formal Methods*
- *Algebraic foundations of Formal Methods*
- *Property oriented specification*
- *Model oriented specification*
- *Multi-paradigm specification*
- *Correct by construction*
- *Correct by verification*
- *Correct by machine checking*
- *Refinement techniques*
- *Programming language semantics*
- *Formalizing distribution, concurrency and mobility*
- *Declarative programming*

The table in appendix A frames all keywords into this two-layered hierarchical body of knowledge[2]. Wherever possible, the entries in the table refer to the SEEK units mentioned earlier on, as well as to some of the units of the CC2001 CS body of knowledge (directly or indirectly) related to formal methods.

---

[2] As it will be discussed in the conclusions, this table is tentative and still far from a definitive answer to the difficult task of building a consensual *ontology* for formal methods.

4 Survey Analysis

The surveyed data have been collected (in abstract-syntax format) in a textual database which was subject to a number of simple "data-mining" operations available from a runnable functional specification of the courses database. The following main analytical projections were identified:

- Survey of courses per topic;
- Survey of courses per notations, notation variants or specification languages;
- Survey of courses per tools.

The enumeration of all courses selected per each projection is given in tabular format in the full version of this paper available from the WWW [14]. Each course is characterized by the following attributes:

Institution — Institution name (or an abbreviation of it).
Ref — Local identification of module in institution (if available / applicable).
Y/S — Year/semester of module, wherever such a time schedule is mentioned or can be safely inferred[3].
Module — Module name.
Contact — Lecturer or contact person.
Topics/Langs/Tools — Acronyms of module topics, (specification) languages, notations and tools. All these entries can be looked up in the glossary of [14].

A brief (quantitative) analysis of these projections follows, in the form of histograms. Concerning the first projection, we have obtained the histogram of Fig. 1. It can be observed that *model-oriented* specification (FM06) is by far the most popular topic in the survey, followed by the teaching of *concurrency* (FM13) and *logical foundations* (FM02). A third group of topics includes *model checking* (cf. FM10), *support for executable specification* (cf. FM14) and formal *semantics* (FM12). Comparatively less widespread is the teaching of *algebraic* approaches to formal specification (topics FM04 and FM05). Last in the list is *multi-paradigm* specification (FM07), a topic whose relevance in industrial case-studies and scientific meetings (eg. FME symposia) is not yet mirrored in the curricula.

Another question we have tried to answer is concerned with whether courses are *focussed* and go in depth into particular subjects, or they tend to spread over many topics in a *light-weight* ("breadth-first") manner. Without further inspection of cross-breedings among topic areas, we found out that 47 courses focus onto one topic area only, 36 courses spread over two topic areas and 21 courses spread over three areas. All other courses remaining are even less focussed.

Concerning the second projection, we have identified 24 notations (or notation variants) and/or (specification) languages, which are listed in [14] ranked by the number of courses which teach or address them[4]. Altogether, we have obtained the histogram of

---

[3] This field proved to be one of the most difficult to fill in due to the variety of academic scheduling systems in Europe (years, semesters, terms, etc.).

[4] It should be mentioned that 37 courses do not refer to any standard FM notation, that is to say, they seem to resort to conventional "pen and paper" mathematics (eg. set theory notation, logic notation etc).

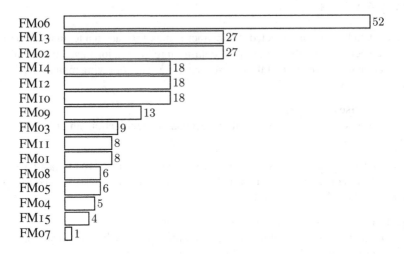

Fig. 1. Number of courses per main topic area

Fig. 2. The popularity of specification languages and methods such as Z [15] and B [1] is consistent with the widespread teaching of model-oriented specification unveiled by the previous projection. The somewhat surprising rôle of functional programming languages such as Haskell [7] and SML [5] is due to their use in animation (rapid prototyping) or to the development of libraries written in such languages which support teaching.

Concerning the third projection, and despite the fact that 65 courses don't mention any support tools in their website description, we have identified 38 tools or (formal specification) libraries, which are listed in [14] ranked by the number of courses which mention them. However, the analysis of the corresponding histogram (Fig. 3) requires some care, as it is not always obvious from website contents which particular tools are being imposed or recommended. Very often, tools are not even mentioned (in particular if they are open source software) and are implicit from the context[5]. Almost half of the tools offer support for model-oriented methods such as B, Z or VDM [4]. The prominent rôle of model checking tools is to be remarked, notably SPIN [6] and UPPAAL [8].

5 Conclusions and Further Work

This report presents the information gathered to date in a survey of FM-courses (on-going action of FME-SoE) in higher education institutions across Europe. Although far from being fully representative, this survey already provides a sample of the target data amenable to multi-dimensional analysis. However, it is lacking consistency in the following respects:

---

[5] For instance, if Haskell is mentioned as a support or specification language, which particular tool — eg. Hugs or GHC (both readily available from http://www.haskell.org/implementations.html) — can one be sure the students use?

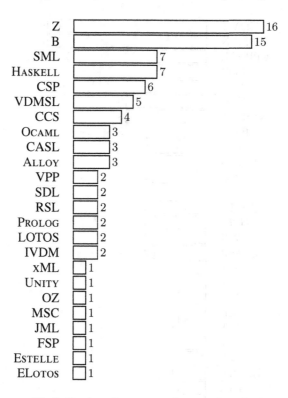

Fig. 2. Number of courses per language/notation

Shortcomings of web-based survey:

- *Availability:* many courses are not available on-line or are password-protected (usually within campus intranets).
- *Temporality*: most websites are "snapshot"-like in the sense that they only show *today*'s data. Elective courses may "exist" but be inactive in the current academic year.
- *WWW dynamics:* URLS are very volatile and change all the time. Therefore, referential integrity can hardly be maintained. (Will the WWW ever be considered an information system as we understand the concept nowadays?)

Shortcomings of sampling method:

- The FME-SoE course sample database is not yet fully representative. In particular, it is geographically asymmetric. Countries such as Germany and Spain, just to mention only two, are far from properly documented.
- The (keyword-based) classification of modules is perhaps too simple. It can be improved once a more effective ontology or body of knowledge is developed.

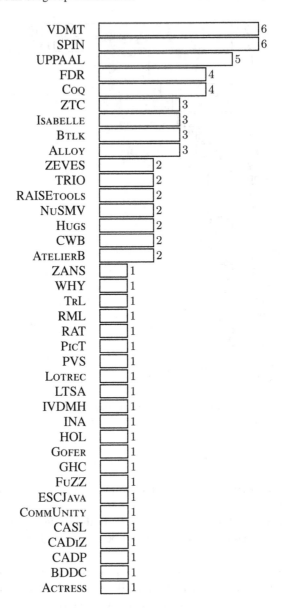

Fig. 3. Number of courses per tool

5.1 Where Are We?

The survey reported in this paper is not yet complete. May it at least serve as a stimulus for course lecturers to advertise their teaching experiences and results. xxx eventually leading to a self-updatable central repository accessible on a "wiki"-basis hosted by FME. The more representative it becomes, the more effective it will be in helping lecturers to cross-compare their teaching and newcomers to adopt particular teaching approaches or styles.

We have, nevertheless, a basis to work on. The information already available can be used to inspect each institution's *thread* of modules. Consistent/successful threads can eventually be selected as prototypical and proposed as (FME) recommended *curricular guidelines*.

Our final concern should be to equip each standard with suitable, FME recommended teaching material (or links to such a material). Like the ACM/IEEE task force have done, we should not aim at proposing a single, standard curriculum, but rather to find our own alternatives in FM curricula. For instance, similarly to the *Imperative-first*, *Objects-first* alternatives in section 7.6 of [12], FM specialists may eventually find evidence that FM introductory courses can be of the classes *Light-FM-first*, *Set-theory-first*, etc. Future collaboration with the ACM/IEEE Task Force on Computing Curricula would be very welcome and beneficial for both sides.

5.2   Need for an FM Ontology

The overall success of FME-SoE will rely on reaching consensus about the FM area of research and teaching: sooner or later, some kind of FM ("meta") *domain analysis* will be required. Ever since the days of Carl Linnaeus (1707-1778), the activity of framing a universe of discourse into classes has always been regarded as essential to the birth of effective science. Addressing this *hot* topic demands effective answers to questions such as

- What is a formal method? The answer found in the Wikipedia, the free encyclopedia, is as follows: *A scientific and engineering discipline of rigorous reasoning about correctness of computer programs, based on the use of symbolic logic.* But perhaps the ultimate target of any formal method (in computing as elsewhere in engineering, as stressed by [10]) could be summed up by a "stamp" such as

which most software houses are unlikely to be able to use for the time being. This entails the need for languages amenable to mathematical reasoning under a careful balance between *descriptive* power and *calculational* (reasoning) power[6].
- What is the borderline between mathematical *foundations* and formal *methods* "as such"?
- What is the borderline between *informal* and *formal* methods? What is a "rigorous" method?

We still have a long way to go.

---

[6] Reference [11] suggests the need for two-layered notations in the style of the "good old" *Laplace transform*.

Acknowledgments. The *FME Subgroup on Education* would like to thank all who have contributed to this survey, particularly Dino Mandrioli and Simão Melo de Sousa whose help was particularly valuable. The anonymous referees also provided a number of helpful suggestions.

References

1. J.-R. Abrial. *The B-book: assigning programs to meanings.* Cambridge University Press, 1996.
2. J. Bowen. World wide web virtual library of formal methods, 2004. Available from `http://www.afm.sbu.ac.uk`.
3. J. Cuadrado. Teach formal methods. *Byte*, page 292, December 1994.
4. J. Fitzgerald and P.G. Larsen. *Modelling Systems: Practical Tools and Techniques for Software Development.* Cambridge University Press, 1st edition, 1998.
5. Michael R. Hansen and Hans Rischel. *Introduction to Programming using SML.* Addison-Wesley, 1999. ISBN 0-201-39820-6.
6. Gerard J. Holzmann. *The Spin Model Checker: Primer and Reference Manual.* Addison-Wesley, 2003. ISBN 0-321-22862-6, 608 pages.
7. S.L. Peyton Jones. *Haskell 98 Language and Libraries.* Cambridge University Press, Cambridge, UK, 2003. Also published as a Special Issue of the Journal of Functional Programming, 13(1) Jan. 2003.
8. Kim G. Larsen, Paul Pettersson, and Wang Yi. UPPAAL in a nutshell. *Int. Journal on Software Tools for Technology Transfer*, 1(1-2):134–152, 1998.
9. K. Fisler (maintainer). Formal methods education resources, 2002. Website hosted by the Department of Computer Science, Worcester Polytechnic Institute. Available from `http://www.cs.indiana.edu/formal-methods-education/`.
10. D. Mandrioli. A few preliminary thoughts about education on formal methods within (university) curricula, 2003. Working document available from the FME-SoE website.
11. J. N. Oliveira. "Bagatelle in C arranged for VDM SoLo". *Journal of Universal Computer Science*, 7(8):754–781, 2001. Special Issue on *Formal Aspects of Software Engineering* (Colloquium in Honor of Peter Lucas, Institute for Software Technology, Graz University of Technology, May 18-19, 2001).
12. The Joint ACM/IEEE-CS Task Force on Computing Curricula. Computing curricula 2001: Computer Science — Final Report. Technical report, Association for Computing Machinery and IEEE Computer Society, December 2001.
13. The Joint ACM/IEEE-CS Task Force on Computing Curricula. Computing curriculum - Software Engineering. Technical report, Software Engineering Education Knowledge (SEEK), February 2004. Public Draft 3.1.
14. FME Subgroup on Education. A survey of formal methods courses in european higher education, 2004. Web version (HTML) available from `http://www.fmeurope.org/` ↦ Formal Methods ↦ Education.
15. J. M. Spivey. *The Z Notation — A Reference Manual.* Series in Computer Science. Prentice-Hall International, 1989. C. A. R. Hoare.

A   Tentative Body of Knowledge for Formal Methods

The table which follows provides a classification for all the keywords employed in the survey (see the glossary in [14]). Wherever possible, the entries in the table refer to the SEEK units mentioned earlier on, as well as to some of the following units of the CC2001 CS body of knowledge (directly or indirectly) related to formal methods:

- DS1. *Functions, relations, and sets*
- DS2. *Basic logic*
- DS3. *Proof techniques*
- DS5. *Graphs and trees*
- PF3. *Fundamental data structures*
- PF4. *Recursion*
- AL2. *Algorithmic strategies*
- PL5. *Abstraction mechanisms*
- PL7. *Functional programming*
- PL9. *Type systems*
- PL10. *Programming language semantics*
- IS3. *Knowledge representation and reasoning*
- IS5. *Advanced knowledge representation and reasoning*
- SE5. *Software requirements and specifications*
- SE6. *Software validation*
- SE10. *Formal methods* [elective]

	Ref.	Topics	CC2001	SEEK04
FOUNDATIONS				
FM01	*Set-theoretic/topological foundations of Formal Methods*			
	DMat	Discrete Maths (ZF set theory, functions, relations, graphs, trees etc)	DS1	FND.mf.1,FND.mf.5
	FixP	Lattice and Fixed Point Calculus		
	ScTD	Scott Theory of Domains		
FM02	*Logical foundations of Formal Methods*			
	FOL	First-order logic (proof techniques, etc)	DS2, DS3	FND.mf.2, CMP.fm.8
	HL	Hoare Logic		
	LamC	(Typed) Lambda Calculus		
	TL	Temporal Logic		
	LTL	Linear Time Temporal Logic		
	CTL	Computation Tree Logic		
	TLA	The Temporal Logic of Actions		
FM03	*Type-theoretic foundations of Formal Methods*			
	TT	Type theory and type systems	PL9	
	PolyT	Polytypism and genericity		

FM04	Algebraic foundations of Formal Methods			
	AIS	Algebraic structures, initial/final algebras		FND.mf.11
	MPC	Mathematics of Program Construction (inc algorithmic problem solving, algebra, category theory)		
FORMAL SPECIFICATION PARADIGMS				
FM05	Property oriented specification			
	ADT	Abstract Data Types (initial algebra specification, etc)		
	CASL	The Common Algebraic Specification Language		
FM06	Model oriented specification			
	ASM	Abstract State Machines		CMP.fm.2
	FPT	Formal program techniques: pre-/post-conditions, invariants, proofs, verification, etc.	SE10	MAA.md.2
	B	B-Method		CMP.fm.2
	VDM	Vienna Development Method		CMP.fm.2
	VDMSL	VDM Standard Language		
	VPP	VDM++		
	IVDM	Irish School of VDM		
	RSL	RAISE Specification Language		
	OZ	Object-Z Specification Language		
	Z	Z-Notation		CMP.fm.2
	Alloy	Alloy		
FM07	Multi-paradigm specification			
	MPS	Integration concerns, multi-paradigm specifications		
CORRECTNESS, VERIFICATION AND CALCULATION				
FM08	Correct by construction			
	AoP	Algebra of Programming, relational calculus		CMP.fm.4, EVO.ac.7
FM09	Correct by verification			
	PV	Program verification	SE10	MAA.md.4
	BDD	Binary decision diagrams		

FM10	*Correct by machine checking*			
	MC	Model Checking		MAA.md.4
	ATP	Automated Theorem Proving		
	TFM	Testing with formal methods		
FM11	*Refinement techniques*			
	ARef	Algorithm refinement, loop invariants, etc		CMP.fm.6, CMP.fm.7
	DRef	Data refinement		CMP.fm.6, CMP.fm.7
	RC	Refinement Calculus		CMP.fm.6, CMP.fm.7
	RefB	Refinement in B		CMP.fm.6, CMP.fm.7
FORMAL SEMANTICS				
FM12	*Programming language semantics*			
	AS	Action Semantics		
	ASe	Algebraic Semantics	PL10	
	FS	Denotational and Operational Semantics	PL10	
	AbsI	Abstract interpretation	PL5	
FM13	*Formalizing distribution, concurrency and mobility*			
	PA	Process algebras		
	CCS	Calculus of Communicating Systems		
	CSP	Communicating Sequential Processes		CMP.fm.2
	PiC	Π-calculus		
	Petri	Petri Nets		
	FSP	Finite State Processes		
	MSC	Message Sequence Charts		
	LOT	LOTOS		
	ELOT	Enhanced LOTOS		
	Estelle	Estelle		
SUPPORT FOR EXECUTABLE SPECIFICATION				
FM14	*Declarative programming*			
	FP	Functional Programming	PL7	
	Haskell	Haskell		
	SML	The Standard ML Programming Language		
	CAML	The CAML Language		
	Prolog	Prolog		

OTHER TOPICS				
FM15				
	AL	Algorithms and Complexity	AL2	
	SA	Software Architecture		
	JML	Java Modelling Language		
	Safety	Safety Analysis Techniques		

Author Index

Börger, Egon   65

Carro, Manuel   85
Christianson, Bruce   47

da Rosa, Sylvia   17
Davey, Neil   47
Davies, Jim   185
Duke, Roger   124

Faucou, Sébastien   166
Fernández-Iglesias, Manuel J.   153

Habrias, Henri   166
Herranz, Ángel   85

Lau, Kung-Kiu   1
Li, Yanhui   225
Llamas-Nistal, Martín   153
Loomes, Martin   47

Mandrioli, Dino   214

Mariño, Julio   85
Martin, Andrew   185
Miller, Tim   124
Moreno-Navarro, Juan José   85

Oliveira, J.N.   235
Ostroff, Jonathan S.   107

Paige, Richard F.   107
Pepper, Peter   140

Reed, Joy N.   32
Robinson, Ken   203

Simpson, Andrew   185
Sinclair, Jane E.   32
Strooper, Paul   124

Xu, Baowen   225

Zhang, Yingzhou   225